THE PSYCHOLOGY OF LEARNING AND MOTIVATION

Advances in Research and Theory

VOLUME 2

CONTRIBUTORS TO THIS VOLUME

R. C. Atkinson

David Birch

Howard K. Kendler

Tracy S. Kendler

Frank A. Logan

R. M. Shiffrin

THE PSYCHOLOGY OF LEARNING AND MOTIVATION

Advances in Research and Theory

EDITED BY KENNETH W. SPENCE
AND JANET TAYLOR SPENCE

UNIVERSITY OF TEXAS, AUSTIN, TEXAS

Volume 2

1968

ACADEMIC PRESS New York • London

COPYRIGHT © 1968, BY ACADEMIC PRESS, INC.
ALL RIGHTS RESERVED
NO PART OF THIS BOOK MAY BE REPRODUCED IN ANY FORM,
BY PHOTOSTAT, MICROFILM, RETRIEVAL SYSTEM, OR ANY
OTHER MEANS, WITHOUT WRITTEN PERMISSION FROM
THE PUBLISHERS.

ACADEMIC PRESS, INC.
111 Fifth Avenue, New York, New York 10003

United Kingdom Edition published by
ACADEMIC PRESS, INC. (LONDON) LTD.
24/28 Oval Road, London NW1 7DD

LIBRARY OF CONGRESS CATALOG CARD NUMBER: 66-30104

Second Printing, 1971

PRINTED IN THE UNITED STATES OF AMERICA

LIST OF CONTRIBUTORS

R. C. Atkinson, Stanford University, Stanford, California
David Birch, University of Michigan, Ann Arbor, Michigan
Howard K. Kendler, University of California, Santa Barbara, California
Tracy S. Kendler, University of California, Santa Barbara, California
Frank A. Logan, University of New Mexico, Albuquerque, New Mexico
R. M. Shiffrin, Stanford University, Stanford, California

223820

PREFACE

The second volume in this serial publication continues with the objective for which the work was conceived. That objective has been to provide a forum in which workers in this field could write about significant bodies of research in which they are involved. The operating procedure has been to invite contributions from interesting, active investigators, and then allow them essentially free rein and whatever space they need to present their research and theoretical ideas as they see fit. The result of this invitation has been a collection of papers in these first two volumes which are remarkable for the nature of their integrative summation, since the usual response to this challenge has been a presentation of a series of experimental results integrated around some particular problem and theory. With the current space limitations in professional journals, there has been no recognized forum for communication of such lengthy, integrative reports which give a sustained overview of a particular problem or theory. And therein lies the potentially unique contribution of annual research volumes such as the present one.

About four years ago, Kenneth and Janet Spence sensed the need for an annual publication which would cover the broad spectrum of topics in learning and motivation. Through their efforts, in concert with those of the publisher, the present serial was conceived. Regrettably, Kenneth Spence was never to see in print even the first product of his editorial labors; he was struck down by cancer in January, 1967, shortly before the first volume appeared. After his unfortunate and untimely death, the decision was made to try to carry on with the ideals and objectives of this work. Accordingly, Gordon Bower was invited to share with Janet Spence editorial responsibility for its continuation. To this end plans have been made for the third and fourth volumes, and a number of distinguished investigators have accepted invitations to write research papers. The first two volumes seem indeed to be fulfilling the unique form of scientific communication which Kenneth Spence envisaged.

A serial publication such as this must be prepared to move where the research workers of a field take it. It must be responsive to the diverse trends on the current research scene, and not become committed to a particular tradition or viewpoint regarding what are "important" scientific problems. The former and current editors were and are fully aware that conceptual revolution and change reflect the vitality of a science that is progressing, and that the important scientific problems of tomorrow probably will not be the same as those of yesterday. Part of this expanding vitality of the field will inevitably appear in the definitional scope of the terms *learning* and *motivation*, and consequently in the range of topics discussed in a volume labeled by these categories. We cannot forecast whither this publication will be taken by its future contributors, but we shall always strive for contributions that are informative, provocative, and of first-class quality.

March, 1968

GORDON H. BOWER
JANET TAYLOR SPENCE

CONTENTS

CONTENTS OF VOLUME 1

INCENTIVE THEORY AND CHANGES IN REWARD[1]

Frank A. Logan

UNIVERSITY OF NEW MEXICO
ALBUQUERQUE, NEW MEXICO

I. Introduction

Of the basic phenomena encountered in the experimental analysis of the learning process, perhaps none has proved to be so intractable to an even temporarily satisfying theoretical description as that of experimental extinction. The closest was probably Pavlov's (1927) original postulation of an internal inhibitory process which, as every introductory psychology student is supposed to know, was suggested by such other

[1] This research was supported in part by grants from the National Science Foundation. Louis Gonzalez supervised the laboratory during the time these data were collected, and ran many of the subjects. In addition, Christopher Bennett, Alfred Coscina, Douglas Gibson, Albert Gonzales, and Eli Padilla assisted in collecting the data.

phenomena as spontaneous recovery and disinhibition. But when Hull (1943) attempted to formalize this approach within a more general and systematic behavior theory, difficulties became apparent. These are generally familiar, having been recited extensively in the literature (e.g., Gleitman, Nachmias, & Neisser, 1954; Koch, 1954), and while defenses and adjustments could be made, the superstructure required to support Hull's original account of experimental extinction would certainly lack parsimony.

Furthermore, there has been a trend among many contemporary learning theorists to reanalyze the distinction between learning and performance, particularly with reference to the concept of reinforcement. The emerging view is that learning, per se, results from a simple contiguity of the events being associated while reinforcement affects performance in a motivational manner. The contiguity principle was presaged by Guthrie (1934), but his system did not include the motivational flavor of more recent approaches; Tolman's (1932) theories were highly motivational, but were also heavily burdened with cognitive-sounding constructs. Intellectual descendents of both of these approaches, together with representatives from the several branches of the Hullian family tree, are more or less independently converging on a theoretical rapprochement.

One direction of convergence is apparent in some of my own work (e.g., Logan, 1960; Logan & Wagner, 1965) and is clearly evident in the writings of Cofer and Appley (1964), Miller (1963), Mowrer (1960), Seward (1956a, 1956b), F. D. Sheffield (1966), and Spence (1956, 1960). To be sure, there are important differences among these various approaches and none, in my opinion, has yet hit upon the key which will start the next round of fruitful theorizing on a grand scale. But the "new look of learning" must imply a new look at extinction; this paper attempts to outline several features of the problem and presents some relevant new data.

A. Incentive Effects in Partial Reinforcement

Let me begin by dogmatically asserting the language to be followed here. This language was visible in Hull's (1952) last version of his theory and has been elaborated more extensively by Spence (e.g., 1956). The critical words are "habit," "incentive," and "drive," which are here symbolized respectively sHr, sINr, and D. These combine multiplicatively to determine excitatory potential which, in turn, is reflected in performance as measured in various ways. Habit refers to a more or less permanent association between a stimulus and a response acquired gradually on the basis of contiguous occurrence of the events in question. Incentive is a learned motivational factor scalable both upward and downward to reflect the anticipated reward level based on contiguous experience of reward following a stimulus-response event. Drive is a temporary state property of the organism based in primary form upon conditions of deprivation or noxious stimulation and, in secondary form, upon stimuli previously associated with aversive states of affairs.

Considering instrumental reward conditioning within this language system, original acquisition results in at least two learning processes: habit and incentive. Under some conditions or reinforcement, drive may also be changed. Correspondingly, extinction could result from loss of habit, a loss of incentive, or a change in drive; probably all will be implicated in some situations. The particular purpose of this paper is to reflect upon the extent to which extinction involves changes in incentive motivation and the basic contention is that other accounts of extinction phenomena need to take incentive factors explicitly into consideration.

This last contention, together with the rationale of the present experimental approach, can be developed in the context of the familiar partial reinforcement effect on extinction (PREE): e.g., a rat that is given food reward on only part of the trials that he runs down an alley persists longer in running when reward is no longer given than a rat initially rewarded every trial. Let us first consider the early Hull-Sheffield (V. F. Sheffield, 1949) account of this phenomenon. Nonreward is assumed to produce a persisting aftereffect which, at least with reasonably short intertrial intervals, is present on the succeeding trial; partially rewarded rats encounter these nonreward stimuli during acquisition and learn to run in the presence of their aftereffects because doing so is sometimes rewarded. Continuously reinforced rats, in contrast, encounter these stimuli for the first time during extinction and suffer thereby a generalization decrement in *habit*. This approach emphasizes the rapidity of extinction following continuous reinforcement rather than the slowness of extinction following partial reinforcement. Particularly in view of the recent elaborations and evidence provided by Capaldi (1966), the aftereffects analysis is not only a logically necessary part of the PREE story but an empirically demonstrable one.

However, the aftereffects analysis does not make any explicit statements about incentive motivation. Presumably, insofar as incentive is elicited by the instrumental stimuli (including the aftereffects of reinforcement and nonreinforcement), a change in them would also produce a generalization decrement in incentive motivation. That is to say, continuously reinforced rats should have little incentive to run in the presence of the aftereffects of nonreinforcement and the performance decrement should also reflect this motivational change. But the rate at which incentive is decreased by further nonreinforcements is not specified nor even considered by an aftereffects analysis.

A more recent account of the PREE is provided by frustration theory (e.g., Amsel, 1962; Spence, 1960). Anecdotally, everyone is familiar with the fact that failure to receive an anticipated reward results in "frustration." The essence of the more formalized version is that frustration contributes to the state of drive motivation and that, like all drives, frustration drive has an associated drive stimulus with which overt responses may be associated. Furthermore, frustration is assumed to be a learnable drive so that it may occur in anticipatory fashion en route to a goal where primary frustration has been experienced. These basic assumptions account for the PREE as follows: continuously rewarded rats will be frustrated at the outset of extinction and will, on subsequent trials, begin to anticipate frustration. Although this added frustration drive increases total motivation, and might thereby increase performance, the initial unconditioned response to the frustration drive stimuli is assumed to be incompatible with the typical instrumental response. Extinction following continuous reinforcement reflects the occurrence of such competing responses in usual performance measures such as speed of locomotion. Partially reinforced rats, on the other hand, have encountered nonreward during acquisition, have thus experienced anticipatory frustration, and have been rewarded for continuing to respond in the presence of these conditioned frustration drive stimuli; hence, they continue to perform even though also frustrated during extinction.

Two factors are involved in the frustration theory account of the PREE: extinction produces an increase in *drive* (at least for the continuously reinforced rats) but the resulting change in the drive stimulus results in a loss of *habit* and the introduction of competing habits. Interestingly enough, frustration is assumed to occur only when and only so long as incentive motivation as an expectation of reward exists, yet explication of how partial reinforcement affects the level of incentive and the persistence of incentive during extinction have not yet been explicitly formulated. Inclusion of these rules is necessary for a complete frustration theory.

One might attempt to derive the properties of incentive motivation by assuming it to be mediated by a classically conditioned response mechanism such as the fractional anticipatory goal response (r_g-s_g). One specific version of this assumption is that the instrumental stimuli and the feedback stimuli from the instrumental response serve to elicit r_g and that the dynamism properties of s_g feed into the total motivational complex. On such an assumption, the laws of classical conditioning should provide the appropriate rules since r_g is assumed to be conditioned according to Pavlovian principles. Some comments on this approach are given in the next section.

B. Re r_g-s_g as the Mechanism of Incentive Motivation

In spite of the apparent appeal in employing the fractional anticipatory goal response as the mediating mechanism for incentive, there are several reasons for questioning the adequacy and generality of this approach. It may be of heuristic value to outline these reservations, and they also provide conceptual justification for the empirical analysis to be reported.

1. The first problem is strictly logical within the theory. Drive motivation (D) should affect the performance of any response, including r_g. Hence, D would be embedded within incentive motivation if the r_g-s_g analysis is followed. Accordingly, D would enter twice in determining instrumental performance (once in energizing the habit for r_g, and again in energizing the habit for the instrumental response itself). Of course, the theory could be changed in these respects so as to restrict the energizing role of drive to anticipatory goal responses, but an analysis would have to indicate how drive effects can be handled entirely through incentive motivation. (For an attempt at such an analysis, see Black, 1965.) For example, adding an irrelevant drive can increase performance (Kendler, 1945), but it is not immediately apparent how this could happen if r_g is selectively energized by drives (Spence, Bergmann, & Lippitt, 1950).

2. A second problem concerns the fact that r_g-s_g is also used, appropriately I believe, as the mediating mechanism for secondary reinforcement. A dual role for r_g-s_g in both incentive motivation and secondary reinforcement is not necessarily bad in its own right, but there appear to be asymmetries in secondary reinforcement and secondary motivation that would preclude this approach. These asymmetries warrant a brief aside.

Although less powerful and persistent than one might hope, secondary reinforcement is a readily demonstrable phenomenon when an originally neutral stimulus is paired with a *positive* reinforcement such as food (e.g., Zimmerman, 1957). In contrast, the weight of evidence indicates that a neutral stimulus paired with a *negative* reinforcement such as the termination of electrical shock, does not acquire learned reinforcing properties (e.g., Nefzger, 1957). There is an inverse asymmetry in the case of learned drive: stimuli paired with the onset of an aversive event acquire secondary motivating properties (e.g., Miller, 1948) while those associated with an increase in deprivation drives apparently do not (e.g., Novin & Miller, 1962). In short, as viewed in the format of a 2×2 matrix, hunger-food is effective for secondary reinforcement but not secondary motivation; pain-fear is effective for secondary motivation but not secondary reinforcement.

These asymmetries can be rationalized by attending to the response components of the events in question and assuming that *all* learning consists of S-R associations. The deprivation drives are not normally response-produced (e.g., one simply becomes hungry over time without making any special drive-inducing response) and hence there is no learnable response component to the deprivation drives; primary reinforcement based on these deprivation drives, however, is response-produced (e.g., the consummatory responses of eating, drinking, copulating) and hence there is a learnable response mechanism for secondary reinforcement. On the other hand, the pain-fear drive does contain learnable response components (arousal in the sympathetic branch of the autonomic nervous system) which can mediate secondary motivation, but primary reinforcement based on this drive is not response-produced (i.e., the aversive state simply terminates) so that no response mechanism for secondary reinforcement exists.

This analysis is not only consistent with the best available evidence in each case, but it also offers promise of rationalizing other perplexing facts. People will fast before Thanksgiving dinner, or eat pretzels while drinking beer, in each case "suffering" some increase in drive so as better to enjoy the consummatory reward. But a normal person will not, as the saying goes, hit his head against a wall because it feels so good to stop. There is no secondary motivation while there is greater secondary reinforcement associated with at least moderate increases in deprivation drives; the converse is true of stimulation drives.

This analysis shows that r_g-s_g is a useful mechanism for secondary reinforcement since it can account for the difference in the effects of positive and negative reinforcement as primary bases for learned reinforcement in a manner that is consistent with the difference between appetitional and aversive drives as primary bases of learned motivation. From the point of view of incentive motivation, however, positive and negative reinforcement do *not* appear to show any significant differences. Both are effective in conditioning and maintaining instrumental responses (see, e.g., Bower, 1960) and quantitative details concerning choice behavior as a measure of relative incentive effects appear comparable (e.g., Kaplan, Kaplan, & Walker, 1960). Accordingly, we may reasonably conclude that incentive motivation is controlled by the same type of process in positive and negative reinforcement. Were this process mediated via r_g-s_g in the case of positive reinforcement, an analogous response would have to be postulated for negative reinforcement (see, e.g., "relief" in Mowrer, 1960). The undesirable by-product of such an approach would be a learnable response mechanism for secondary reinforcement based on primary negative reinforcement, which would be contrary to the best available evidence on this issue.

3. An assortment of difficulties for r_g-s_g as a mediating mechanism

for incentive arise if one pays strict attention to the data in the relevant situations. As a specific illustration, the interstimulus-interval function in classical conditioning shows an optimum at somewhere between a half and one second; the delay of reinforcement gradient does not show such nonmonotonicity. As another example, Egger and Miller (1963) have recently shown that the later stimuli in a sequential chain of conditioned stimuli preceding an unconditioned stimulus do not come to control conditioned responses. As secondary reinforcers, only the early stimuli are effective. This should mean that r_g would not be evoked by the stimuli arising late in the instrumental behavior chain, although the common assumption in this regard is that incentive motivation increases progressively as the goal is approached. The detailed laws of classical conditioning have not yet been systematically applied to the incentive construct within a theory and hence the extent to which inconsistencies would be detected is not fully known. However, special problems would almost certainly arise from such realizations as that conditioned responses occur with some probability while incentive motivation must be present on every trial.

4. An empirical source of disillusionment concerns the attempts to identify salivation as a component of r_g and to obtain supporting evidence by recording and/or manipulating salivation during instrumental conditioning. By and large, the results of these efforts have not been very encouraging (see, e.g., Lewis & Kent, 1961) although a few suggestive results have been reported (e.g., Shapiro, 1962). It may be granted that salivation has been used simply to illustrate the logic of an r_g-s_g mechanism; r_g as an intervening variable need not be physiologically localized and hence the failures with salivation are indeed not crucial. But to many observers, the salivation illustration is simply too good: the necessary features (e.g., a learnable component of the goal response that is not incompatible with the instrumental response) are present and it ought to work better.

5. Finally, an approach in which incentive motivation is mediated by a response mechanism is most appropriate for a theory utilizing a cybernetic-feedback type of analysis, especially if incentive is assumed to contribute to the general motivational level (but see Trapold, 1962, for contrary evidence). Indeed, this is the context in which it is typically employed (e.g., Miller, 1963; Mowrer, 1960; F. D. Sheffield, 1966; Spence, 1960). In these analyses, the organism is assumed somehow to be behaving; feedback from his behavior is available and is, through prior conditioning, associated with the incentive-mediating response mechanism which, in turn, fosters either continuation of the ongoing behavior or change, presumably toward a more optimal level. Miller and Sheffield have, somewhat differently, included response habits on which to base the choice of responses. Although this type of approach has a

great deal of appeal and most probably indicates the direction of future theorizing, it does not readily permit incentive motivation to act selectively at the instant of choice. This difficulty is most obvious at the moment of initiation of a response, but actually recurs continuously during a behavior chain.

To emphasize the difficulty in the context of response initiation, one might postulate that the organism covertly scans the domain of possible responses, receives internal and external feedback from each of these, and selects the one with which the most vigorous r_g is associated. In its simplest and most visible form, this type of behavior is seen in the VTE behavior of rats at a choice point in a maze (Spence, 1960; Tolman, 1932). Even in that context, however, a complete theory must postulate additional storage and comparative mechanisms that enable the organism to select the optimal response. For example, a rat rewarded differentially in both arms of a T-maze might happen to orient toward the arm containing the smaller reward. The feedback cues available in that orientation elicit some r_g, but the rat must be assumed to have the capacity to withhold continuation of that response; he must be assumed to store that level of r_g while orienting toward the other arm where the there-appropriate r_g is in turn elicited; following these orientations, the r_g's must be compared so that their relative strengths can determine choice. These molecular details have not been explicitly incorporated into a behavior theory of even this simple situation, much less the more complex, freer situations where, for example, the rat is choosing a speed of locomotion. It seems improbable that any organism has the time or resources to make momentary decisions on the basis of implicit monitoring of all possible courses of action.

It is, of course, possible that a sufficiently molecular analysis will ultimately show that this approach is realistically tractable. At the present time, however, it appears preferable to conceptualize incentive motivation as specific to different S-R events and immediately given as a basis for choice before the choice is made. Feedback from prior behavior is certainly a component of the total stimulus complex in which decisions occur but incentive motivational differences among the responses to be made must be available in advance. That is to say, the r_g associated with the feedback from the response in the *next* instant is important as a secondary reinforcer and to help guide the ensuing behavior, but this feedback cannot possibly be present at the actual moment of choice before the response is made.

C. Rationale

On the basis of the above arguments, the view adopted here is that incentive motivation is a fundamental process like habit (i.e., it is not mediated) that changes according to mathematical rules as a result of experience. Each quantitative value of reward is presumably associated with an incentive value toward which incentive motivation approaches as a limit. That is to say, incentive motivation has some value before any trial; if the reward encountered on that trial has an associated incentive value differing from the existing level, then some change occurs toward the level appropriate to the reward received. The simplest such model would assume that the change is a constant fraction of the discrepancy, and that the same rule applies whether the change is an increase or a decrease in incentive motivation.

Existing data suggest that this simple model is not correct, at least with respect to the incremental and decremental rates. Were these rates identical, then the net incentive value of varied reward would always be equal to the mean of the incentive values of the rewards involved; this implication has not been confirmed (e.g., Logan, 1960, 1965). The best interpretation of these data at the moment is that the incremental rate is greater than the decremental rate, at least under varied reward. That is to say, if incentive increases toward a higher level on each trial with a large reward and decreases toward a lower level on each trial with a small reward, the running average level will exceed the mean of the separate levels only if the former rate is greater than the latter. In short, incentive motivation appears to be gained faster than it is lost.

It is still possible, however, that these rates of change in incentive motivation are state characteristics of the organism and are not subject to modification by prior experimental conditions. It is this question to which the present research is addressed. Specifically, is the rate at which sINr changes modifiable?

The approach begins with a definitional assumption: other things (such as exposure) being equal, choice between two alternative courses of action reflects their *relative* incentive value. In practice, holding "other things equal" is difficult: the organism may have a position, brightness, or similar preference over and above any incentive effects. In principle, however, choice depends on relative momentary excitatory potential as mainly determined by incentive differences based on prior reward experiences.

Suppose, then, that a rat is given a choice between two alternatives, one continuously and the other partially rewarded. The rat should learn to select the continuously rewarded alternative (see e.g., Davenport, 1963). This direct comparison establishes, by definition, the relative incentive value of the alternatives: sINr is greater following 100% than 50% reward.

Suppose further that after the rat has faced these alternatives and has demonstrated his preference, he is then confronted with extinction conditions in *both* alternatives. Should incentive motivation decrease at the same relative rate in both alternatives in spite of their different prior reinforcement history, preference should decrease monotonically toward indifference. However, should incentive motivation decrease more rapidly after continuous reinforcement, preference should temporarily reverse to the initially 50% alternative. To repeat: after rats have learned to select a 100% in preference to a 50% alternative, will there be a (temporary) reversal of preference when both are continuously nonreinforced during joint extinction? If so, incentive motivation must persist longer after partial than after continuous reward and thus the rate of change in sINr must not be invariant.

The approach to be described followed this general rationale. Rate of change in sINr was evaluated by the rate of change in preference following a change in the reward conditions. In order to make the conclusions as general as possible, several conditions of changed reward were studied. In each case, however, the same logic of monitoring choice behavior provided the rationale for inferring incentive motivational effects.

II. Method

A. Subjects

The *S*s were 232 hooded rats predominantly bred in the colony maintained by the Department of Psychology of the University of New Mexico. Additional rats from one replication of several of the studies were discarded when it subsequently became apparent that the strain had become so highly inbred at that time that the data were unusually insensitive to reward effects. Other rats were excluded because they showed such strong position/brightness preferences that no variability in their early choice behavior occurred; still others were deleted at random to equate N's for analysis and to ensure appropriate counterbalancing. The inclusion of these discarded data would, of course, add noise to the graphic presentation of the results but would not, in fact, alter any of the conclusions.

Age, sex, and source of the rats were counterbalanced across the conditions within any study. These are not reported because subanalyses failed to indicate any significant interactions with these factors. During the experimental treatments all *S*s were maintained in individual cages with water freely available. They were maintained on approximately 12 gm per day of laboratory chow given immediately after each day's session.

B. Apparatus

Two apparatuses were employed, half the *S*s in each study normally running in each apparatus. These consisted of pairs of parallel straight alleys, differing principally in that one pair was 4 feet and the other 8 feet long. All doors in the short apparatus were fully automated; the goal box door in the long apparatus was manually operated. In each apparatus, one alley was black and the other white, confounded with position. Speeds were recorded from reciprocal-reading clocks that started with the breaking of photobeams located approximately 3 inches outside the start door and stopped with the breaking of photobeams located inside the food cups; these were individually converted into feet per second for treatment.

Rats were confined in the goal section of the alley after completing the response. Food reward consisted of 45-mg Noyes pellets. These were delivered immediately upon breaking of the food-cup photobeam by Davis feeders pulsed at a rate of about six per second. Rats were removed after consuming the reward or after about 10 seconds on nonreward trials.

C. Procedure

*S*s were preadapted to the appropriate apparatus on an adjusting shaping schedule. First, groups of four rats were permitted freely to explore the maze for approximately 30 minutes with all doors open and with food pellets available in the food cups. This exploration was followed by individual magazine training in the goal sections of each alley with CRF programmed on the food-cup photobeam. By the time training proper began, each *S* was eating readily from each food cup and had adapted to the sound of the feeding mechanism.

Rats were run in squads of four on a rotating basis, producing a somewhat variable intertrial interval averaging after the initial trials about 3–4 minutes. Six trials per day were run, the first four trials being forced according to one of the following patterns rotated over blocks of 4 days: RRLL, RLLR, LRRL, LLRR. The fifth trial was then a free-choice trial providing the basis for observation of preference, followed by a final forced trial opposite in direction to that chosen on the fifth trial.

The assigned reward conditions simply prevailed from the beginning of training proper. When partial reinforcement was scheduled in any alley, a preassigned sequence was followed that distributed six reinforcements over the 12 trials in that alley during each block of 4 days. The sequence was designed to ensure that each ordinal trial position received equal frequency of reinforcement. Specifically, for example, half of the choice trials would be programmed for reinforcement if that alternative were chosen.

The competing reward alternatives were counterbalanced across alleys in each study. There was a slight initial preference for the black alley, but the terminal data did not depend importantly on which alley received which reward.

III. Experimental Designs and Results

A. Experiment 1. Joint Extinction Following Partial and Continuous Reinforcement

The first experiment followed the design described in the introduction. Sixteen rats were given a large reward every trial on which they ran down one alley (100% 9A) and were given the same large reward on an irregular half of the trials that they ran down the other alley (50% 9A). These conditions prevailed for a relatively large number of training trials (42 days at six trials per day, totaling 126 trials in each alley before extinction), the expectation being that the combination of a large reward and prolonged training would maximize the chance that the continuously reinforced response would undergo relatively rapid extinction. It will be recalled that the rats would be expected to show a temporary reversal of preference if incentive motivation following partial reinforcement persists longer than that following continuous reinforcement.

The results are shown in Fig. 1, the wide-lined curve showing the percent choice of the continuously reinforced alley during the last 12 days of original acquisition and throughout 36 days of joint extinction. It is apparent that no reversal occurred. The curve became somewhat unstable during the later stages of nonreinforcement but never dropped below the 50% level. This result indicates that incentive motivation did not persist longer in the partial-reward alley.

One possible complication with this interpretation of the results of this design arises from the concept of the generalized partial reinforcement effect (Brown & Logan, 1965). This effect refers to the fact that an instrumental response that is, in its own right, reinforced continuously may nevertheless show increased resistance to extinction if a similar response has received partial reinforcement. Persistence trained in one situation tends to generalize to similar situations. Evidence that such a phenomenon occurred with respect to the instrumental performance measure in the present design is also depicted in Fig. 1 by the narrow-lined curves connecting solid points. These show the response speeds separately for the continuously and partially reinforced responses by the rats encountering both conditions and given a choice between them. It is clear that there was little difference in the speed measure during extinction, the rats running, if anything, somewhat faster in the alley that had been continuously reinforced.

This phenomenon is emphasized by observing the solid narrow-lined curve connecting open points in Fig. 1 which shows the speed of responding during extinction by a control group given only continuous reinforcement in a single alley. It is clear from comparing the two solid curves

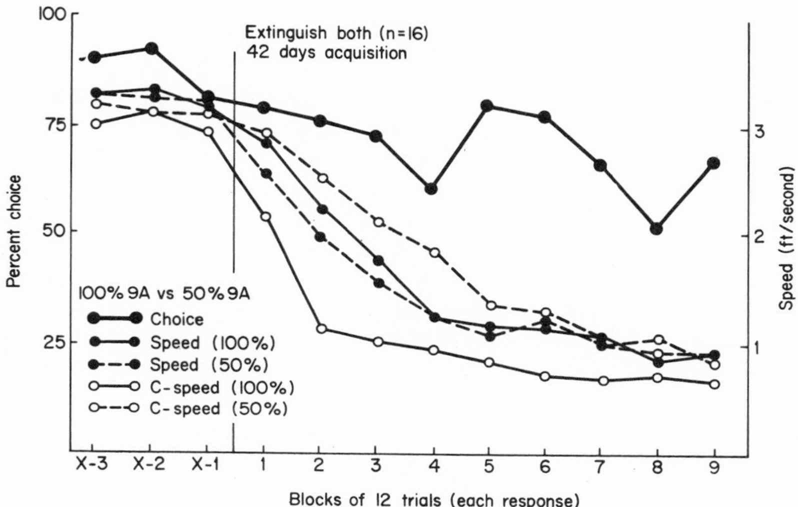

FIG. 1. Choice behavior during joint extinction following initial training with partial and continuous reinforcement in two alternative alleys. Graphed are the last 12 of 42 days of acquisition and 36 days of extinction. Speed data in the two alleys are also depicted, together with the speeds of control groups that received only partial or only continuous reinforcement before extinction.

that extinction proceeded more rapidly when no other response was included that was trained with partial reinforcement. A converse effect can also be seen in Fig. 1 by referring to the dashed narrow-lined curve connecting open points, which shows running speed during extinction following partial reinforcement for a control group that did not also encounter joint extinction of a continuously reinforced response. The apparent greater resistance to extinction following partial reinforcement when extinguished separately was evaluated statistically by determining for each rat the trial block on which his speed first fell below the midpoint between his individual asymptotes at the end of training and extinction. The difference was highly significant by the Mann–Whitney U Test ($z = 4.26$, $df = 49$, $p < .01$).

Accordingly, it must be recognized that two generalization effects on instrumental performance are embedded in the joint extinction design, the one being increased resistance to extinction following continuous reinforcement and the other being reduced resistance to extinction following partial reinforcement. Whether these effects are indeed critical for the conclusion suggested by the choice data depends upon the conceptual basis for the generalization effects themselves. If they represent incentive motivational effects, then the choice data are clearly biased against finding any differences in preference during joint extinction. If, however, the generalization effects represent transfer of instrumental performance factors, such as running habits in the presence of cues of nonreinforcement, then the preference data are uniquely sensitive to changes in incentive motivation. Although this latter interpretation seems at least equally probable, additional studies were run to search for possible differential incentive effects.

B. Experiment 2. Reacquisition Following Original Training with Partial and Continuous Reinforcement

A somewhat different approach to the question of whether or not extinction has differential effects on incentive motivation following partial and continuous reinforcement arises in the context of reacquisition. Since performance during extinction differs radically following these training conditions, the effects on incentive might differ in a way that could be detected by the reintroduction of reward. Specifically, for example, if continuously reinforced rats stop instrumental performance rapidly because of other-than-incentive factors such as a generalization decrement in habit, then they might have more residual incentive motivation than partially reinforced rats who persist longer in making the instrumental response. Hence, reacquisition might progress at different rates following extinction after initial training with partial or continuous reinforcement.

To evaluate this possibility, the control groups shown in Fig. 1 were run for an additional 60 trials with reward again present. Reacquisition conditions were run under continuous reinforcement for some rats and under partial reinforcement for others in order to control for possible generalization decrements due to change from the original training conditions. The results are plotted in Fig. 2. It is apparent that all groups reacquired the running response rapidly, and somewhat more rapidly with continuous than with partial reinforcement during this stage of the experiment. But no noticeable differences occurred during reacquisition as a residual from the original acquisition reinforcement conditions. Accordingly, in spite of dramatic differences in instrumental performance during extinction following partial and continuous reinforcement, there are no apparent differences in the persisting effects of nonreinforcement insofar as these can be seen in instrumental performance after reintroduction of reward.

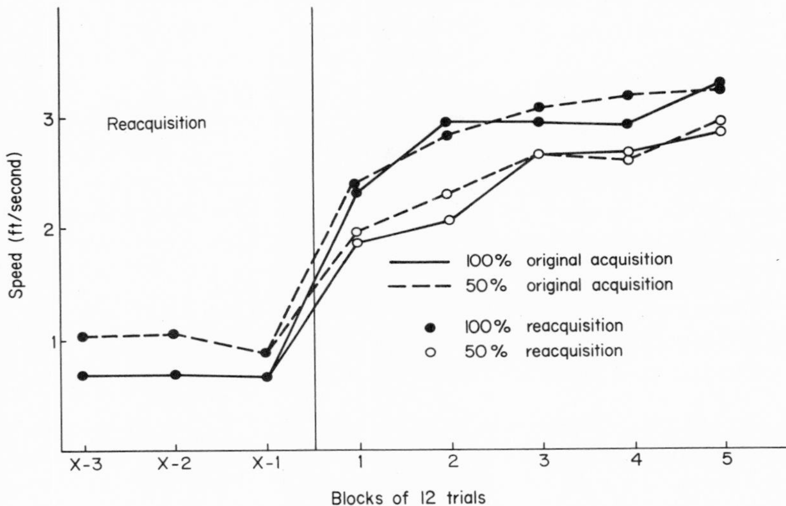

FIG. 2. Speeds during reacquisition by groups originally trained with either partial or continuous reinforcement and split after extinction to receive reacquisition training with either partial or continuous reinforcement. Graphed are the last 12 trials of extinction (the earlier data being shown as the control groups in Fig. 1) and 60 trials of reacquisition.

C. EXPERIMENTS 3 AND 4. REVERSAL OF CHOICE FOLLOWING PARTIAL AND CONTINUOUS REINFORCEMENT

In an attempt to minimize the possible role of generalization effects, a between-groups design was employed to compare the rates of loss of incentive motivation following partial and continuous reward. Two groups of rats received a large reward in one alley, one group receiving the reward on every trial (100% 9A) and the other group receiving the large reward on an irregular half of their trials in that alley (50% 9A). *Both* groups received a small reward *continuously* (100% 1A) in the other alley. The selection of these amounts of reward was intended to ensure that both groups would initially prefer the large-reward alternative, although presumably the incentive basis for this preference would be somewhat greater with continuous than with partial reinforcement.

After clear evidence of such preference for the larger reward was apparent (28 days at six trials per day), extinction conditions were initiated in the large-reward alley for both groups. The small reward was still given to both groups on every trial in the alternative alley. Accordingly, both groups would be expected ultimately to come to prefer the

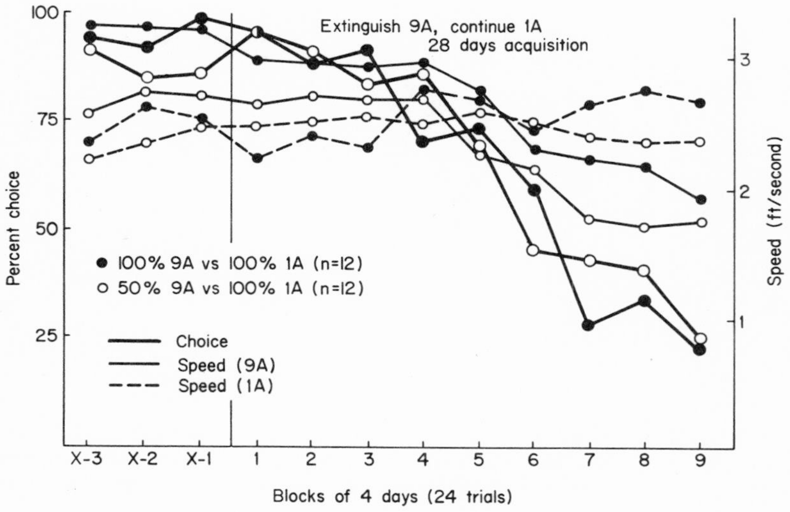

FIG. 3. Choice behavior during reversal by groups initially given partial or continuous large reward opposed to continuous small reward, and then extinguished in the large-reward alternative. Graphed are the last 12 of 28 days of acquisition and 36 days following the change. Speeds for each group in each alternative are also depicted.

small-reward alley since it was now pitted against no reward. By using this procedure, the incentive motivation that persisted in the large-reward alley during extinction could be monitored relative to that maintained in the small reward alley. If incentive motivation persists longer following partial reinforcement, reversal toward a small reward should be slower following partial large reward than following continuous large reward.

The results of this experiment are shown graphically in Fig. 3. The wide-lined curves again show percent choice of the originally large reward alley, beginning during the last 12 days of exposure to the original conditions and proceeding through 36 days during which extinction prevailed in that alley. It is apparent that reversal was not particularly rapid for either group and that there were no noticeable differences in the rate at which reversal took place. Accordingly, even in this between-groups design, there is no evidence that incentive motivation persisted longer following partial than continuous reinforcement.

Because some possible generalized partial reinforcement effects may also arise in this differential-reinforcement procedure, especially following a relatively small amount of discrimination training (Brown & Logan,

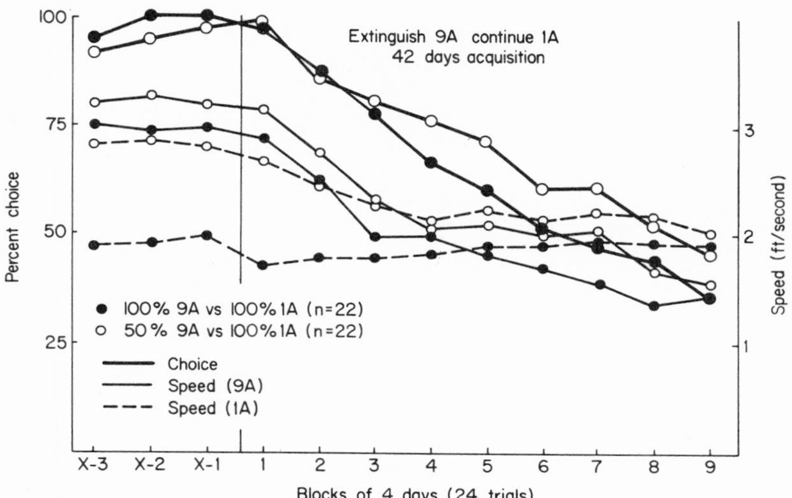

FIG. 4. Choice behavior following a replication of the conditions shown in Fig. 3 except that 50% overtraining was given before extinction of the large-reward alternative. Graphed are the last 12 of 42 days of acquisition and 36 days following the change. Speeds for each group in each alternative are also depicted.

1965), the procedure was repeated with new rats who were given sufficient overtraining to minimize further any generalization effects. Specifically, 42 days under the original reward conditions were given before the large-reward alley underwent extinction. This represents 50% overtraining beyond that given the previous groups in this design; otherwise, the procedures were identical.

The results are shown in Fig. 4. The choice data are depicted by the wide-lined curves and, although the partial group remained somewhat above the continuous group during the later portions of the extinction phase, this difference was absolutely quite small and did not approach statistical significance. Again, the evidence suggests that incentive motivation did not persist longer following partial reinforcement than following continuous reinforcement, at least insofar as this is reflected in the rate at which this persisting incentive is able to compete successfully with the incentive produced by a continuous small reward.

Attention to the speed data also shown in Fig. 4 reveals several relevant results. Comparing the two solid curves, it can be seen that asymptotic running speed was greater with partial large reward than with continuous large reward, and that this difference persisted during extinction. Thus, although perhaps attenuated in this design, the partial reinforcement effects on both acquisition and extinction were evident in the instrumental response speed measures even though no differential incentive-motivational effects were found in choice. A new finding of potential significance is seen by comparison of the two dashed curves in Fig. 4, which show the running speed of the two groups to the small reward. There was a clear and statistically significant difference in their running speeds at the end of original training, the group receiving partial reinforcement in the other alley running faster for the small reward than the group receiving continuous reinforcement in the other alley ($t = 5.62$, $df = 43$, $p < .01$).

There are two alternative interpretations of this speed difference. On the one hand, it could be argued that a small reward suffers more by contrast with continuous large reward than with partial large reward. Fortunately, this interpretation can be ruled out by attending to performance in the small-reward alley during extinction in the large-reward alley. The group that had received continuous large reward maintained a relatively steady speed in the small-reward alley while the group that had received partial large reward gradually slowed down in the small-reward alley. This suggests that the faster speed to the small reward by the latter group resulted from some facilitating performance effect generalizing from the partial-reward alley.

A reasonable account may be referred to as the *generalized frustration effect*. The presumption would be that being forced to run in the small-reward alley is somewhat frustrating because of the experience of a large reward in the other alley (i.e., the reward for entering the start box varies between large and small eventual reward). If the large reward is given on only part of the trials, the rat also experiences anticipatory frustration in that alley where he sometimes receives a large reward for running. The resulting tendency to run in spite of anticipatory frustration should generalize to the small-reward alley and the added frustration drive should contribute to instrumental performance there. In contrast, the group receiving continuous large reward experiences anticipatory frustration only when forced to run in the small-reward alley where running is never reinforced with a large reward. Their instrumental performance therefore reflects a more nearly perfect discrimination of the reward conditions.

D. The Overtraining Extinction Effect

A number of studies (e.g., North & Stimmel, 1960) have recently appeared suggesting that overtraining of an instrumental response may lead to reduced resistance to extinction of that response compared with smaller amounts of training. This phenomenon, then, is another instance in which differential rates of change in incentive motivation might possibly be detected. Evidence against such an interpretation can be seen by comparison of Figs. 3 and 4. It will be recalled that the only difference between these studies concerned the number of training trials given prior to extinction of the large-reward alley. Hence, if incentive motivation decreased more rapidly following overtraining (with either partial or continuous reward) then the reversal in Fig. 4 should have been faster than that in Fig. 3. It is clear that no such difference occurred, reversal of preference being essentially equally gradual in both instances. Examination of the speed curves, however, *does* show a more precipitous decline after overtraining. But there is no evidence that the overtraining extinction effect represents changes in the rate of extinction of incentive motivation.

E. Experiment 5. Effect of Amount of Reward on Resistance to Extinction of Incentive Motivation

Recent evidence (e.g., Hulse, 1958) indicates that, at least after a substantial amount of training, instrumental extinction proceeds more rapidly with large as compared with small rewards. Experiment 5 was designed to determine whether this phenomenon might reflect an effect on the rate of change in incentive motivation. Furthermore, since the amount-of-reward effect on extinction appears to be specific to continuous reinforcement, partial reward conditions were also included.

Two groups of rats received a large reward in one alley and a small reward in the other alley, one group receiving both of these rewards continuously and the other group receiving both of these rewards on an irregular 50% partial reinforcement schedule. After 42 days of acquisition under these conditions, both alleys were subjected to joint extinction. Consistent with the logic developed previously, if extinction of incentive motivation proceeded more rapidly following the large as compared with the small reward, preference should show a temporary reversal toward the small-reward alley.

The results are shown in Fig. 5. The heavy-lined curves show the choice data for the two groups separately, and it is clear that no reversal occurred. Instead, both curves drifted gradually toward indifference in response to continued nonreinforcement. Attention to the speed curves does reveal that the rate of extinction as measured by instrumental performance was greater following continuous large reward than following continuous small reward, and that this differential rate of extinction did not occur comparing partial-large against partial-small rewards. The speed data are thus consistent with those obtained in between-group designs, but again the choice data do not indicate that these effects are based on differential rates of change in incentive motivation.

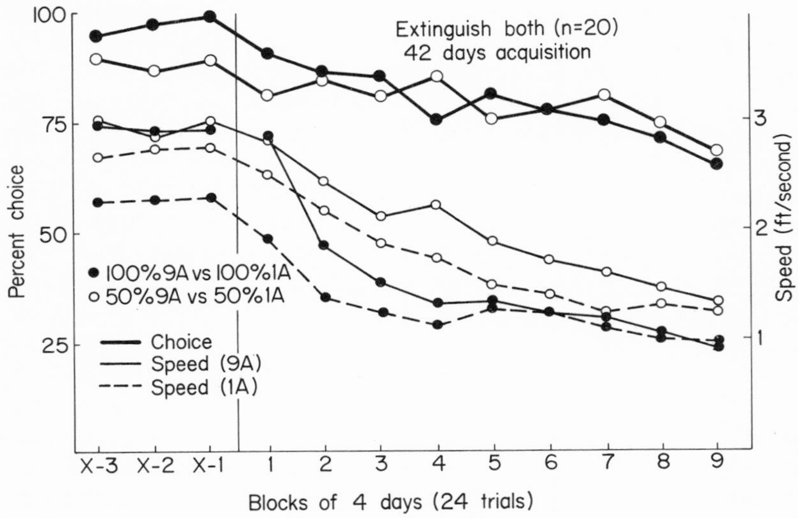

FIG. 5. Choice behavior during joint extinction following initial training with a large reward in one alternative and a small reward in the other. One group received both rewards continuously and the other group received both rewards on an irregular half of their trials in each alley. Graphed are the last 12 of 42 days of acquisition followed by 36 days of joint extinction. Speeds for each group in each alternative are also depicted.

The data in Fig. 5, incidentally, afford an additional confirmation of the comparison of extinction rates following partial and continuous reward as studied in Experiments 1, 3, and 4. In this case, if *differential* incentive persisted longer for the partial group than the continuous group, choice should have dropped more slowly toward indifference. The close overlap of the choice curves in Fig. 5 indicates that no such rate changes were involved.

F. EXPERIMENT 6. INCENTIVE CONTRAST

The phenomenon of incentive contrast has had a somewhat rocky history. The term refers to the possibility that the effective incentive value of a particular amount of reward depends in part upon the context in which it is embedded. Specifically, a small reward might have less incentive value if the subject is accustomed also to receiving a larger reward in the same or a similar situation and, conversely, a large reward might have still greater incentive value if given in a context containing smaller rewards. In short, the incentive motivation produced by a reward may be relative rather than absolute.

There are reasonable a priori grounds for anticipating such a phenomenon. A reward, after all, is a stimulus which must be perceived by the subject. In principle, therefore, the laws of perception should apply as much to reward stimuli as to any other, and one pervasive perceptual principle is that of contrast. The size, weight, intensity, etc. of stimuli are known to be perceived in relation to the context (Sherif, Taub, & Hovland, 1958), including events occurring somewhat previously in time. This argument would lead one to suspect that some contrast effects might be found in the area of incentive motivation.

It is, however, important to distinguish clearly between a reward as a stimulus event and the hypothetical construct of incentive motivation. Scaling the incentive value of different rewards might, at first thought, appear to be a psychophysical problem and indeed, certain gross similarities are evident. For example, a constant absolute increase in the amount of reward produces a progressively smaller increase in incentive motivation the larger the amounts involved (Logan, 1965). However, the "perceived size" of the reward, while perhaps a necessary precurser of its incentive value, is not necessarily equivalent to incentive motivation. For example, a rat might be able to detect the difference between 20 and 30 pellets of reward when viewed as stimuli, but the latter might not produce greater incentive motivation than the former. In short, incentive value is a property of some stimuli, namely rewards, which should be distinguished from the cue value of such stimuli.

Early evidence suggesting incentive contrast was provided independently by Crespi (1944) and Zeaman (1949). These investigators trained hungry rats in a simple instrumental running response first with either a large or a small amount of food reward. Subsequently, the reward sizes were switched, and performance not only changed in the appropriate directions but appeared to overshoot the appropriate levels. That is to say, the rats that were shifted from a small to a large reward not only increased in running speed, but ran faster than the rats that had been trained initially with the larger reward; conversely, the rats that were shifted to the smaller reward at least temporarily ran slower than the rats initially trained with the smaller reward. These data suggested that the new value of reward contrasted with the earlier value that the rats had been accustomed to receiving.

These results have been criticized (Spence, 1956) on the grounds that the original training may not have been carried fully to asymptote and that the group shifted to the larger reward may have run faster not because of any incentive contrast effect but because additional habit was being acquired during the postshift trials. Subsequent studies have tended to favor this interpretation; a number of studies are now available (e.g., Ehrenfreund and Badia, 1962) indicating that the upward shift in amount of reward does not always produce the overshoot seen in the earlier data. These latter studies, however, may also be criticized because the larger reward employed has probably been near or at the upper limit of potential incentive value. That is to say, a large reward might appear still larger by contrast with concurrent or preceding smaller rewards, but if the incentive value of the large reward is already maximal, any such contrast would not appear in instrumental performance.

Other studies that might reveal an incentive contrast phenomenon have employed a concurrent exposure to different amounts of reward. For example, Bower (1961) and Goldstein and Spence (1963) gave rats a small reward in an alley of one color and a large reward in another alley. The performances of these rats were separated for the two alleys and compared with control rats receiving all of their training with either the large or small reward. These results have been consistent in showing no contrast effect with respect to the large reward although some of the data suggest that performance with a small reward may be inferior if the rats are concurrently encountering a large reward in a similar situation. The same possible criticism with respect to the upper limit of incentive applies and, in addition, there is the question of the extent to which incentive effects generalize between the situations so as to provide a basis for contrast. The unresolved issue is the degree to which the situations would have to be similar for different rewards to show any effective contrast as opposed to complete discrimination of the rewards appropriate to the different situations.

The limiting case of similarity, of course, is to give different rewards in the same situation. This procedure of varied reward has been studied most systematically by Beier (see Logan, 1960) but the inability to infer the incentive value of the rewards separately makes any interpretation based on contrast highly speculative. However, suggestive analyses in favor of such a phenomenon were reported.

Some data bearing on this issue were presented in Fig. 4. Rats received a large reward in one alley and a small reward in the other alley followed by extinction in the large-reward alley while the small reward continued. If one refers to the running speed in the small-reward alley when it was initially paired with a large reward and subsequently paired with no reward, it is apparent that no differences appeared. That is to say, the rats ran as well toward one pellet reward when they were receiving nine pellets in the other alley as when they were receiving nothing in the other alley. This presumably indicates that incentive was more or less perfectly discriminated and that no contrast effects, upward or downward, occur in this situation.

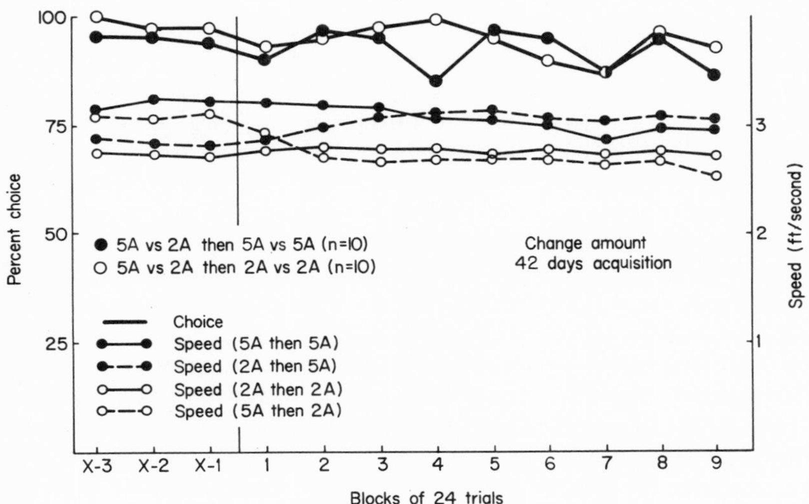

FIG. 6. Choice behavior after reward was equalized following initial training with differential reinforcement. Equalization was achieved by increasing the small reward for one group and by decreasing the large reward for the other group. Graphed are the last 12 of 42 days of acquisition followed by 36 days with equal rewards. Speeds for each group in each alternative are also depicted.

Experiment 6 was intended to study the possibility of an incentive contrast effect within the context using the within-groups design permitting observation of choice behavior. Two groups were initially given a relatively large reward (5A) in one alley and a relatively small reward (2A) in the other alley. The choice of these amounts was intended to ensure some initial preference for the larger reward but still leaving room both above and below the initial values for possible incentive contrast effects to be detected. Following 42 days of acquisition under these conditions, the amount of reward was equated in the two alleys. This was accomplished for one group by increasing the reward in the one alley from two to five pellets; for the other group, the reward in the other alley was decreased from five to two pellets. If the alleys subjected to a change in amount of reward should show incentive contrast effects, preference should at least temporarily reverse to the alley originally containing the small reward. For the one group, that alley was shifted to five pellets which could contrast above the five pellets continued in the other alley; for the other group, that alley continued at two pellets while the other alley could be contrasted below that level because of reduction to two pellets.

The results of this study are shown in Fig. 6. The wide-lined curves show that choice behavior continued to reveal a quite strong preference for the alley originally containing the larger reward, even though the rewards were now equated. Clearly, no tendency for reversal of preference occurred. Appropriate changes did occur in the speed measures corresponding to the changes in amount of reward, and small but statistically insignificant elation and depression effects were obtained. The changes observed in the instrumental response measure, however, apparently do not reflect incentive motivational factors.

G. Experiment 7. Rate of Increase in Incentive Motivation

The previous studies in this series have concentrated primarily on possible changes in the rate at which incentive motivation is lost. Possible effects on the incremental rate are, of course, of equal importance. Instrumental studies showing such an effect are not available, but a likely candidate would be partial reinforcement. It is known that classically conditioned responses shift gradually following a change from partial to continuous reinforcement (Spence & Trapold, 1961) and a similar phenomenon might occur with respect to incentive motivation.

Experiment 7 sought to evaluate this possibility. Two groups of rats received an intermediate-sized reward (3A) continuously in one alley; one group received nothing in the other alley and the second group received partial large reward (50% 5A). The choice of these values was based on our earlier work (Logan, 1965) on quantifying incentive motivation, since 3A would be expected to be preferred, at least to some extent, to 50% 5A.

Following 42 days of acquisition under these conditions, both groups were given the large reward (5A) continuously in the one alley while 3A was continued in the other alley. Thus, preference should reverse toward the alley now containing five pellets (although the degree of preference over three pellets would not be expected to be complete), and interest resides in the rate at which this reversal takes place. If the group increased from nothing to five pellets acquired that level of incentive motivation more rapidly than the group accustomed to partial-five pellets, then reversal could occur more rapidly in the former group.

The results are plotted in Fig. 7. It is clear that the groups attained different levels of preference during the original 42 days of acquisition, thus making the rate comparisons somewhat difficult. Even so, however, there is no indication that the group shifted from partial to continuous took longer to reverse than the group shifted from nothing to continuous large reward. If anything, the latter obtained, presumably reflecting the initial difference in preference. Hence, these data do not suggest that the incremental rate parameter for incentive motivation is modified by prior reinforcement history.

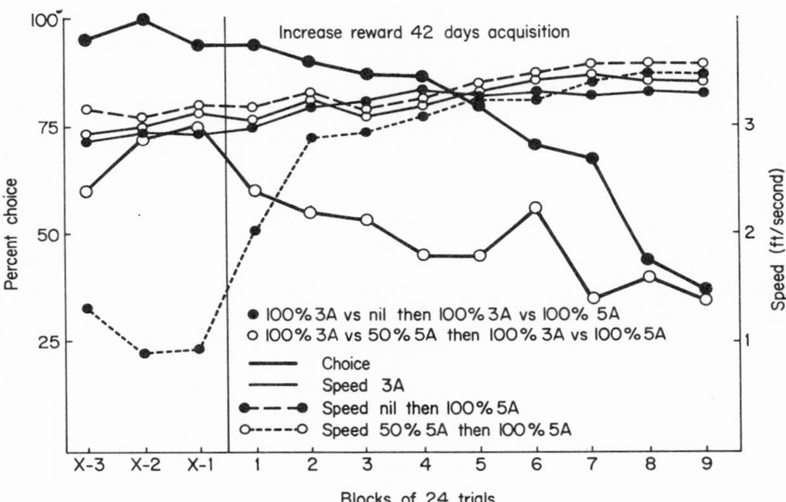

FIG. 7. Choice behavior during reversal when a relatively small reward was initially pitted against either nothing or partial reinforcement with a relatively large reward and was subsequently pitted against continuous reinforcement. Graphed are the last 12 of 42 days of acquisition followed by 36 days for reversal. Speeds for each group in each alternative are also depicted.

IV. Discussion

Changes in incentive motivation are essential aspects of contemporary theories of learning, but little explicit attention has been paid to the rate at which such changes take place. Were incentive motivation mediated by a response mechanism such as r_g-s_g, then the laws of classical conditioning would suffice to describe incentive change effects. However, since reasonable questions can be raised about a mediational approach to incentive motivation, the present research program attempted to evaluate the question empirically.

Incentive motivation is only one of the conceptual determinants of instrumental performance, and hence cannot be measured directly. Nevertheless, it is assumed that choice between two alternatives that are otherwise equivalent can be used to index their *relative* incentive values. Accordingly, changes in choice behavior were monitored following a variety of changes in reward, including partial reinforcement, overtraining, and amount of reward. In each case, the choice data failed to reveal any effect of these procedures on the rate at which incentive motivation changed. Simultaneous measurements of the speed of instrumental responding showed effects which, while somewhat attenuated, were consistent with those found in between-group designs. They are also consistent with the results of the extensive series of studies by Amsel (1967) using the speed measure in closely related within-subject experiments.

The implication, then, is that the rate of change in incentive motivation is a state parameter of the subject and is not affected by prior reinforcement history.

As for any conclusion of this potential significance, other types of procedures and other species of subjects should be studied before generality can be assumed. Indeed, several reservations might be noted in the results of the present program. Most obviously, generalization effects between the two alleys may have been sufficiently great that evaluation of their independent properties could not be assessed. This possibility has been mentioned earlier and data suggesting this problem were noted. However, the fact that appropriate changes in response speed did occur in many of the studies combined with the recognition that consistent differences have been obtained in earlier studies using these procedures make this reservation about the conclusion somewhat doubtful.

Perhaps a more critical problem concerns the sensitivity of the choice measure to transitory changes in incentive motivation. The gradual reversals of preference obtained in all of the studies suggests that the choice response includes some habit factors over and above any innate brightness/position preferences and the prevailing reward conditions. This is most evident in Experiment 6 (Fig. 6) where choice behavior continued with little change even after the rewards had been equalized in the two alleys. That is to say, choice habits acquired on the basis of initial differences in reward tended to persist when no other basis for preference existed. It is possible, therefore, that these habits cannot be overcome rapidly enough to show the temporary effects that changed rewards are having on incentive motivation. In short, changes in preference may lag behind changes in incentive motivation.

This problem cannot be resolved within the context of these studies, and must temper the conclusion accordingly. However, it would seem reasonable to expect that, were conceptually significant effects involved, some suggestion of these would have appeared somewhere in the total pattern of results. Thus, if rats indeed lose incentive motivation faster following continuous than partial reinforcement, one would expect that they would reach a stage in which incentive had extinguished in the one alley while some incentive remained in the other and that their choice of behavior would reflect this fact. In no case were there indications of such phenomena.

Less significant effects on incentive motivation may have occurred. Specifically, for example, the initial incentive value following continuous reinforcement is greater than that following partial reinforcement. It would be possible for the relative rate of loss of incentive motivation to be somewhat faster in the former procedure, but not sufficiently faster to cross the latter in order to motivate a reversal of preference. This possibility can be tested by using conditions which initially produce more nearly equal incentive levels but which differ in the pattern of reinforcement experienced.

It is also possible that more radical initial conditions may affect the rate of change in incentive motivation. For example, Solomon has found that dogs given preliminary exposure to unavoidable, inescapable electric shocks subsequently may have difficulty learning to escape from shock in another situation. This could mean that the development of incentive motivation based on primary negative reinforcement is affected by prior experimental history, although it is also possible that such training has simply changed the initial response hierarchy to primary motivation. In any event, the researches reported covered a wide range of effects that are familiar in the learning literature and failed to implicate incentive motivation as a major factor in the observed phenomena. Alternative analyses of these, for example, the frustration account of the partial reinforcement effect, are thus indirectly supported.

The general conclusion suggested by these results is that the assumption of invariant rates of change in incentive motivation is a tenable one. When the incentive value of the reward received after a response differs from the preexisting incentive motivation for that response, an appropriate change occurs at a rate that is more or less independent of prior experimental history. With specific reference to extinction, continued nonreinforcement results in a loss of incentive to respond, but the rate at which this decrease occurs does not differ with prior reinforcement conditions. Confidence in this conclusion will depend, of course, on the success enjoyed by further development of a quantitative model of incentive motivation incorporating this assumption.

V. Summary

The rate at which incentive motivation changes in response to a change in the reward conditions was evaluated empirically by use of a choice procedure with rats as subjects. Two alternatives initially received different conditions of reinforcement followed by a change in the conditions for one or both alternatives. The procedures studied were selected from effects familiar in the literature of learning, including the effects on extinction of partial reinforcement, amount of reward, and overtraining. Changes in both amount and probability of reward were also studied. In no case was choice behavior affected by these changes in the manner that would be expected if the rate at which incentive motivation changes had been significantly affected.

During forced trials, running speeds reflected most of the familiar phenomena of simple instrumental performance measures. Several novel results were also obtained in the speed data, notably a reduction in the partial reinforcement effect when extinction is conducted jointly with a continuously reinforced response, and a generalized frustration effect reflected in faster running for small reward when combined with partial as compared with continuous large reward. In general, the speed data confirmed that the rats were performing appropriately to the conditions of reinforcement in each alternative.

Reservations about the generality of the choice procedure were noted, especially the possible generalization effects between the alternatives and the observable persisting habits of choice. Nevertheless, the consistency of the results suggests the conclusion that the rate of change in incentive motivation is an invariant state parameter of the subject and is not significantly affected by prior reinforcement history.

References

Amsel, A. Frustrative nonreward in partial reinforcement and discrimination learning: Some recent history and a theoretical extension. *Psychological Review*, 1962, **69**, 306–328.

Amsel, A. Partial reinforcement effects on vigor and persistence. In K. W. Spence and J. T. Spence (Eds.), *The psychology of learning and motivation: Advances in research and theory*, Vol. 1. New York: Academic Press, 1967. Pp. 1–65.

Black, R. W. On the combination of drive and incentive motivation. *Psychological Review*, 1965, **72**, 310–317.

Bower, G. H. Partial and correlated reward in escape learning. *Journal of Experimental Psychology*, 1960, **59**, 126–130.

Bower, G. H. A contrast effect in differential conditioning. *Journal of Experimental Psychology*, 1961, **62**, 196–199.

Brown, R. T., & Logan, F. A. Generalized partial reinforcement effect. *Journal of Comparative and Physiological Psychology*, 1965, **60**, 64–69.

Capaldi, E. J. Partial reinforcement: An hypothesis on sequential effects. *Psychological Review*, 1966, **73**, 459–477.

Cofer, C. N., & Appley, M. H. *Motivation: Theory and research.* New York: Wiley, 1964.

Crespi, L. P. Amount of reinforcement and the level of performance. *Psychological Review,* 1944, **51**, 341–357.

Davenport, J. W. Spatial discrimination and reversal learning based upon differential percentage of reinforcement. *Journal of Comparative and Physiological Psychology,* 1963, **56**, 1038–1043.

Egger, M. D., & Miller, N. E. When is a reward reinforcing?: An experimental study of the information hypothesis. *Journal of Comparative and Physiological Psychology,* 1963, **56**, 132–137.

Ehrenfreund, D., & Badia, P. Response strength as a function of drive level and pre- and post-shift incentive magnitude. *Journal of Experimental Psychology,* 1962, **63**, 468–471.

Gleitman, H., Nachmias, J., & Neisser, U. The S-R reinforcement theory of extinction. *Psychological Review,* 1954, **61**, 23–33.

Goldstein, H., & Spence, K. W. Performance in differential conditioning as a function of variation in magnitude of reward. *Journal of Experimental Psychology,* 1963, **65**, 86–93.

Guthrie, E. R. Reward and punishment. *Psychological Review,* 1934, **41**, 450–460.

Hull, C. L. *Principles of behavior.* New York: Appleton, 1943.

Hull, C. L. *A behavior system.* New Haven: Yale University Press, 1952.

Hulse, S. H., Jr. Amount and percentage of reinforcement and duration of goal confinement in conditioning and extinction. *Journal of Experimental Psychology,* 1958, **56**, 48–57.

Kaplan, R., Kaplan, S., & Walker, E. L. Individual differences in learning as a function of shock level. *Journal of Experimental Psychology,* 1960, **60**, 404–407.

Kendler, H. H. Drive interaction: I. Learning as a function of the simultaneous presence of the hunger and thirst drives. *Journal of Experimental Psychology,* 1945, **35**, 96–109.

Koch, S. Clark L. Hull. In W. K. Estes, *et al., Modern learning theory.* New York: Appleton, 1954. Pp. 1–176.

Lewis, D. J., & Kent, N. D. Attempted direct activation and deactivation of the fractional anticipatory goal response. *Psychological Reports,* 1961, **8**, 107–110.

Logan, F. A. *Incentive.* New Haven: Yale University Press, 1960.

Logan, F. A. Decision making by rats. *Journal of Comparative and Physiological Psychology,* 1965, **59**, 1–12 and 246–251.

Logan, F. A., & Wagner, A. R. *Reward and punishment.* Boston: Allyn & Bacon, 1965.

Miller, N. E. Studies of fear as an acquirable drive: I. Fear as motivation and fear-reduction as reinforcement in the learning of new responses. *Journal of Experimental Psychology,* 1948, **38**, 89–101.

Miller, N. E. Some reflections on the law of effect produce a new alternative to drive reduction. In M. R. Jones (Ed.), *Nebraska symposium on motivation.* Lincoln, Nebr.: University of Nebraska Press, 1963. Pp. 65–112.

Mowrer, O. H. *Learning theory and behavior.* New York: Wiley, 1960.

Nefzger, M. D. The properties of stimuli associated with shock reduction. *Journal of Experimental Psychology,* 1957, **53**, 184–188.

North, A. J., & Stimmel, D. T. Extinction of an instrumental response following a large number of reinforcements. *Psychological Reports,* 1960, **6**, 227–234.

Novin, D., & Miller, N. E. Failure to condition thirst induced by feeding dry food to hungry rats. *Journal of Comparative and Physiological Psychology,* 1962, **55**, 373–374.

Pavlov, I. P. *Conditioned reflexes.* (Translated by G. V. Anrep.) London and New York: Oxford University Press, 1927.

Seward, J. P. Reinforcement and expectancy: Two theories in search of a controversy. *Psychological Review*, 1956, **63**, 105–113. (a)

Seward, J. P. Drive, incentive, and reinforcement. *Psychological Review*, 1956, **63**, 195–203. (b)

Shapiro, M. M. Temporal relationship between salivation and lever pressing with differential reinforcement of low rates. *Journal of Comparative and Physiological Psychology*, 1962, **55**, 567–571.

Sheffield, F. D. A drive induction theory of reinforcement. In R. N. Haber (Ed.), *Current research in motivation.* New York: Holt, 1966. Pp. 98–121.

Sheffield, V. F. Extinction as a function of partial reinforcement and distribution of practice. *Journal of Experimental Psychology*, 1949, **39**, 511–526.

Sherif, M., Taub, D., & Hovland, C. I. Assimilation and contrast effects of anchoring stimuli on judgments. *Journal of Experimental Psychology*, 1958, **55**, 150–155.

Spence, K. W. *Behavior theory and conditioning.* New Haven: Yale University Press, 1956.

Spence, K. W. *Behavior theory and learning.* Englewood Cliffs, N.J.: Prentice-Hall, 1960.

Spence, K. W., Bergmann, G., & Lippitt, R. A study of simple learning under irrelevant motivational-reward conditions. *Journal of Experimental Psychology*, 1950, **40**, 539–551.

Spence, K. W., & Trapold, M. A. Performance in eyelid conditioning as a function of reinforcement schedules and change in them. *Proceedings of the National Academy of Sciences of the U.S.*, 1961, **47**, 1860–1868.

Tolman, E. C. *Purposive behavior in animals and men.* New York: Century, 1932.

Trapold, M. A. The effect of incentive motivation on an unrelated reflex response. *Journal of Comparative and Physiological Psychology*, 1962, **55**, 1034–1039.

Zeaman, D. Response latency as a function of the amount of reinforcement. *Journal of Experimental Psychology*, 1949, **39**, 466–483.

Zimmerman, D. W. Durable secondary reinforcement: Method and theory. *Psychological Review*, 1957, **64**, 373–383.

SHIFT IN ACTIVITY AND THE CONCEPT OF PERSISTING TENDENCY[1]

David Birch

UNIVERSITY OF MICHIGAN
ANN ARBOR, MICHIGAN

I. Introduction

A day in the life of any organism, as recorded by an observer, would be composed of the environmental events the organism was exposed to and the sequence of activities in which he engaged. A more complete log for the day would also include the time at which the environmental events and the activities began and ended. Such a protocol is much too complex to be dealt with in detail by existent psychological theories, but it does

[1] Portions of this research were supported by a grant, NSF G-19217, from the National Science Foundation. Much of the conceptual analysis that appears in this chapter is based on a theory of motivation developed in collaboration with my colleague, John W. Atkinson, and currently in preparation as a theoretical monograph. The author also wishes to acknowledge the contributions of Dr. Guy J. Johnson, William Timberlake, and Fred P. Valle who took part in planning and executing various phases of the research and Douglas Coombs who assisted in data collection. Dr. Johnson participated as a USPHS Post Doctoral Fellow and Mr. Timberlake as a National Science Foundation Pre-Doctoral Fellow.

lie within the aspirations of several (see, for example, Barker, 1963; Barker & Wright, 1954; Lough, 1960). The contents of this chapter were instigated partly by similar long-range aspirations but offer the results of research on a problem smaller in scope and hopefully with more manageable theoretical and experimental characteristics.

The problem chosen for study is shift in activity. It is apparent that the protocol referred to earlier is a compilation of shifts in activity as well as a sequence of activities. In the work to be presented, single shifts in activity have been isolated out of the total flow of behavior by contriving experimental situations in which clearly defined ongoing and alternative activities can be identified. These situations have been used to obtain data showing the effects of certain characteristics of both the ongoing and alternative activities on the time taken for a shift in activity. It might be expected (Birch, 1966a) that the point in time when a shift in activity occurs will be sensitive to variables affecting the strength of the tendency for the ongoing as well as for the alternative activity.

The time data, certainly not unlike the traditional measures of persistence and latency of responses, are the subject matter for the models of action and the theories of psychological processes that are taken up in the chapter. Several models, some with variations, were used against the data. In the course of these efforts one issue emerged as primary; namely, what happens to the disposition of an organism to engage in an activity when the environmental instigation for that activity ceases? Put in the language of tendencies the question becomes, "Does a tendency, once aroused, persist?" This issue defined another set of theoretical and experimental problems and some initial efforts on them are also included in the chapter.

II. Nature of a Shift in Activity

Consider an organism engaged in some activity A. Consider further what would happen if the organism were presented a signal for an alternative incompatible activity B while he was still engaged in activity A. He might continue to engage in activity A or he might shift to activity B. The time taken for such a shift in activity is either the latency of B or the persistence of A, depending on whether the experimenter has his interest focused on the onset of activity B or the cessation of activity A (Atkinson, 1964; Birch & Veroff, 1966). Shift in activity is the more general problem embracing the special problems of both latency and persistence.

This view of the primacy of shift in activity as a topic for study is based on the premise that living organisms are always doing something. If this premise is correct, theoretical and experimental analyses will be better if our thinking is in terms of shifts in activity rather than in terms of the onset and cessation of activities. Thus, it would be more appropriate to conceive of activities giving way to or being replaced by other activities than of activities beginning and ceasing. By so thinking it becomes very clear that the time measure of concern will be influenced by characteristics of both the ongoing and alternative activities. The time it will take for a shift from activity A to activity B should be positively related to the strength of support for activity A and negatively related to the amount of instigation for activity B. The actual time measure obtained in any specific case will be determined by the interplay between these effects.

A. Previous Research

1. *Experimental*

The emergence of shift in activity as a pivotal topic in the analysis of molar behavior is a natural outgrowth of much previous research on learning and motivation. Richter (1922) observed rats over extended periods of time and gained information on the activities engaged in by the rats and the effects of various conditions of deprivation and stimulation on these activities. In some respects the research of Allison (1964) is an extension of that of Richter. Using pair comparison presentations, Allison allowed rats the opportunity to divide a time period between two chambers offering possibilities for eating, interacting with a litter mate of the same sex, or enjoying commerce with a hardware cloth object. Like Richter, he was interested in activities as the basic unit of study; unlike Richter, however, he used his measures to define the strength of an individual differences parameter, motive for food, for the rats.

One of the very few experiments that was designed to study a variable affecting a shift between two well-defined activities was carried out by Jensen (1963). Jensen gave rats either 40, 80, 160, 320, 640, or 1280 rewarded bar press trials and then offered them the option of pressing the bar for pellets or of eating the same pellets from a dish. The data, presented in terms of the mean percentage of all pellets eaten that were obtained by bar pressing, show that the bar-pressing activity was directly affected by the degree of bar-pressing training. What makes this study of shift in activity of special interest is that Jensen made sure that all *S*s were eating freely from the dish before he made the bar available. Thus, a well-defined shift in activity from eating pellets out of a dish to pressing a bar for pellets was attained.

Shifts in activities are sometimes found to complicate the interpretation of experimental findings. Two examples of this in which effects of deprivation were under investigation will illustrate the point. Stellar and

Hill (1952, p. 101) in a study of thirst comment as follows: "It is clear that rats get drawn away from their drinking many times during a test period, but the stronger their thirst, the more they persist in drinking without interruption and the sooner they return to it afterward. That these interruptions represent some positive interference with the thirst drive rather than only temporary satiation is clear. When rats stop drinking, they do something else. Most commonly, the first major break in drinking is spent in vigorous washing and grooming. At other times, the rat scratches itself, sniffs about the cage, or chews on the wire mesh. Late in the drinking period, it may sleep. With mild deprivations, these competing activities appear early in the course of drinking and last relatively long times. With severe deprivations, they appear late, and little time is given to them. The rate of water intake, then, is the outcome of both the strength of the thirst drive and all the tendencies the animal has to do other things in the drinking situation." Similarly, Cotton (1953) analyzed speed of running in a straight runway with and without competing responses (presumably with and without shifts in activity) and reports that the effect of food deprivation on the speed of running is greatly reduced when trials involving competing responses are not included in the calculations.

2. *Theoretical*

On occasion special theoretical effort has been devoted to the role of the ongoing activity in certain situations. This was the case for vicarious trial-and-error behavior as dealt with by Muenzinger (1938), Tolman (1939), and Spence (1937, 1960) in the framework of discrimination learning in animals. These investigators gave systematic attention to the determinants of choice point behavior and the way in which this behavior influences subsequent choices. The behavior of an organism on a trial of a discrimination learning problem can be viewed as a shift in activity if the ongoing activity is defined as the behavior at the choice point and the shift in activity is considered to be displayed in the choice. Special treatment was afforded the ongoing activity by Estes (1950) also, who gave full recognition to the importance of that activity in determining the latency and rate of response. In a later section where conceptual analyses are undertaken, we shall draw on Estes' proposals to frame an hypothesis about the processes underlying a shift in activity.

B. Defining Characteristics

In the research to be reported in this chapter, simple instances of shifts in activity have been isolated for study. The simplest case is one based on only two activities as introduced at the beginning of this section. An organism is engaged in activity A and while so occupied is exposed continuously to stimulation inviting him to engage in activity B, which is incompatible with A. At some later point in time activity A is observed to give way to activity B.

Let us begin the analysis of this simple shift in activity with a definition: If activity A is occurring rather than activity B, the organism will be said to be in state A rather than in state B. States correspond directly to coded activities. More specifically the statement, "The organism is in state A at moment m" means that a continuously occurring process has resulted in support for activity A at moment m. If the organism remains in state A for the time interval m to $m + n$, it is implied that the process has led to a sequence of results that has supported activity A throughout this interval. When the organism shifts to activity B, he is said to move into state B, and it is implied that the process has resulted in support for activity B at this time. The latency measure tells how long it took for the process to produce a change from state A to state B, but no observations display this process to us. The unavoidable conclusion from a shift in activity, however, is that the output of the process must have changed over time and we can justifiably expect theories to give answers to questions about how and why such changes might take place.

It was pointed out earlier that the time taken for a shift in activity could be expected to be a function of characteristics of both the ongoing and alternative activities. In the next section experiments are reported which demonstrate that this is the case. One of the experiments will be presented in detail because the data provide the substance for the conceptual analysis of shift in activity to be offered later in the chapter.

III. New Experiments on Shift in Activity

The first requisite for a shift in activity experiment is that one clearly identifiable activity be pitted against another clearly identifiable activity. Although all organisms, human and animal, participate in shifts of activity and are thereby proper subjects for study, human beings with their special verbal and cognitive processes make observations particularly difficult. An experimenter needs to know what activity is ongoing and when that activity is supplanted by a particular alternative. Human beings engage in the covert activities of thinking and talking to themselves as well as overt activities and can accomplish shifts in activity without an observer knowing it. Lower organisms may also engage in covert activities but surely with less facility and prevalence. Rats were chosen in preference to human beings for use in the present experiments largely for these reasons.

A. Preliminary Studies

1. *Selection of Activities*

Preliminary experimentation showed that eating food and exploring a novel and complex environment would serve as suitable activities. In one experiment (Timberlake & Birch, 1967) rats were given food to eat in one chamber and simultaneously offered the option of exploring another chamber. See Fig. 1 for a diagram of this apparatus. For one

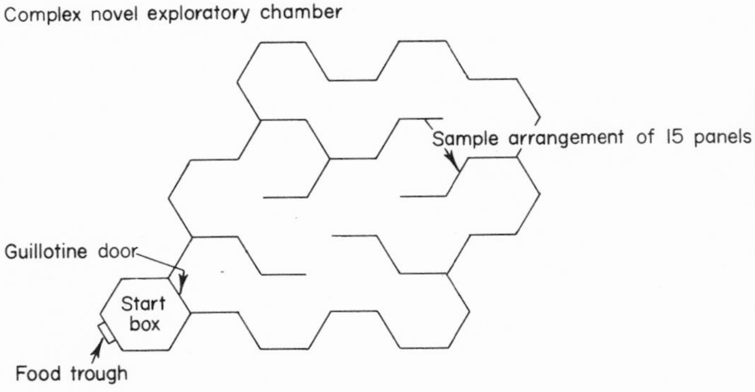

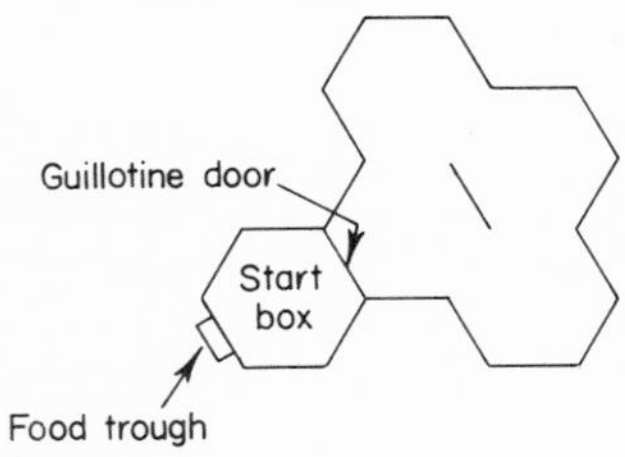

Fig. 1. Diagram of apparatus used for shift in activity experiments.

group, N = 10, the alternative chamber was somewhat less than 2 feet in diameter and empty, and for the other group, N = 8, it was over 3 feet in diameter and contained 15 panels the arrangement of which was varied from trial to trial. On each trial *S* was placed in the proper exploratory chamber for a 2-minute adaptation period, returned to its home cage for another 2 minutes, and then placed in the food chamber with the door to the alternative chamber open. The food chamber contained more than enough wet mash to satiate *S*. All *S*s were 22 hours hungry when tested and generally began to eat promptly. A stopwatch was used to measure the time from when *S*'s feet touched the food chamber floor until its whole body entered into the exploratory chamber. At this point a door was lowered to prevent retracing and *S* was allowed 2 minutes to explore. *S*s received 16 trials given at one trial per day.

The group with the complex and novel exploratory chamber was quicker to leave the eating chamber than the group with the simple and non-novel chamber on all 16 trials. The average latency was 8.72 minutes for the first group and 13.73 minutes for the second, and these two values differ significantly ($p < .025$). Both groups increase their time spent in the eating chamber across the 16 trials. On the first trial, for example, the simple non-novel group stayed about 2 minutes and the complex novel group about 15 seconds. On day 16 the two groups averaged approximately 18 and 15 minutes, respectively.

Two major ends were accomplished in this experiment. It was shown, first, that two degrees of complexity and novelty would yield differentially attractive alternative activities to eating, and, second, that eating was an admirable ongoing activity in that it was clearly codeable and it continued for an appreciable period of time.

2. *Sensitivity of the Time Measurement*

In another preliminary study, in which I was assisted by Douglas Coombs, an attempt was made to assess the sensitivity of the shift in activity time measure, based on eating and exploring, to the effects of simple experimental manipulations. For this experiment an exploratory chamber was placed adjacent to the goal box of a straight runway. *S* was presented with 100 .045-gm Noyes pellets in the goal box and was free to shift from eating to exploring at any time. The time spent in the goal box and the number of pellets consumed were investigated as a function of the number of acquisition trials on the runway and whether *S* ran to the goal box or was placed directly into it on a test trial.

Sixteen male hooded rats approximately 3 months old were used in the experiment. Runway training was given in the morning and tests in the afternoon. Six massed runway trials, each rewarded by two .045-gm pellets, were administered to each *S* on 9 consecutive days. Following the day's training *S* was returned to its home cage for its daily food ration (as much as *S* consumed in $1\frac{1}{2}$ hours of free feeding). Two hours after food was removed from the home cage, *S* was returned to the runway for a single test trial. Two types of test trials, running and placement, were administered with half of the total group receiving each type each day.

As training proceeded, the time spent eating and the number of pellets eaten increased significantly. The average time spent eating for the running and placement trials combined at the beginning of runway training (i.e., the first 4 days) was 251 seconds whereas at the end (i.e., on the last 4 days) it was 361 seconds. Similarly, the mean number of pellets eaten increased from 42 to 62 over this period. The placement and running conditions had no differential effects on either measure early in training. At the end of training, however, *S*s were spending more time eating and were eating a larger number of pellets when placed directly into the goal box than when they ran into it. These effects were evaluated statistically by Wilcoxen's test for matched pairs and were significant ($p < .05$) with each measure. The mean values were as follows: 39 pellets and 236 seconds for placement at the beginning of training, 72 pellets and 403 seconds for placement at the end, 44 pellets and 265 seconds for running at the beginning of training and 53 pellets and 319 seconds for running at the end.

These data substantiate the earlier finding that eating is a reliable and prolonged activity for rats. Even when deprived for only 2 hours, some *S*s consumed all 100 pellets, placing an additional 4.5 gm of food into their stomachs. That *S*s would replace eating by exploring before exhausting the pellets on some occasions is consistent with the shift in activity paradigm and confirms the efficacy of exploration as an alternative activity to eating. It is of further interest that the shift in activity was influenced by the amount of runway training and by whether *S* ran or was placed into the goal box. Assuming that these manipulations affected the tendency to eat and not the tendency to explore, it would appear that runway training strengthens the tendency to eat and that this tendency is stronger under placing than running. The latter finding suggests the hypothesis that under some conditions running to food might actually decrease the tendency to eat. Such speculations, however, are pertinent to the concept of persisting tendency and belong to a later part of the chapter.

B. Main Experiment

1. *Design and Hypotheses*

On the basis of results from the preliminary studies it was possible to proceed with a shift in activity experiment in which characteristics of both activities were manipulated together.[2] Eating and exploring were chosen as the ongoing and alternative activities, respectively. Two levels

[2] William Timberlake was responsible for all data collection in this experiment and assisted with the data analyses.

of each variable were combined factorially in the experiment as shown in Table I. *S*s were either 2 or 21 hours deprived of food and were offered either a simple or complex alternative chamber to explore. If the time taken to shift from eating to exploring is a function of the strength of tendency for both activities and if the experimental conditions impose the different strengths of tendency properly, Group 21-S should take the most time to supplant eating with exploring. This is because in Group 21-S the greater strength of tendency for eating due to the 21 hours' food deprivation is combined with the less potent instigation for exploring

TABLE I

Expected Pattern of Results in Terms of Time to Shift Activities for Groups Differing Systematically in Support for the Ongoing Activity and Instigation to the Alternative Activity

		Instigation to alternative exploratory activity		
		Low (simple, non-novel)		High (complex, novel)
Support for ongoing eating activity	High (21 hours dep.)	Group 21-S	>	Group 21-C
		∨		∨
	Low (2 hours dep.)	Group 2-S	>	Group 2-C

arising from the simple, non-novel chamber. In Group 2-C the opposite combination of conditions obtained and this group should show the least time to shift activities. By similar argument the shift times for the other two groups, 21-C and 2-S, should fall between the times for Groups 21-S and 2-C, but no definitive statement about the ordering of these intermediate groups is possible. This pattern of inequalities to be expected from the data for the four groups is represented in Table I.

2. *Method*

Fifty-three naive hooded rats began pretraining at 80–90 days of age. Seven *S*s were discarded during pretraining for failure to leave the food chamber or refusal to eat 4 days in succession. The final sample of 46 was distributed with 11 *S*s in each of the 21-hour deprivation groups and 12 *S*s each in the 2-hour deprivation groups.

The basic apparatus was the same as that used in the first preliminary experiment by Timberlake and Birch (1967). A schematic diagram of this apparatus appears in Fig. 1. The food chamber was in the shape of a regular hexagon, $10\frac{1}{2}$ inches on the short diagonal measure, and was formed by plywood panels 6 inches wide and 8 inches high. A hole, $3\frac{3}{4}$ inches wide by 3 inches high and $1\frac{1}{4}$ inches off the floor, was cut in the back wall, giving *S* access to a feeding trough attached to the outside of the wall. Another hole, 3 inches wide and $3\frac{1}{2}$ inches high, was cut in the wall opposite the back wall to give *S* an entrance to the exploratory chamber. A guillotine door controlled by a photosensitive relay, which operated when *S* had moved $4\frac{3}{4}$ inches out of the food chamber and thereby broke a light beam, prevented *S* from reentering the food chamber.

The exploratory chamber was either simple, non-novel, and 4 hexagons in size or complex, novel, and 15 hexagons in size. The smaller exploratory chamber contained a single panel placed $10\frac{1}{2}$ inches outside the doorway which partially blocked *S*'s view from the food chamber. The larger chamber contained 15 panels in an arrangement that was varied in groups of 3 panels before every trial with the restrictions that 1 panel always block *S*'s view from the food chamber (the same panel as was present in the simple exploratory chamber) and that no part of the chamber be completely separated from another part. A hardware cloth screen lay across the top of the apparatus to confine *S* and a bed sheet was stretched above that to minimize room cues. A ventilator system provided constant masking noise and all recording instruments were placed in an adjacent room.

At the beginning of the 18 days of pretraining *S*s were housed in individual cages outside the experimental room and placed on a feeding schedule in which they were allowed to eat solid food in their home cages for 1 hour and 15 minutes each day. *S*s were handled daily and beginning with day 9 this handling took place on a table top covered with sawdust. On days 15 and 16 the food trough to be used in the food chamber was placed on the table top, filled with wet mash (one-half food powder and one-half water) and presented to the *S*s. All *S*s ate from the trough on both days. After random assignment to either the simple, non-novel or the complex, novel exploratory condition on day 17, each *S* individually was allowed to investigate the appropriate chamber for 2 minutes on that day and the next with the door to the start box closed.

At the end of pretraining, *S*s in the two exploratory condition groups were further assigned to one of the deprivation conditions, 2 or 21 hours. The experiment was carried out in three replications with sample sizes 15, 14, and 17. Although all groups could not be represented equally in all replications, this assignment was approximated and the numbers for the groups ranged between three and five in each replication.

Trials were administered one per day for 15 days. To begin each trial *S* was taken from its home cage and placed directly into the appropriate exploratory chamber for 2 minutes of adaptation and/or curiosity arousal. During the next 2 minutes *S* was weighed and returned to its home cage and then placed in the food chamber with the door to the exploratory chamber open. The food trough contained more wet mash than *S* was able to take in. The total time *S* remained in the food chamber was recorded on a standard electric timer which *E* started by closing a knife switch at the same time he deposited *S* on the food chamber floor and which *S* stopped by breaking the light beam on the other side of the doorway in the exploratory chamber. Breaking the light beam also caused the retrace door to lower, and *S* was given opportunity for exploration during the next 2 minutes before being returned to its home cage. *E* left the experimental room immediately after placing *S* in the food chamber.

A second time measure was obtained from *S* in the food chamber. This measure was devised to record the time *S* spent in the immediate vicinity of food and thus to estimate the time *S* spent eating as distinct from the total time *S* spent in the food chamber. In the first replication this eating time measure was attained by use of an electric field set up inside the food trough which, when disturbed by *S*'s head, would close a relay and operate a Hewlett–Packard electronic clock. This system proved less reliable than desired, however, and was replaced by a photocell system in which the light beam was located inside the food chamber $1\frac{3}{4}$ inches above the floor and $1\frac{1}{4}$ inches from the food trough for the last two replications.

3. *Results and Conclusions*

Results using the measure of the total time *S* spent in the food chamber before shifting to the exploratory activity will be considered first. A plot of the mean time of shift in activity in seconds for the four groups across the 15 days of the experiment may be seen in Fig. 2. Two aspects of the data stand out most clearly in this plot. First, there is a marked increase in the amount of time spent in the food chamber over the 15 days although the values for all groups from day 7 on appear to be without any appreciable trend. Second, the ordering of the groups is quite in line with expectations with Group 21-S the slowest to leave the food chamber, Group 2-C the quickest, and Groups 21-C and 2-S about in the middle. It is interesting to note that this ordering holds even during the first 6 days before the time values had stabilized. One additional aspect of the data is also important. By day 7 all groups were spending appreciable amounts of time in the food chamber; even Group 2-C, the group quickest to shift activities, was averaging approximately 8 minutes with the food.

The main purpose of this experiment was to obtain data which would help to evaluate the joint effects of characteristics of both the ongoing and alternative activities on the time it takes to shift from one activity to another. With this in mind it was decided to concentrate attention on the time measures obtained over the last 9 days of the experiment when

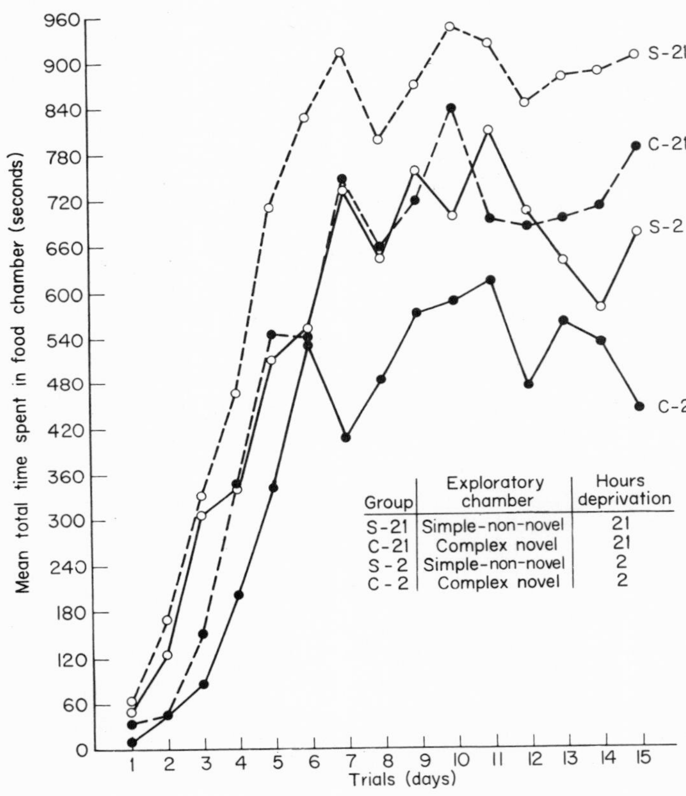

FIG. 2. Total time spent in food chamber for groups differing in food deprivation and complexity of exploratory chamber.

performance had stabilized. It was also decided to analyze medians determined from the scores from the last 9 days for each *S* to circumvent the difficulty of skewness to be found in the distribution of time scores. Examination of the data showed a few scores that were unusually brief (i.e., 2–39 seconds) for which it seemed impossible to argue that a well-defined ongoing activity of eating was present. These scores were not used in arriving at the medians.

The means and variances for the four groups calculated from these medians are presented in the left column of Table II. It is apparent from Table II, and from Fig. 2, that *S*s spend more time in the food chamber when deprived 21 hours than when deprived 2 hours and more time when the exploratory alternative is simple and non-novel than when it is complex and novel. Analysis of variance shows that both main effects are significant ($p < .05$). Furthermore, very close to zero interaction between time of deprivation and the degree of complexity of the exploratory chamber is found in the data. The difference in mean time

TABLE II

Means and Variances of the Median Times in Seconds over the Last 9 Days for the Total, Food-Orienting, and Nonfood-Orienting Activities

	Total time		Food-orienting time		Nonfood-orienting time	
Group	Mean	σ^2	Mean	σ^2	Mean	σ^2
21-S	863	72,845	658	35,246	194	6,990
2-S	721	73,260	538	44,241	160	2,790
21-C	721	40,432	612	33,622	111	8,572
2-C	562	9,279	444	7,573	102	2,773

spent in the food chamber for 21 as opposed to 2 hours deprivation when the exploratory chamber is simple and non-novel is 142 seconds and it is 159 seconds when the alternative chamber is complex and novel. When evaluated by analysis of variance, this interaction yields $F = 0.015$, $df = 1, 42$. Thus, there appears to be no reason why an hypothesis of simple additivity between the effects of food deprivation and degree of complexity of the alternative exploratory chamber should not be retained.

Examination of the second time measure taken in the food chamber, namely, how long *S* spent oriented toward the food, helps explicate this additive relation. Because the recording apparatus for this time measure was unreliable, particularly at the beginning of the experiment, data for some *S*s on some trials are missing. To compensate for these missing data, the 15 days of the experiment were grouped into five sets of three and the median determined for each *S* for each of the five sets. The means of these medians are plotted in Fig. 3 where they appear as the topmost four curves. Visually these data have much the same appearance as those for total time plotted in Fig. 2, particularly as the rank order of the groups is retained. In the middle column of Table II the means and variances for the four groups calculated from the medians of the last 9 days (the measure corresponding to that for the total time spent in the food chamber appearing in the left column of Table II) can be found. Despite the similar appearance of the data for total time and food-oriented time in Table II as well as in Figs. 2 and 3, analysis of variance

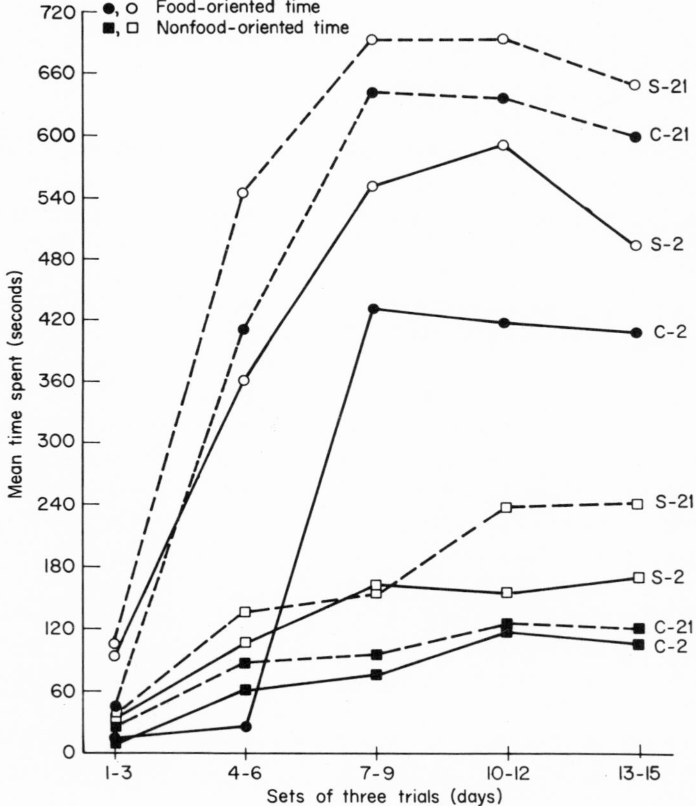

FIG. 3. Food-oriented and nonfood-oriented times for groups differing in food deprivation and complexity of exploratory chamber.

of the food-oriented time yields significance for the deprivation main effect ($p < .025$) but not for the effect of degree of complexity of the exploratory chamber ($p > .10$). No statistical support for an interaction between deprivation and exploratory effects comes from the analysis of variance with $F = 0.201$, $df = 1, 42$. Thus, although there is a hint that the food-oriented time may be affected by the complexity of the exploratory chamber, there is statistical support only for a deprivation effect on this time measure.

The difference between the total time spent in the food chamber and the food-oriented time (call this the nonfood-oriented time) provides additional information of use in interpreting the effects of deprivation and exploratory chamber complexity on the total time spent measure. The four lower curves of Fig. 3 are plots of the course of the nonfood-orienting-time over the period of the experiment and the third column of Table II contains the means and variances calculated from the medians for the last 9 days. Both Fig. 3 and Table II show that the groups are ordered the same on nonfood-orienting time as on food-orienting time except that the two middle groups (2-S and 21-C) have reversed positions. Thus, there is visual evidence that both deprivation and exploratory chamber complexity are pertinent to nonfood-orienting time, but, as was the case with the food-orienting time, only one of the main effects gains statistical support. With the food-orienting time measure, it was deprivation that proved statistically significant; with the nonfood-orienting measure, it is the degree of complexity of the exploratory chamber ($p < .001$). The deprivation main effect is not significant ($p > .10$) nor is the interaction, $F = 0.948$, $df = 1, 42$.

Breaking down the total time *S* spent in the food chamber into two parts, food-orienting time and nonfood-orienting time, gives a basis for interpreting the total time main effects and near zero interaction in terms of a sequence of activities. Despite the intention to obtain a simple shift from eating to exploring, it seems clear that a third activity must be identified. This third activity, whatever it was that *S* was doing during the nonfood-orienting time, was affected by the complexity of the exploratory chamber but not by the degree of deprivation. This pattern of effects is exactly opposite to that for the food-orienting time and argues for the presence of two distinct activities in the food chamber.

The reason for the two activities in the food chamber may be found in the way in which that chamber was constructed. Since the food-dispensing device was located directly opposite the exit door, *S* was not exposed to the visual stimuli of the exploratory chamber while eating. Correspondingly, when *S* turned away from the food he was exposed to the stimuli for exploration but was no longer as strongly stimulated by the food cues. By this analysis *S* was never simultaneously exposed to stimuli with strong instigating values for eating and exploring but only sequentially so exposed. Thus, when *S* shifted activity from eating, typically it was to the other activity in the food chamber, not directly to exploring. From this activity *S* shifted either back to eating or to exploring. With the stimuli instigating eating and exploring functioning sequentially in this way, the additive relationship found for the two effects on the total time spent measure follows naturally.

The presence of a third activity complicates but does not change the basic nature of the shift in activity paradigm. Let eating be identified as activity A, exploring as activity B, and the third, nonfood-orienting activity, as activity X. The data indicate that *S* engages in activity X subsequent to activity A and prior to activity B. Thus, *S* follows one of the sequences AXB, AXAXB, AXAXAXB, etc., depending on how many times a shift in activity occurred from X back to A. In approaching the problem of analysis in the next section, we shall deal conceptually with the simple unitary shift in activity first and then introduce complications in order to come to grips with the data of this section. Several models will be used as vehicles for the analysis and one of our purposes will be to identify and explicate some of the properties shared and not shared by these models.

IV. Conceptual Analysis of Shift in Activity

In an earlier section it was pointed out that a shift in activity from A to B tells only that the organism must have moved from state *A* into state *B*, over the period of observation. The dynamic aspect of this statement is its most important feature. Emphasis is placed on a shift in activity and the change in states that takes place over time (the meaning reserved for the word "dynamic" in the present context). This emphasis is picked up in the analysis to follow where attention will be focused on processes hypothesized to occur in time and to underlie the change in states reflected in the shift in activity.

Two hypotheses about the nature of the process will be considered. The first is that it is discrete with the sequence defined by a random process and the second that it is continuous and strictly deterministic. Stated this way the two hypotheses are quite clearly different. Both, however, are amenable to elaboration and modification that reduce their differences. In addition, the two hypotheses, formulated about unseen processes as they are, do not always lead to different conclusions about what will be observed. Explicating implications of the hypotheses when they are applied to the shift in activity situation and clarifying points of agreement and difference arising from the hypotheses are the aims of this section. To begin with the hypotheses will be simple and pure; complications will be adduced as we proceed.

A. Discrete Random Process Hypothesis

1. *Hullian Theory*

Under the hypothesis of a random process operating on discrete values, the organism is in state *A* or state *B* at a particular moment in time depending on the outcome of a probabilistic process. Embedded in this hypothesis is the idea of values fluctuating over time. For example, in Hullian theory the oscillation function, ${}_SO_R$, is imposed on a stable effective reaction potential, ${}_S\bar{E}_R$, to yield values of the momentary effective reaction potential, ${}_S\dot{\bar{E}}_R$. Whether or not a response will occur at a particular point in time depends on the relation of ${}_S\dot{\bar{E}}_R$ to the reaction threshold ${}_SL_R$. As Hull (1943, p. 308) phrased it, "In such a situation, if the ${}_S\bar{E}_R$ chances to oscillate so as to be above the reaction threshold at the moment of stimulation, overt reaction will occur; if it chances to fall below the reaction threshold, the reaction will not occur." The oscillation function was assumed by Hull to produce a distribution of momentary effective reaction potential values that is approximately normal in form. By this assumption ${}_S\dot{\bar{E}}_R$ jumped discontinuously from one discrete value to another over time but in accord with a normal distribution. Given the parameters of this distribution and the magnitudes of ${}_S\bar{E}_R$ and ${}_SL_R$, the probability of response evocation at any moment in time is easily determined. Similarly, it is not difficult to calculate the probability of occurrence of one of two responses when the necessary parameter values have been specified and the complete distributions for both ${}_S\dot{\bar{E}}_R$'s are above ${}_SL_R$. In this case the probability of either response at any moment is given by the probability that the ${}_S\dot{\bar{E}}_R$ for that response is greater than the ${}_S\dot{\bar{E}}_R$ for the other response.

2. *Stimulus Sampling Theory*

Another example of a discrete random process model for shift in activity is found in stimulus sampling theory. In presenting this theory Estes (1950, p. 95) takes particular note of the role of the ongoing activity by pointing out, "In most formulations of simple learning, the organism is said originally to 'do nothing' in the presence of some stimulus; during learning, the organism comes to make some predesignated response in the presence of the stimulus; then during extinction, the response gradually gives way to a state of 'not responding' again." Later, in presenting the conditional relation between an *R*-class and the elements in an *S*-population, he goes on to say (Estes, 1950, p. 97), "If all behaviors which may be evoked from an organism in a given situation have been categorized into mutually exclusive classes, then the probabilities attaching to the various classes must sum to unity at all times. We consider the organism to be always 'doing something.' If any arbitrarily defined class of activities may be selected as the dependent variable of a given experiment, it follows that the activity of the organism at any time must be considered as subject to the same laws as the class under consideration."

Beginning with the conception of a population of stimulus elements that is sampled repeatedly over time, stimulus sampling theory identifies the occurrence of a particular response with the drawing of a sample that dictates the occurrence of that response. The parameter of central importance in this theory is the probability that any given stimulus element is connected to the response in question. In the simple two-response case where every element of the population is conditioned to one response or the other, the probability of either response at any moment in time is based directly on the proportion of elements that is conditioned to that response.

At the level of the earlier discussion of activities A and B and their corresponding states, the Hullian theory and the stimulus sampling theory are not distinguishable. Both would give meaning to the phrase "the probability that the organism is in state A at moment m" but they would do so from different bases. In Hullian theory the meaning would be derived from the probability that the ${}_S\dot{\bar{E}}_R$ for response (activity) A was greater than the ${}_S\dot{\bar{E}}_R$ for response (activity) B at moment m. In stimulus sampling theory, the probability that the organism is in state A at moment m would be interpreted in terms of the proportion of elements connected to responses A and B in the sample drawn at moment m, with the proportion in the sample governed by the proportion in the population. This kind of equivalence in the two approaches has been illustrated by the parallel derivations made for latency of response. Estes (1950) started from stimulus sampling and used probability theory to derive an equation for latency while Spence (1954) began with the Hullian postulates and used the same probability theory to arrive at a comparable latency equation.

B. Continuous Deterministic Process Hypothesis

The second hypothesis about the process determining a shift in activity is that it is continuous and strictly determined. If an organism is engaged in the ongoing activity A at the beginning of the interval of observation, it means that he is in state A. Being in state A means in turn that the tendency to engage in activity A is greater than the tendency to engage in activity B at this time; i.e., $T_A > T_B$. When the organism shifts from activity A to activity B, it must be that the dominance relation between T_A and T_B has changed such that now $T_B > T_A$. The inescapable conclusion is that the strength of T_A or T_B or T_A and T_B must have changed during the time interval, and the second hypothesis states that these changes are continuous and strictly determined. This hypothesis leads to models concerned with how long it will take for the changing T_A and T_B to reverse dominance rather than the probability of a shift from state A to state B at each moment in time.

Working within the framework of the second hypothesis, Atkinson and Birch (1967) have proposed a specific theory to account for the changing strength of tendencies. Portions of the theory and a number of the general implications of this conceptual scheme can be found in Atkinson (in press). This theory begins with the fundamental premise mentioned earlier that living organisms are always engaged in some activity and that the basic problem in the analysis of action is to account for shifts in activity. Changing dominance relations among tendencies are responsible for shifting activities and a new construct, force, is introduced to account for changes in the strength of a tendency.

Forces change the strengths of tendencies and there are two kinds of forces, instigating and consummatory. Environmental stimuli are said to have instigating force properties and function to increase the strength of tendencies. Thus, the sight, smell, and taste of food result in the application of an instigating force that increases the strength of the tendency to eat. Neutral stimuli can gain instigating force properties through the processes of conditioning and learning. On the other hand, the source of the consummatory force, which functions to decrease the strength of a tendency, is found in the expression of the tendency in action. For example, an organism engaged in the activity of eating is said to be expressing the tendency to eat and as a result is subjected to the effects of a consummatory force.

If conditions are such that both an instigating and a consummatory force are operating on a tendency (as, for example, should be the case in eating where the organism is exposed to the instigating stimuli from the food at the same time he is expressing the tendency to eat), the change in the strength of the tendency will be affected by both. The basic postulate of the theory, written in differential equation form, is

$$\frac{dT}{dt} = {}_{S}F - {}_{R}F \tag{1}$$

This equation states that the rate of change in the strength of a tendency, T, over time, t, is given by the difference between the values for the instigating force, ${}_{S}F$, and the consummatory force ${}_{R}F$.

The change in T can be large or small and positive or negative, depending on the values of ${}_{S}F$ and ${}_{R}F$. It is hypothesized further that the consummatory force depends on two factors, the consummatory value of the activity and the strength of the tendency being expressed. The consummatory value, c, of an activity is the extent to which one unit of the activity is capable of reducing the strength of the tendency and activities are conceived to differ in their consummatory values. For example, drinking one drop of a 32% sucrose solution would be expected to have more consummatory value with respect to the tendency to drink sucrose solutions than drinking one drop of a 4% solution. The consummatory force depends on the product obtained by multiplying together the consummatory value of the activity and the intensity with which the activity is being expressed. Written as an equation this relation is

$$_RF = c \times T \tag{2}$$

Instigating force, $_SF$, in contrast, is assumed to be constant for constant stimulus conditions during the interval of observation.

When $_RF$ is replaced by its equivalent, $c \times T$, the basic postulate for change in the strength of a tendency over time becomes

$$\frac{dT}{dt} = {_SF} - c \times T \tag{3}$$

Integrating this differential equation yields

$$T = T_I \times e^{-ct} + \frac{_SF}{c}(1 - e^{-ct}) \tag{4}$$

which specifies the value of T for every point in time. In general, T begins at an initial value, T_I, and heads monotonically in a negatively accelerated fashion toward an asymptote, $_SF/c$. Whether T rises to the asymptote or falls to it depends on the relative magnitudes of T_I and $_SF/c$. Figure 4 illustrates the kinds of paths that T might take over time as determined by Eq. 4.

Discussion thus far has concerned the fate of a tendency when it is being affected by instigating and consummatory forces simultaneously. This occurs when the tendency is dominant and therefore being expressed in action. Another case of special interest is that in which a tendency is not dominant, and therefore not expressed, but is being influenced by an instigating force from the environment. Here

$$\frac{dT}{dt} = {_SF} \tag{5}$$

only because the presence of a consummatory force depends on the expression of the tendency.[3] Integrating this differential equation produces the equation for a straight line,

$$T = T_I + {_SF} \times \mathrm{t} \tag{6}$$

Thus, the basic postulate stated in Eq. 1 leads to the expectation that, as time passes, the tendency supporting an ongoing activity A will rise or decline from an initial value, T_{AI}, toward an asymptotic value,

[3] This discussion ignores the important role that indirect consummatory forces, often called substitution effects, must play in any complete presentation of this theory. These effects are treated by Atkinson and Birch (1967) but are omitted in this chapter in order to retain simplicity.

$_SF_A/c_A$, while the tendency for the alternative activity B will increase in strength linearly from its initial value, T_{BI}, at a rate equal to $_SF_B$. The time taken for a shift in activity is the time it takes the initial dominance relation $T_{AI} > T_{BI}$ to change to $T_B > T_A$ as a result of the operation of the instigating and consummatory forces that are present.

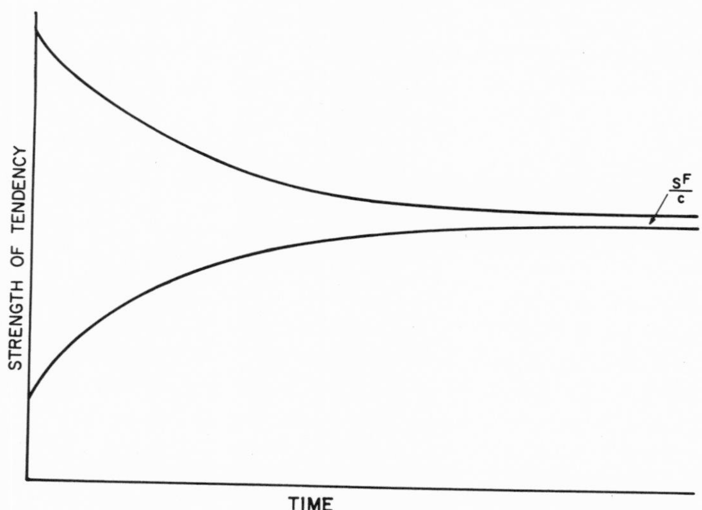

FIG. 4. Examples of the course of the strength of a tendency over time when it is subjected to both instigating and consummatory forces.

C. Application of the Hypotheses to Shift in Activity

It will be convenient to apply the hypothesis of a continuous deterministic process to shift in activity before doing so for the discrete random process hypothesis. Conclusions derived from the two hypotheses will then be compared.

1. *Continuous Deterministic Process Model*

As has been pointed out, a shift in activity from A to B implies that initially $T_{AI} > T_{BI}$ but that subsequently $T_B > T_A$. This, of course, means there is a point in time at which $T_A = T_B$ (call this $T_{AF} = T_{BF}$ to designate the relation between the tendencies at this final point in time just prior to the shift in activity) and we are interested in this time value. From Eqs. 4 and 6 we know

$$T_A = T_{AI} \times e^{-c_At} + \frac{_SF_A}{c_A}(1 - e^{-c_At})$$

and

$$T_B = T_{BI} + {}_SF_B \times t$$

The relation $T_{AF} = T_{BF}$ takes on one of two forms depending on whether or not T_{AF} is known. If T_{AF} is known, we substitute for T_{BF} from Eq. 6 to obtain

$$T_{AF} = T_{BI} + {}_SF_B \times t$$

This equation may be solved for t, yielding

$$t = \frac{T_{AF} - T_{BI}}{{}_SF_B} \tag{7}$$

If T_{AF} is not known, we must substitute from both Eqs. 4 and 6 which produces

$$T_{AI} \times e^{-c_At} + \frac{{}_SF_A}{c_A}(1 - e^{-c_At}) = T_{BI} + {}_SF_B \times t$$

Unfortunately, this equation does not yield a solution for t. However, two special cases are interesting and useful. These two special cases are illustrated alongside the general case in Fig. 5 where an arrow marks the point of shift in activity in each example.

The leftmost panel (a) of Fig. 5 shows two examples of the general case, one where $T_{AI} > {}_SF_A/c_A$ so that T_A declines toward asymptote and the other where $T_{AI} < {}_SF_A/c_A$ so that T_A rises. The middle panel (b) illustrates the special case where T_A has stabilized at asymptote (i.e., $T_{AI} = T_{AF} = {}_SF_A/c_A$). This case yields a solution for t; namely,

$$t = \frac{\dfrac{{}_SF_A}{c_A} - T_{BI}}{{}_SF_B} \tag{8}$$

The second special case, where ${}_SF_B = 0$, leads to the plot shown in the third panel (c) of Fig. 5. Here

$$t = \frac{1}{c_A} \ln \left[\frac{T_{AI} - \dfrac{{}_SF_A}{c_A}}{T_{BI} - \dfrac{{}_SF_A}{c_A}} \right] \tag{9}$$

Certain conclusions hold for the general and specific cases alike. For example, conditions favoring a weak T_A or a strong T_B will produce a small value for t. The opposite set of conditions will lead to a large t. Thus, if the initial tendency supporting activity B is strong or if the instigating force on T_B is large, less persistence of the ongoing activity A is to be expected than if T_{BI} were weak or ${}_SF_B$ small. A short duration of activity A can also result from a weak initial T_A, a small instigating force on T_A, or a large consummatory value for activity A.[4]

The concept of persisting tendency is implicitly an essential element of this theory. It is only because tendencies are assumed to persist, that is, that they retain whatever strength they have unless changed by stimuli or responses, that differential initial values for T_A and T_B are

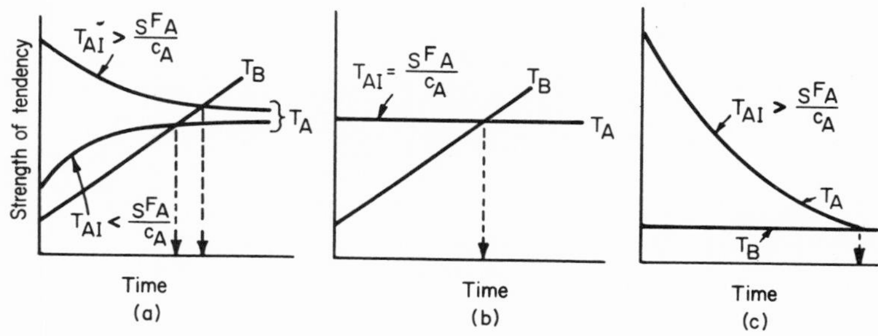

FIG. 5. Three cases derived from tendency theory illustrating the dynamics of a shift in activity.

possible. Even more important, it is only because tendencies are assumed to persist that the continued exposure to a stimulus with instigating force properties will result in an increase in the strength of a tendency. The theory built on the hypothesis of a continuous deterministic process is dynamic because its focus is on tendencies changing in strength over time; the assumption of persisting tendencies is the cornerstone of the theory.

2. *Discrete Random Process Models—Fixed Probabilities*

Various possibilities, differing in complexity and character, arise from the discrete random process hypothesis. The specification of two states, *A* and *B*, and the probability that the organism is in the one or the other at any given moment in time starts the theory but two questions demand answers very quickly. First, what kind of random process is to be proposed? The answer to this question must include a statement about the criterion to be met in order that activity shift. Second, are the parameters of the process conceived as fixed or changing throughout the

[4] Throughout this chapter the time to execute a shift in activity is ignored. This is an important problem and the models presented here can only be expected to be appropriate if execution time is small or if differences are evaluated between conditions where execution times can be considered equal.

interval of observation? Unless the parameters are fixed, a further statement as to how the parameters change in time must be made. The discrete random process hypothesis has freedom with respect to both questions—there is nothing about the hypothesis per se that dictates an answer to either. Table III shows the possibilities that arise from some answers to these questions.

a. Single Instance Criterion. Probably the most simple discrete random process model is the one where fixed probabilities for the states are combined with a sampling process that yields a single determination (either

TABLE III

EXAMPLES OF ASSUMPTIONS ABOUT PROBABILITIES OF STATE EVENTS AND THE CRITERION FOR SHIFT IN ACTIVITY THAT LEAD TO DIFFERENT DISCRETE RANDOM PROCESS MODELS

Probabilities	Criterion set by
Fixed	Single instance of event
Fixed	r Instances of event
Fixed	Gambler's ruin
Changing	Single instance of event
Changing	r Instances of event
Changing	Gambler's ruin

a state A or a state B event) at each moment in time and a criterion that produces a shift in activity with the occurrence of the first state B event. An organism engaged in ongoing activity A, thereby described as being in state A, will continue to engage in activity A only so long as the moment-to-moment sampling process continues to place him in state A each time. As soon as a sample yields a state B event, he will enter state B and his activity will shift. In the language of stimulus sampling theory, the organism will remain in state A so long as the stimuli sampled are connected to the responses of activity A and will switch to state B with the first stimulus sampled that is connected to the responses of activity B. Similarly, in Hullian theory the shift from activity A to activity B occurs the first time the ${}_S\dot{\bar{E}}_R$ for activity B exceeds the ${}_S\dot{\bar{E}}_R$ for activity A.

The derivation of the expected number of samples to be drawn before the shift in activity is well known and straightforward. In fact, it is the same form as that given by Estes (1950) and Spence (1954), and the resulting expression can be written as $E(n) = (1/p_B)$. When multiplied by k, the average time required to draw a sample, this expression gives the expected duration of activity A,

$$t = \left(\frac{1}{p_B}\right) k \tag{10}$$

Actually, this random process generates a geometric distribution (Feller, 1957; McGill, 1963) with the mean given above and a variance of

$$\left(\frac{p_A}{p_B{}^2}\right).$$

b. r Instances Criterion. If the criterion for a shift in activity is set such that r instances of the state B event must occur before the organism moves into state B (instead of the one such event that was sufficient in the first model) a more elaborate model results. The distribution of the number of samples that must be drawn in order to reach the criterion is the negative binomial (Feller, 1957; La Berge, 1962) which has a mean of (r/p_B) and a variance of $r(p_A/p_B{}^2)$. The expected time for a shift in activity from A to B is thus

$$t = \left(\frac{r}{p_B}\right) k = \frac{r}{p_B\left(\frac{1}{k}\right)}$$

Note that $(1/k)$, the sampling rate, properly appears in the denominator because its meaning is tied to that of p_B not to that of r.

c. Gambler's Ruin. Another discrete random process model for shift in activity is to be found by analogy with the classic problem of a gambler's ruin. The time it takes for a shift in activity from A to B can be viewed formally as the same as the duration of a simple game of chance in which the gambler is playing against an infinitely rich adversary. Consider a game in which the outcome of each bet may be a win, a loss, or a tie and, using the notation of Feller (1957, p. 334), let α, β, and γ be the probabilities for these events, respectively. Further, let the value of a win be $+1$, a loss -1 and a tie 0. The gambler begins with resources of amount z and plays until his resources are exhausted. Our interest is in how long he will be able to play and in the conditions of the game that will lead to his ruin.

Following Feller (1957, p. 318), the probability of the gambler's ruin when playing against an infinitely rich adversary can be written $q_z = 1$ if $q \geqslant p$ and $q_z = (q/p)^z$ if $q < p$ where $q = \beta/(1-\gamma)$ is the probability that the gambler's holdings will be reduced by one unit on a bet and $p = \alpha/(1-\gamma)$ is the probability that his holdings will increase by one unit as a result of a bet. Considering only conditions where $q > p$ (i.e., where $\beta > \alpha$) so that ruin is assured, the expected duration of the game is $z/(\beta - \alpha)$ (Feller, 1957, p. 448). The variance of the duration is

$$\frac{4\alpha\beta(1-\gamma)z}{(\beta-\alpha)^3}$$

To use the gambler's ruin as an analogy to shift in activity, the following identifications need to be made: z corresponds to the criterion, r, in the discrete random process model previously presented and α, β, and γ are the probabilities that the processes operating in time result in a movement of one unit away from the criterion (α), a movement of one unit toward the criterion (β), or no movement with respect to reaching the criterion (γ). The shift in activity from A to B occurs when the initial advantage of A over B, symbolized by z, is overcome by the results of the random process involving α, β, and γ. The parameters β and γ have their counterparts in the discrete random process models already considered but α adds something new. This parameter permits the event of a given moment to result in an increase in the distance required to reach criterion, as would be the case if the supports for activity A were strengthened or those for activity B weakened by the event.

A comparison of the form of the expression that results from viewing shift in activity as analogous to a gambler's ruin,

$$t = \frac{z}{(\beta-\alpha)\left(\frac{1}{k}\right)} \tag{11}$$

with the expressions derived already

$$t = \frac{r}{p_B\left(\frac{1}{k}\right)} \quad \text{and} \quad t = \frac{T_{AF} - T_{BI}}{{}_SF_B}$$

shows them to be nearly identical. It will take a very special experiment, one we do not have at present, to determine whether events can increase the distance to criterion and, if so, whether these effects are best interpreted as decreasing the denominator as in

$$t = \frac{z}{(\beta-\alpha)\left(\frac{1}{k}\right)}$$

or as increasing the numerator as in

$$t = \frac{T_{AF} - T_{BI}}{{}_SF_B}.$$

3. *Comparisons of Formal Characteristics of the Models*

This is a good place to pause and make some additional comparisons among the models. All three equations above are clearly similar in one respect—there is an inverse relation between t and the parameters that determine the approach to the criterion. For the model derived from the continuous deterministic process hypothesis, the parameter is ${}_SF_B$, the instigating force functioning to increase the strength of T_B; for the models resulting from the discrete random process hypothesis the parameters are p_B, the probability that a state B event will obtain at any moment in time, and α and β, the probabilities that the distance to the criterion will be increased or reduced by the events of a given moment. In each case the parameters are assumed constant for the period of observation.

One main difference among the equations is that an explicit reference to the ongoing activity A appears only in the expression derived from the continuous deterministic process hypothesis. Provisions for possible influences of characteristics of activity A on the time taken for a shift in activity are not found in the other two equations. The equation

$$t = \frac{T_{AF} - T_{BI}}{{}_SF_B}$$

has the form of a ratio between the influence of T_{AF}, as modified by T_{BI}, and that of ${}_SF_B$. Something of a similar ratio would appear in the other equations if r and z were conceived to be functions of characteristics of the ongoing activity A. These parameters set the criterion for the shift in activity. If r and z were made functions of the characteristics of activity A such that they were large when there was strong support underlying the occurrence of activity A and small when the support was weak, the three equations would become more alike in meaning.

A second main difference in the expressions is also located in the numerator and concerns whether a nonzero initial level of support for alternative activity B is allowed for. Conceptions of a criterion requiring r state B events before the organism moves into state B or that z distance be overcome before a shift in activity will occur has implicitly included a mechanism that tallies up the events as they occur. Accordingly, it is feasible to think of a nonzero level of support for activity B in the sense that the actual occurrences of some events have reduced the overall requirement of r or z occurrences. If this possibility of a reduced r or z value due to a nonzero level of support for activity B is permitted for the beginning of the interval of observation, the functional meaning of T_{BI} will be included in the meanings of r and z.

Thus, these two points of difference among the equations can be resolved by conceiving r and z to be determined by the difference in the final level of support for activity A and the initial level of support for activity B. In fact, when this step is taken, the equations become formally identical with the criterion of shift located in the numerator and the rate of approach to the criterion in the denominator. Precedent for thinking of the criterion of response as approachable is found in a part of La Berge's (1962) theoretical treatment of reaction time. La Berge proposes that the facilitating effect of set (e.g., as derived from instructions) on reaction time may be interpretable in terms of the organism's having a headstart on meeting the criterion of response. However, no explicit recognition is given to the possible role of the ongoing activity in La Berge's formulation, a point specially stressed in the Atkinson–Birch theory based on the continuous deterministic process hypothesis.

4. *Comparisons of Meanings of the Models*

The three equations, though formally identical, do differ in meaning. The concept of tendency, and particularly that of persisting tendency, is central to the model based on the continuous deterministic process hypothesis. The models built on the discrete random process hypothesis do not include the concept of persisting tendency. Tendencies are sufficient for action and herein lies the most distinctive difference in meaning in the two formulations. In the former, tendencies are conceived as continuously present and modifications in the relative strengths of tendencies are responsible for activity shifts. In the latter, action is dependent on the moment-to-moment result of the random sampling process, and there is no carryover effect from one moment to the next.

There are, however, interpretations that can be given to the concept of tendency in the discrete random process model of the r criterion type. For example, it is easily shown that the expected number of samples required to reach criterion goes from $(1/p_B)r$ at the beginning of sampling to $(1/p_B)r - 1$ after one sample has been drawn to $(1/p_B)r - 2$ after two samples to, in general, $(1/p_B)r - s$ after s samples have been drawn, so long as $s \leqslant r$. This sequence is linear in the interval $s \leqslant r$; the function becomes negatively accelerated and approaches asymptotically to 0 as s continues beyond r. Figure 6 illustrates this relation, $E(n) = (1/p_B)r - s$, for $r = 10$ and $p_B = .5$.

The reduction in $E(n)$ could be associated with the growth of something. The "something" might be as little as registering the approach to the criterion on a counter or as much as a tendency with a set of postulated properties. In the latter case the concept of tendency would be introduced to account for the reduction in $E(n)$, and $E(n)$ would be said to decline because the tendency supporting alternative activity B was growing. This tendency would have properties similar to those attributed to the tendency in the continuous deterministic model.

Thus, some of the initial differences between the discrete random process and the continuous deterministic process models begin to

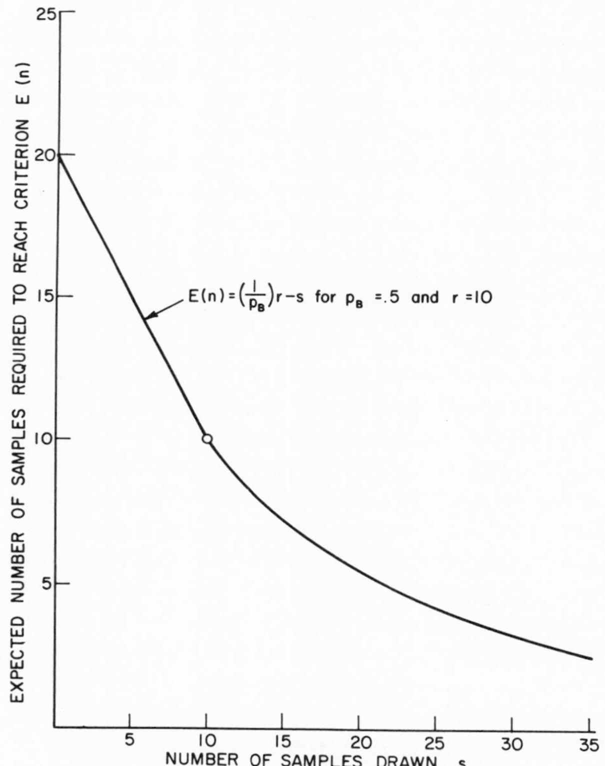

FIG. 6. Reduction in the expected number of samples required to reach criterion as a function of the number of samples already drawn.

disappear. Three of the models are not only identical in their mathematical form but they also share some common meanings for their parameters, even to the extent that the concept of tendency can be defined in each. An important issue, but not necessarily one that distinguishes between the two classes of models, is whether the concept of tendency is only a numerical index of approach to a criterion or whether it has a central role to play in theory with more extensive implications for behavior. A second important issue is generated by the necessity for any model eventually to deal with the fact of variability in behavior. The discrete random process models approach this issue by including a probability mechanism as a part of the genesis of action. The continuous deterministic process model does not include such a mechanism and must make additional commitments if it is to encompass group data or repeated measures from the same individuals under nonconstant conditions.

The continuous deterministic process hypothesis holds that tendencies are always present at some strengths and that the effects operating on tendencies are continuous so long as applications of the instigating and consummatory forces are continuous. If these forces are applied discontinuously over an interval of time, however, the overall picture of a tendency will be one of discontinuous changes. In other words a continuously changing tendency is contingent on uninterrupted applications of the instigating and consummatory forces. Furthermore, labeling the process deterministic means that the process, when operative, is not subject to any inherently random effects; that is, the process itself is not governed by a random mechanism. The line being drawn in this discussion is between the nature of the process when it is functioning and the methodological problems of observation and control that specify when and how the process is functioning. The position represented by the continuous deterministic process model is that all individuals would yield identical data if the variables and their values were the same for all. If individuals differ in the strength of their initial tendencies for the ongoing and alternative activities or in their values for instigating and consummatory forces, these differences need to be assessed and taken into account. It is also possible that over an extended time interval the application of an instigating force is not continuous but rather sporadic and unsystematic, and it may be convenient to summarize such effects in probability terms. Probability theory might assist in summarizing in a similar way the appearance of a consummatory force over a time interval in which the tendency was not expressed continuously. Thus, the continuous deterministic process model is amenable to a stochastic appendage and, in fact, must include a treatment of error in order to be brought into contact with data. However, the heart of the model resides in its nonstochastic characteristics. The extent to which probability considerations have to be introduced is an indication of the extent to which the methodology is still unsatisfactory and the dictum is that it should be improved.

5. *Discrete Random Process Models—Changing Probabilities*

In working with the discrete random process hypothesis we have confined our attention to models in which the value of p_B, the probability of a state B event at a given moment, was assumed constant for the interval of observation (see Table III). There is no reason why this assumption need be made. As a matter of fact, there are good reasons in both Hullian and stimulus sampling theory to propose a systematically changing p_B. The problem is to specify the way in which p_B is changing. In the model presented under the continuous deterministic process hypothesis, instigating and consummatory forces are postulated to change the strength of tendencies, $(dT/dt) = {}_SF - {}_RF$. The instigating force is assumed to remain constant over the interval of observation while the consummatory force is assumed to depend on the expression of the tendency and to change proportionally with the strength of the tendency being expressed. The constant of proportionality is called the consummatory value of the activity.

It is also quite natural to look to the effects of engaging in an activity for reasons why p_B might not remain constant over time in the models derived under the discrete random process hypothesis. Both Hullian and stimulus sampling theory emphasize the role that learning can play in determining p_B. In the former an increase in ${}_SH_R$ has a direct effect on the value of ${}_SE_R$ and thus on p_B; in the latter learning is conceived as a process of reconnecting stimulus and response elements, a process that is expected to change p_B under proper conditions. Both theories also make a place, although certainly a less noticeable one, for other ways of changing p_B. Of most interest to us are the proposals by Estes (1958, 1959) that the population of stimulus elements changes as a function of deprivation and satiation and the possibility in Hullian theory that D might be reduced by an activity—as, for example, if D were based primarily on food deprivation and the activity were eating.

Estes (1958) added two sets of cues, one for deprivation and the other for satiation, to the already well-discussed sets of cues for the controlled signal and the extraneous stimuli. As an organism is deprived, the satiation cues decrease in effectiveness while the deprivation cues gain predominance. Correspondingly, it is to be expected that as an organism engages in a consummatory activity the opposite relations will obtain with the number of cues for satiation increasing while those for deprivation are decreasing. By these postulates the composition of the population of cues on which p_B is based changes continually since an organism is always either engaged in a particular activity or deprived of the opportunity to engage in it.

Knowing the character of the response elements connected to these additional stimulus elements permits an assessment of possible changes in p_B. One might assume that deprivation cues are most strongly connected to the consummatory activity since the consummatory activity has unfailingly occurred in the presence of these cues in the past.

Similarly, it is probably reasonable to assume that satiation cues are most strongly connected to activities other than the consummatory activity since these are the cues present when the consummatory activity is supplanted by other activities. Under these assumptions p_A, the probability of a state A event (i.e., an event supporting the ongoing activity A) would decrease as activity A continued because the population of elements would be shifting from deprivation to satiation. The probability of a state B event, $p_B = 1 - p_A$, would, of course, be increasing during this period. As Estes (1958) states, the particular functions describing these effects need to be determined empirically.

Similar consideration can be given to another effect of the ongoing activity on p_B within the context of Hullian theory. If the primary drive D is based on deprivation, it is to be expected that engaging in the appropriate consummatory activity will reduce D. A reduced D means the difference between ${}_SE_R$'s will be diminished which implies in turn an increased p_B. This is seen most easily by recalling (Hull, 1943, p. 245) that ${}_SE_R = {}_S\bar{H}_R \times \bar{D}$ where

$$\bar{D} = \left(\frac{\dot{D} + D}{\dot{D} + M_D}\right)100$$

and D is the value of the dominant primary drive, $\dot{D}$ the aggregate strength of all the nondominant primary drives active at the time, and M_D the physiological drive maximum. Assuming $\dot{D}$ and M_D remain constant, $\bar{D}$ decreases directly with decreasing D. Thus, for fixed ${}_S\bar{H}_R$'s the difference in ${}_S\bar{E}_R$'s for activities A and B,

$$({}_SE_{R_A} - {}_SE_{R_B}) = ({}_S\bar{H}_{R_A} \times \bar{D}) - ({}_S\bar{H}_{R_B} \times \bar{D}) = ({}_S\bar{H}_{R_A} - {}_S\bar{H}_{R_B}) \times \bar{D},$$

decreases with decreasing $\bar{D}$ to a minimal value set by the value of

$$\left(\frac{\dot{D}}{\dot{D} + M_D}\right)100.$$

The precise form of the reduction in p_A and corresponding gain in p_B depends on the function describing the decline in $\bar{D}$, an empirical matter, and the oscillation function.

Considerable maneuvering room is available to the discrete random process models when possibilities for shifting composition of the stimulus populations and for altered values of $\bar{D}$ are entertained. Actually, this freedom is often not needed or even welcome in dealing with the broader aspects of data. We shall see this in the next section when we use the models against the basic shift in activity data reported earlier in this chapter.

6. *Applications of the Models*

a. Discrete Random Process. Analyses of the shift in activity data strongly indicate that the time spent in the food chamber before *S* entered the exploratory chamber was determined by both the degree of food deprivation and the complexity of the exploratory chamber. These analyses also showed that the total food chamber time was not homogeneous in that the food-orienting time was affected mainly by food deprivation and the nonfood-orienting time mainly by exploratory

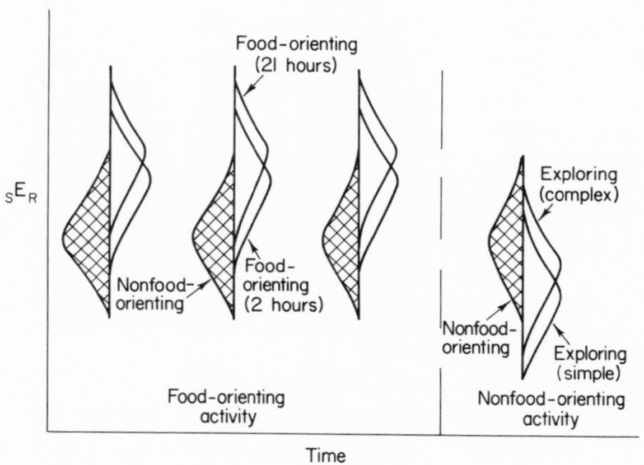

FIG. 7. Sequence of activities from food orienting to nonfood-orienting to exploring as represented in Hullian theory with fixed values for ${}_SE_R$'s.

chamber complexity. It was concluded that *S* did not shift activities directly from eating to exploring but went through a third intermediate activity. Figure 7 illustrates how this sequence might be diagrammed using the oscillation function and fixed values of ${}_SE_R$'s.

The left portion of the figure depicts the two deprivation groups during the period when the food-orienting activity is occurring. The ${}_SE_R$ for the 21-hour group is shown above that for the 2-hour group and both of these ${}_SE_R$'s are placed above the ${}_SE_R$ for the nonfood-orienting activity, assumed common to the two deprivation groups. With fixed values for the ${}_SE_R$'s this arrangement holds until the random process produces a shift in activity. An average of 491 seconds is taken for the shift in the 2-hour group and 635 seconds in the 21-hour group. After the shift to the nonfood-orienting activity, a new arrangement holds in which the ${}_SE_R$ for exploring is pitted against the ${}_SE_R$ for the ongoing nonfood-orienting activity in each group. For convenience the ${}_SE_R$ for the nonfood-orienting activity has been kept at its previous location and the two new

${}_{S}E_{R}$'s for the complex and simple exploratory chamber groups placed somewhat below and in that order. This configuration remains until the random process produces a shift to exploring. For the complex exploratory chamber group, an average of 106 seconds pass before the shift and for the simple exploratory chamber group 184 seconds. This presentation has been made uncomplicated by considering only the food-orienting

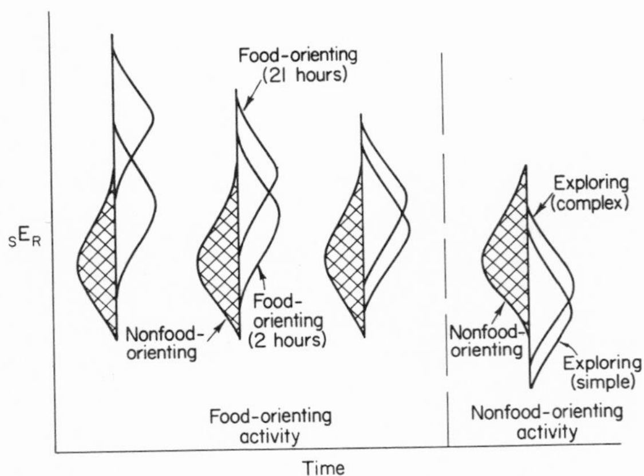

FIG. 8. Sequence of activities from food orienting to nonfood-orienting to exploring as represented in Hullian theory when D is assumed to decline as a result of the food-orienting activity.

activity to nonfood-orienting activity to exploring sequence and ignoring the possibility that S might return to the food one or more times before leaving the food chamber. The random process model can be extended to encompass more complex sequences, but we shall not pursue the matter here because such extensions do not assist in distinguishing among models in regard to the present data.

Instead, we shall turn briefly to Fig. 8 where an example in which ${}_{S}E_{R}$'s are assumed to change over time is presented. Again the left portion of the figure shows the situation when the food-orienting activity is occurring and the right portion after the shift to the nonfood-orienting activity. While the food-orienting activity is going on, the ${}_{S}E_{R}$'s for that activity are assumed to decrease because eating is assumed to reduce D. The result is that the overlap between the nonfood-orienting activity distribution and the food-orienting activity distributions increases with time and, equally important, the difference between the two deprivation groups disappears with time spent eating. In the equations presented earlier these effects would appear through the introduction of continuously changing values for the probabilities, p_B or α and β, over time.

Diagrams similar to those of Figs. 7 and 8 could be constructed for the stimulus sampling version of the random process model. Fixed or changing p_B (or α and β) would be conceived in terms of fixed or changing populations of elements and the connections they have with responses. In the case of both theories, Hullian and stimulus sampling, the refinements embodied in the changing values of p_B; however intuitively reasonable they may be, go beyond the minimum required to account for the present data.

b. Continuous Deterministic Process. We shall oversimplify the continuous deterministic process model also as we apply it to the present data. We shall assume that no instigating forces are being applied to the tendencies for exploring the alternative chamber while the food-orienting activity is ongoing but that they begin their application when the nonfood-orienting activity begins. This means that the exploratory tendencies remain at their initial levels as long as the food-orienting activity is occurring. We shall assume the levels to be somewhat different with the tendency to explore the complex chamber stronger than the tendency to explore the simple chamber as a result of the 2 minutes of exposure given prior to each day's test. We shall also assume that the tendency for the food-orienting activity does not change after the shift from that activity to the nonfood-orienting activity because *S* removes himself from the stimuli with the major instigating force properties for eating. At the same time, the instigating force for the tendency to engage in the nonfood-orienting activity should increase when *S* begins that activity and our assumptions reflect this.

Figure 9 represents the processes hypothesized to occur in the continuous deterministic process model for the sequence of activities from food orienting to nonfood-orienting to exploring. The curves are adjusted to fit the obtained time values. In the top panel of Fig. 9 the shifts in activity for the two 21-hour groups are presented. The groups do not differ in the time taken for the first shift in activity which occurs when the linearly growing tendency for the nonfood-orienting activity reaches the tendency for the food-orienting activity which is falling to its asymptote defined by $_{S}F/c$. When activity shifts, the tendency for the nonfood-orienting activity begins to rise to its $_{S}F/c$ asymptote and the tendencies to explore the alternative chamber begin to grow linearly. The tendency to explore rises more rapidly in the group for which the exploratory chamber is complex than in the group for which it is simple and, as Fig. 9 illustrates, the first group shifts from the nonfood-orienting activity to exploring more quickly. Exactly the same kinds of processes are pictured for the two 2-hour groups in the lower panel of Fig. 9. The difference between these functions and the ones above arise because the 2-hour groups are assumed to begin the time interval with a less strong tendency to engage in the food-orienting activity than the 21-hour groups.

The functions pictured in Fig. 9 correspond to the equations presented earlier for the continuous deterministic process model. Derivations from

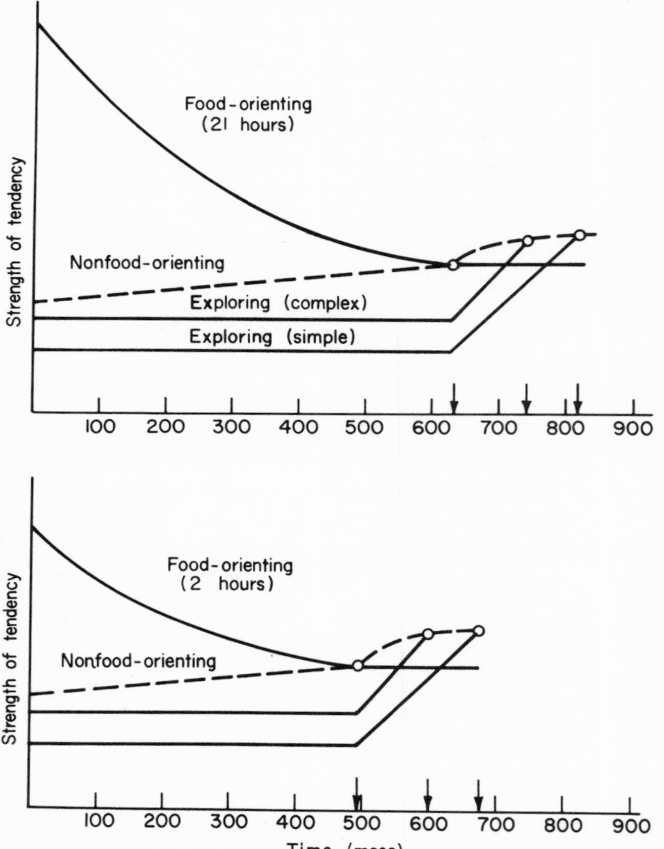

FIG. 9. Hypothesized processes for the sequence of activities from food orienting to nonfood-orienting to exploring according to the continuous deterministic process model.

these equations are certainly consistent with the time data just as were the derivations from the equations for the discrete random process models. These time data make the point strongly that characteristics of the ongoing activity as well as those of the alternative activity need to be considered in models of action. Under the continuous deterministic process hypothesis, we have presented a model that inherently gives equal and explicit attention to both activities since shift in activity is defined by the changing dominance relation between the tendencies to engage in the ongoing and alternative activities. The models based on the discrete random process hypothesis draw more attention to the role of the alternative activity than to that of the ongoing activity, but we have indicated that these models also include provision for effects from both activities and illustrated how they might be expanded to encompass such effects.

We found that the equations for all the models, at least under special conditions, were very similar. There are, however, fundamental differences embedded deeply within the models that should not be ignored simply because certain equations share a common form. One fundamental difference, the one we wish to devote the next section to discussing, is in the treatment of the function of a stimulus and the implications this has for a concept of persisting tendency.

V. Concept of Persisting Tendency

Some theories are stimulus bound (Atkinson, 1964; Atkinson & Cartwright, 1964). For example, Hull (1943, p. 109) in discussing response evocation says, "Now, it is assumed that *the immediate causes of an event must be active at the time the event begins to occur*. But at the time a habit action is evoked, the reinforcing event may be long past, i.e., it may no longer exist; and something which does not exist can scarcely be the cause of anything. Therefore, reinforcement can hardly be the direct or immediate cause of an act. We accordingly conclude that the immediate cause of habit-mediated action evocation must be a combination of (1) the stimulus event and (2) a relatively permanent condition or organization left by the reinforcement within the nervous system of the animal." Similarly, Estes (1950, p. 96) states, "For analytic purposes it is assumed that all behavior is conditional upon appropriate stimulation" and (p. 97) "If a set of x elements from an S are conditioned to (i.e., have the conditional relation to) some R-class, R_1, at a given time, the probability that the next response to occur will be an instance of R_1 is x/S."

We will term a theory stimulus bound if it permits a response to occur only if an eliciting stimulus is present at that moment; that is, if the "cause" of the response is to be found in stimuli. The theory presented under the continuous deterministic process hypothesis is not stimulus bound. In this theory activities are "caused" by tendencies, not by stimuli. Furthermore, tendencies are postulated to persist until changed by forces acting on them. Stimuli, if they have instigating force power, are treated as agents that can increase the strength of tendencies rather than as events necessary for the evocation of behavior. Action is tied directly to tendencies and only indirectly to stimuli.

Three points with experimentally testable consequences stand out in regard to the postulated persisting tendency.

1. A tendency with some baseline strength should be increased in strength by the application of a stimulus with appropriate instigating force value.

2. A tendency that has been increased in strength should retain its new level of strength even after the stimulus with instigating force value is removed. This implies that a tendency aroused in one situation will carry over and be expressed in another situation.

3. The strength of a tendency should grow as a function of the time of exposure to a stimulus with instigating force power since the force applied at each moment in time boosts the strength of the tendency over the level there at that moment.

A. Experimental Evaluation

In this research we have attempted to assess the strength of a tendency by measuring the intensity of an activity while it is going on instead of by a shift in activity paradigm. To justify this we make use of the assumption introduced earlier in relation to consummatory force that the intensity with which a tendency is expressed is directly proportional to the strength of the tendency being expressed. We chose eating as the activity to be investigated and obtained our measure of intensity by counting the number of pellets of food eaten in a fixed period of time.

Three experiments have been carried out.[5] In all three the same apparatus and basic procedure were employed. Two sets of cages, one used for feeding and the other for testing, contained eight individual cells, 9 inches long, 6 inches wide, and 8 inches high, constructed of plywood walls and masonite floor. Each cell has its own hardware cloth cover. The feeding cages are painted flat white and each cell has an aluminum food trough, 2 inches long by 2 inches wide by $\frac{1}{2}$ inch deep, fastened on the back wall $\frac{1}{2}$ inch above the floor. Water bottles were placed on the covers with the tubes projecting down into the cells. The masonite floor is all one piece and hinged to the cage shells to facilitate cleaning. The testing cages are identical to the feeding cages with two exceptions: they are painted flat black and they do not include aluminum food troughs. Instead, during tests clear glass coasters were in place in the left front corners of the cells.

When *S*s were received from the supplier they were placed into group cages and maintained on an ad libitum food schedule for approximately

[5] The first experiment was carried out by Fred P. Valle, the second by Guy J. Johnson, and the third was a collaborative effort by both.

2 weeks. Two days prior to the experiment *S*s were handled for a few minutes each day. On the first day of the experiment *S*s were moved into individual cages in a standard 60-cage animal rack with water always available but with *no food ever present*. The location of the home rack was considerably removed from the general housing room containing the group cages. The feeding and testing cages were located in still other rooms. The main point of this part of the procedure is that *S*s *never* received food in their individual home cages and they *always* received their daily ration in the special feeding cages. The ration given *S* each day was a mixture of ground Purina lab chow, powdered milk, and Wesson oil in approximately a 10:1:1 mixture.

1. *Experiment 1*

In the first experiment 16 naive, male hooded rats, 140–200 days of age, were used as *S*s. These *S*s were placed in both the feeding and testing cages daily according to the following schedule. At the same time each day a squad of 8 *S*s were transported from their home cages to the feeding cages and allowed to eat freely from an oversupply of their maintenance diet for 90 minutes. They were then returned to their home cages and 120 minutes later placed for 10 minutes in the testing cages where the glass coasters in each cell contained 100 .097-gm Noyes pellets. After testing, *S*s were replaced in their home cages where they remained until the same schedule was repeated the next day. Food was always available in the feeding and testing cages and never available in the home cages. Water was always available in the home cages and in the feeding cages but never in the testing cages after it was found that it moistened the pellets and made impossible an accurate count of the numbers of pellets consumed. This regime was continued for 18 days giving baseline data as to the numbers of pellets *S*s would consume during 10 minutes in the testing cages, 2 hours after having been fed their daily rations in the feeding cages.[6]

On the following day the experimental conditions were instituted. These conditions broke up the 120-minute feeding to testing time interval into two parts. The first part was either 115, 105, 75, or 30 minutes long and it was spent by *S*s in their home cages while the second part, correspondingly, was 5, 15, 45, or 90 minutes and it was spent by *S*s in the feeding cages. During this latter period the feeding cages were empty of all food but water was still available. In order to determine the

[6] For 3 days prior to this period *S*s had been allowed to eat for only 60 minutes in the feeding cages, were returned to their home cages for 180 minutes, and were tested for 30 minutes in the testing cages. This procedure was altered when it became evident that large numbers of pellets were being consumed in the tests, many more than were necessary or desirable for the purposes of the experiment.

assignment of Ss to the four experimental conditions, they were ranked from smallest to largest eaters within each squad on the basis of the mean number of pellets they consumed during the last five baseline days and placed into four groups. The top two eaters from each squad made

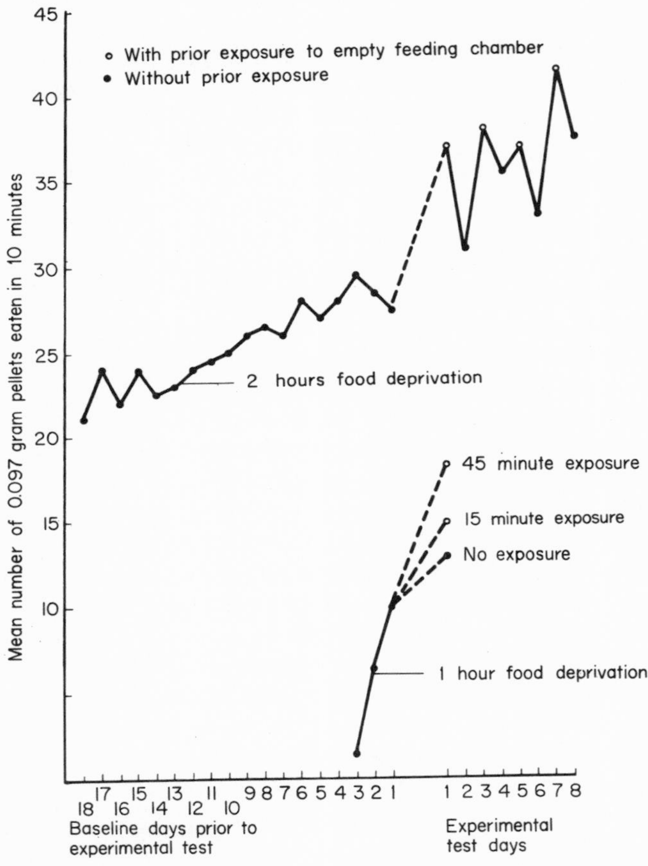

FIG. 10. Number of pellets consumed on baseline and test days by the groups of Experiments 1 and 2 bearing on the concept of persisting tendency.

up the "largest eaters" group and Ss ranked 3 and 4, 5 and 6, and 7 and 8 in each squad were joined to form the remaining three groups. These four groups were entered into a latin square with the four exposure conditions and four experimental testing days to give the design of the study. A total of 8 days were used in this testing phase because each administration of the experimental conditions was separated by a day in which the regular baseline procedure was employed.

The measure of interest is the number of pellets consumed in the 10-minute testing intervals. Figure 10 contains this information in the upper graph plotted in terms of means. The lower graph in Fig. 10 is from the next experiment and should be ignored for the present. It is clear from the upper graph that the mean number of pellets consumed is increasing rather regularly over the 18 baseline days with a peak value of 29 reached on the third to last point. A striking jump in the graph occurs between these baseline days and the days when the experimental conditions are imposed. Furthermore, each of the four experimental test days produces a larger mean number of pellets eaten than the four corresponding baseline days.

In order to evaluate whether exposure to the empty feeding cages affected the eating activity of the *S*s in the test, the overall mean number of pellets eaten on experimental test days 1, 3, 5, and 7 (when exposure was given) were compared with the overall mean number of pellets consumed on days 2, 4, 6, and 8 (when exposure was not given). Fifteen of the 16 *S*s ate more pellets with exposure than without, a result most unlikely on the basis of chance alone. The mean values were 38.5 pellets following exposure and 34.3 pellets following no exposure, values which differ significantly ($p < .05$). Overall average difference scores for the 5, 15, 45, and 90-minute conditions were 3.2, 2.8, 5.8, and 5.0 pellets, respectively. Although these values are suggestive of an effect due to duration of exposure, statistical analysis does not permit such a conclusion. Nor did the other two main effects of the latin square design, amount eaten during the baseline assessment and days of experimental testing, show statistical significance.

The first experiment provided support for two of the three points raised in regard to the concept of persisting tendency. First, *S*'s tendency to eat was strengthened significantly over its baseline by exposure to stimuli with instigating force value for that tendency and, second, the stronger tendency persisted into a new testing situation and was displayed there in the intensity of S's eating. No solid support was realized for the hypothesis that time of exposure to the instigating stimuli is related to the strength of the tendency being instigated.

2. *Experiment 2*

The second experiment in this series utilized a design in which *S*s were not treated with more than one experimental condition. The latin square design of the first experiment served well enough as an initial effort, but examination of the data suggested the possibility that complex interaction effects were contributing to the lack of significance of the main effects, and it was decided to approach the points raised by the persisting tendency hypothesis more simply. To accomplish this the same basic method of the first experiment was employed, but three separate experimental groups, one with no immediately prior exposure to the feeding cages, another with 15 minutes exposure, and the third with 45 minutes exposure, were formed.

*S*s were 30 male hooded rats approximately 60 days old at the beginning of the experiment. They were assigned to individual cages the same day they arrived from the supplier. As in the first experiment, *S*s were housed in a room different from those in which they were fed and tested. The same feeding and testing cages and the same regime of allowing *S*s free access to food for 90 minutes each day were employed in this experiment as in the first. *S*s were maintained on their schedule for 14 days before baseline testing. Two changes in testing procedure were introduced: baseline testing lasted only 3 days and all testing, baseline and experimental, was carried out under 1 hour of food deprivation. *S*s were accustomed to the pellets used in testing by receiving five of them along with their daily rations on each of the 3 baseline testing days. The testing period was 10 minutes as in the first experiment, and all three groups were represented in each testing session.

Results are pictured in the lower portion of Fig. 10. *S*s increased their consumption of the pellets over the 3 days of baseline testing from an average of 1.6 pellets on the first day to 6.7 pellets on the second and 9.9 on the third. The three experimental groups, each with $N = 10$, were formed by assigning *S*s at random, a procedure which resulted in groups with very similar baseline data. In fact, the points plotted in Fig. 10 for the baseline testing are accurate representations of the data for the separate groups as well as for the total. On the experimental testing day *S*s given 45 minutes exposure to the empty feeding cages just prior to testing consumed an average of 18.7 pellets, those given 15 minutes exposure 15.1 pellets, and those given no exposure only 12.9 pellets, as may be observed in Fig. 10. The average gains in the number of pellets eaten on the experimental testing day as compared to the last baseline testing day are 8.5 (45 minutes exposure), 5.3 (15 minutes exposure), and 3.1 (0 exposure). The difference in gain between the 45-minute and zero exposure groups is significant ($p < .05$); other differences among groups do not reach significance.

This experiment, like the first, gives support to the hypothesis that exposure to stimuli with instigating force value for eating will increase the tendency to eat and that the increased tendency will persist after *S*s have been removed from the presence of the instigating stimuli. Once again, however, no reliable support was found for the hypothesis that duration of exposure to stimuli with instigating force properties is a factor in increasing the strength of a tendency.

Some additional data on the effects of exposure to the empty feeding cages in conjunction with 25 hours food deprivation were obtained from the *S*s in this experiment. On the 2 days following the experimental testing day *S*s were given two more baseline tests; the first, again under 1 hour of food deprivation, yielded a mean of 14.5 pellets eaten and the second with *S*s 25 hours food deprived produced a mean of 34.6. The effectiveness of the greater deprivation time on the number of pellets consumed in the test is supported also by the data for individual *S*s which show that 29 out of the 30 *S*s increased their eating when the deprivation time was increased. The latter testing was administered simply by not feeding *S*s their daily rations and then testing them at the usual time.

Following the 25-hour baseline test *S*s were returned to their home cages for 10 minutes and then received their daily ration in the feeding cages. The next day no tests were carried out and *S*s were fed at their usual times. On the day after, the three exposure groups were subjected to the same experimental conditions as previously (i.e., 45, 15, or 0 minutes exposure to the empty feeding cages) and then tested under 25 hours deprivation. The mean increases in the number of pellets consumed in this test over the baseline were 13.4, 10.6, and 4.7 for the three groups ordered in terms of decreasing duration of exposure. The three groups are shown to differ significantly ($p < .01$) when their means are evaluated by analysis of variance, but consistent with the results of the 1-hour testing, the difference between the 15 and 45-minute exposure groups is not reliable. Thus, again we find that exposing *S*s to the empty feeding cages prior to testing produces more eating than not exposing them but that statistically satisfactory evidence for the effectiveness of duration of exposure is lacking.

3. *Experiment 3*

The design of the third experiment of the series takes into account the leads provided by the first two. A total of eight groups were used, each with N = 8. *S*s were male, naive hooded rats approximately 55 days old when obtained from the supplier. Preliminary handling while *S*s remained in group cages continued over 12 days, and *S*s were adapted to the maintenance schedule for 14 days. Twenty-five of the .097-gm Noyes pellets were put into the feeding cages before feeding on days 5 and 6 of adaptation in order to provide *S*s experience with the pellets prior to testing. The major procedural change introduced into this experiment was to place *S*s in the *empty* testing cages for 10 minutes on each of the 14 days of adaptation. This allowed *S*s to be tested with food in the testing cages for the first time on the experimental testing day but under conditions where they had eaten pellets previously and had become familiar with the testing cages. *S*s in seven of the eight groups were tested 110 minutes after feeding (the same interval as used when familiarizing *S*s with the testing cages) for 10 minutes. On the thirteenth day of adaptation *S*s were assessed as to the number of pellets they would eat in their feeding cages under 22 hours of food deprivation to permit adjustments for individual differences during subsequent statistical analyses.

The 110-minute period between feeding and testing on day 15 was used to impose the experimental conditions. Table IV summarizes the treatments for the eight groups. Group (2-0-0) was tested when 2 hours food deprived (actually 110 minutes) with no exposure to the empty feeding cages and immediate placement into the testing cages. Groups (2-10-0), (2-40-0), and (2-70-0) were tested under 2 hour deprivation following 10, 40, and 70 minutes exposure, respectively, and with no return to the home cage but rather immediate transfer from the empty feeding cages to the testing cages. Groups (2-10-30), (2-40-30), and (2-70-30) correspond to the previous three groups in their treatments except that the exposures to the empty feeding cages were given 30 minutes earlier, allowing for a 30-minute delay between exposure and test. This delay period was spent by *S*s in their home cages. Group (26-0-0) was not tested until the following day. On this second testing day all eight groups were made 26 hours hungry by omitting their regular feedings and then tested without exposure to the empty feeding cages and with direct transfer from the home cages to the testing cages. *S*s were organized into squads with each group tested on a day (seven groups on the first day and eight on the second) represented by a single *S*. All *S*s were given their experimental treatments within the same 110-minute period and then tested simultaneously in the eight cell testing cages.

Table V presents the means and variances for the groups in each of their tests, baseline and experimental. Results in terms of mean differences in pellets consumed between the tests and the baseline, adjusted so that the mean for Group (2-0-0) is set equal to 100, are pictured in Fig. 11. Looking first at the data obtained when the *S*s were under 2 hours deprivation we note that (1) Group (2-0-0) consumes considerably fewer pellets than the other six groups, (2) Groups (2-10-0), (2-40-0), and (2-70-0) are ordered in terms of the mean number of pellets consumed, (3) Groups (2-10-30), (2-40-30), and (2-70-30) are not so ordered and (4) the overall level of the 30-minute delay groups is slightly above that of the 0 delay groups. Statistical analyses of these data show that only the differences between Group (2-0-0), with no exposure to the empty feeding cages prior to testing, and the other six groups with some amount of exposure are reliable. A simple test of the difference between the mean for Group (2-0-0) and that for the other six groups pooled is significant ($p < .05$). In addition, the means for four of the other six groups [Groups

TABLE IV

EXPERIMENTAL CONDITIONS IMPOSED DURING THE 110 MINUTES BETWEEN THE END OF THE NORMAL FEEDING PERIOD AND THE BEGINNING OF TESTING

	Minutes spent sequentially in		
Group[a]	Home cages	Empty feeding cages	Home cages
2-0-0	100	0	0
2-10-0	100	10	0
2-40-0	70	40	0
2-70-0	40	70	0
2-10-30	70	10	30
2-40-30	40	40	30
2-70-30	10	70	30
26-0-0[b]	110	0	0

[a] Three digits are used to identify the groups: the first digit tells the hours of food deprivation at testing, the second digit the minutes of exposure to the empty feeding cages, and the third digit the time of delay in minutes from the end of exposure to the beginning of testing.

[b] *S*s in this group were treated the same as those in Group (2-0-0) except that they were not given their regular feeding on the day of testing.

TABLE V

MEANS AND VARIANCES FOR THE NUMBER OF PELLETS CONSUMED DURING THE BASELINE ASSESSMENT, THE FIRST TESTING DAY AND THE SECOND TESTING DAY

	Baseline[a]		First testing day (2-hours deprivation)		Second testing day (26-hours deprivation)	
Group	Mean	σ^2	Mean	σ^2	Mean	σ^2
2-0-0	39.2	126.8	31.0	29.5	50.5	107.2
2-10-0	36.1	38.6	36.0	101.0	52.1	83.4
2-40-0	33.1	59.1	34.8	43.8	53.6	115.5
2-70-0	35.6	75.5	42.9	91.9	53.5	65.8
2-10-30	35.0	78.8	39.5	58.2	54.1	53.4
2-40-30	35.9	39.1	36.5	123.0	52.2	79.5
2-70-30	32.9	71.4	40.6	102.0	54.1	72.9
26-0-0	35.2	73.0	—	—	40.4	73.8

[a] Baseline assessment occurred in the feeding cages under 22-hour food deprivation.

(2-10-0) and (2-40-30) are the exceptions] lie outside the 95% confidence interval set up around the mean for Group (2-0-0); namely, 100.0 ± 8.8. Differences among the six groups with exposure whether with respect to amount of exposure or to delay between exposure and testing, are not statistically significant.

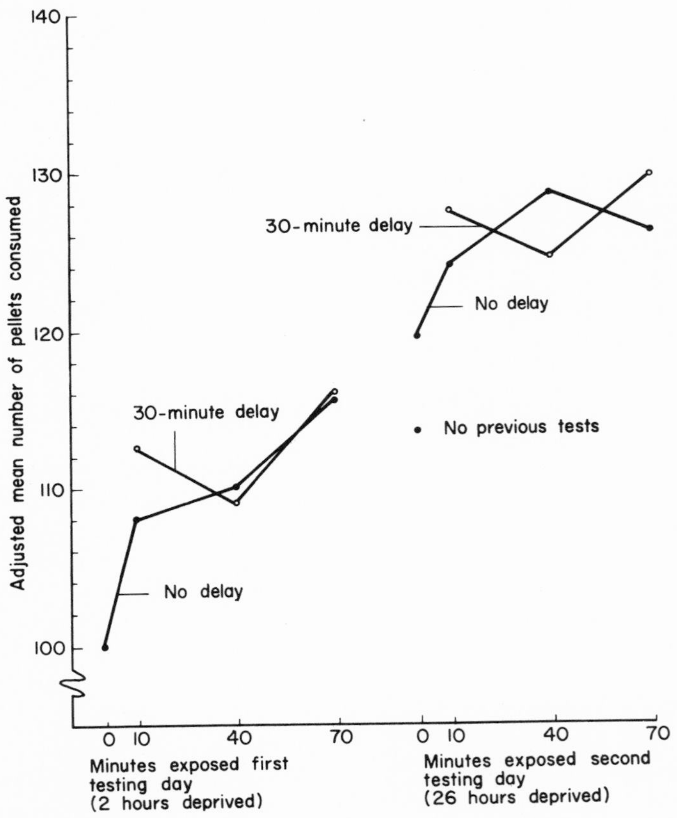

FIG. 11. Vigor of eating in groups differing in amount of exposure, exposure to testing delay interval, and degree of deprivation.

Similar conclusions follow from the data obtained from these groups under 26 hour food deprivation, as shown in Fig. 11 for the second testing day. The mean for the six exposure groups pooled differs significantly ($p < .05$) from that for Group (2-0-0), and the 95% confidence interval around the Group (2-0-0) mean (119.4 ± 5.0) excludes the means for all groups except Group (2-10-0). Differences among exposure groups do not approach significance, but it should be recalled that these groups were all treated alike (0 duration of exposure and 0 delay) on the second testing day.

The data are informative on two additional points. First, Group (26-0-0), tested for the first time on the second testing day, consumed more pellets (113.3) than did Group (2-0-0) on its initial test (100.0) but the fewest pellets of all the eight groups on the second testing day. Both results are statistically significant, the first when evaluated by simple analysis of variance ($p < .05$) and the second by the 95% confidence interval set up around the Group (26-0-0) mean (113.3 ± 5.0) which excludes the means for all of the other seven groups. The second point relates to the overall effect of the second test under 26-hour deprivation. As may be observed in Fig. 11, each of the seven experimental groups tested under 2-hour deprivation on one day and under 26-hour deprivation the next consumes a larger mean number of pellets the second day. The generality of this effect is emphasized by noting that 53 of 56 *S*s increased the number of pellets they ate from the first to the second test. That this effect is not due to the change in deprivation alone but also to the fact of a previous test is shown by the lesser mean for Group (26-0-0) as compared to the means for the other seven groups on their second day of testing.

Putting together the results from all three experiments, we may conclude:

1. The tendency for rats to eat pellets is strengthened over a baseline determined from the degree of food deprivation by exposure to stimuli with instigating force value for the eating tendency.
2. The eating tendency retains its enhanced strength from one situation to another even over a 30-minute interval.
3. The tendency to eat is strengthened more by 26-hour than by 2-hour food deprivation in a setting that is designed to afford few stimuli with instigating force value for eating.

A conclusion about the effect of duration of exposure to stimuli with instigating force value for eating must be brought forward more tentatively. In all three experiments a trend that related greater eating during the test to longer exposure to the empty feeding cages was observable, but in none of the experiments was the effect satisfactory statistically.

B. Commentary

1. *Persisting Tendency and the Data*

The first two findings, that the tendency to eat will persist well beyond the time when the instigating stimulus was present and that the tendency to eat can be strengthened by exposure to stimuli with instigating force value, are quite consonant with the theory about tendencies presented in this chapter. The third finding, that the tendency to eat was stronger after 26-hour food deprivation than after 2-hour deprivation, should surprise no one. What is of interest here revolves around the question of why this should be the case.

Within the framework of the tendency theory, deprivation is a period of time in which an organism is exposed to stimuli with instigating force value for some tendency without opportunity to engage in activities which would reduce that tendency.[7] Each occurrence of a stimulus with instigating force value is postulated to boost the level of tendency and, of course, 26 hours of exposure to instigating stimuli should result in a stronger tendency than 2 hours of exposure. This can be seen to be the case in the present experiments; Group (26-0-0) ate significantly more pellets than Group (2-0-0) during initial testing even though care was taken to reduce as much as possible the contribution of extraneous instigating stimuli to the tendency to eat. It should not be overlooked, however, that *S*s in Group (2-0-0) ate approximately 3 gm of food in the test while those in Group (26-0-0) ate only .9 gm more. An increase of approximately 1 gm of food eaten as a result of an additional 24 hours without food is not impressive. Note also that *S*s in the other six groups, those deprived for 2 hours but exposed to the instigating stimuli of the empty feeding cages, consumed very nearly the same amount of food as *S*s in Group (26-0-0), a finding which highlights further the crucial role of instigating stimuli in determining strength of tendency. The suggestion from these data is very strong: Exposure to stimuli with instigating force value in the absence of expression of the resulting tendency serves to increase the strength of a tendency and deprivation is effective only to the degree that it subjects the organism to such exposure.

The failure of duration of exposure to the empty feeding cages to exert greater command over the data than it did needs careful scrutiny. It is not a necessary part of the theory that tendencies grow continuously with exposure to stimuli with instigating force value; it was so proposed, however, and that proposal should be evaluated.

An unwarranted assumption may have been made in designing the experiments. Theoretically, under continuous exposure to an instigating stimulus the tendency will approach an asymptote defined by the ratio of the instigating force (${}_SF$) to the consummatory value (c). A tendency can be expected to *increase* in strength over this time period only if this

[7] This interpretation of deprivation follows rather directly from the Atkinson–Birch theory and was used as a point of departure for the present experiments. Studies by Birch, Burnstein, and Clark (1958) and Brown and Belloni (1963) contain other relevant theoretical and methodological background.

ratio stays high enough. If $_SF$ were to decrease in value over the time period, as would be expected if extinction were occurring, the asymptote could fall far enough that the tendency would not rise appreciably or it might even decline as time of exposure increased. Thus, it may be in the present experiments that the instigating force of the empty feeding cages declined over the 15, 40, 45, and 70 minutes of exposure to such an extent that one had no right to expect sizeable differences in the final level of tendency for the exposure conditions. Finding ways to preserve the instigating force value of a stimulus as it is operating on the strength of a tendency will help to bring this potential factor to test.

A second reason for the relative ineffectiveness of duration of exposure could be that instigating stimuli have their effects only during onset. An assumption to this effect would destroy expectation of differences among exposure groups since each was placed into the empty feeding cages only once. At the same time it would not allay a concern that the trend between duration of exposure and strength of tendency as observed in each of the experiments needs to be accommodated.

Both suggestions as to why duration of exposure was not found to be more effective than it was should be elaborated to take into account a most reasonable possibility that stimuli other than those of the feeding cages might acquire instigating force value. The sights and sounds of cage doors and certainly the cues from picking up and carrying the animals are present as potential instigating stimuli. Perhaps the duration of exposure to the empty feeding cages simply is not a powerful enough manipulation when it is imposed on a background of these other instigating forces.

2. *Persisting Tendency and the Theory of Action*

Persisting tendencies originate with stimulation but, once aroused, exist independently of stimulation. This is not a postulate about tendencies that is customarily made in behavior theory, but it is one that is integral to the molar theory of action outlined in this chapter. [See Birch (1966b) for an example in which the analysis of certain aspects of the verbal control of nonverbal behavior in children is based on the concept of persisting tendency.] The postulate that tendencies can persist over time, even in the absence of any observable stimulation for them, releases the theorist from the obligation to hypothesize stimuli when he is unable to identify them. It is sufficient that he locate the events external to an organism's nervous system that produce changes in the strengths of tendencies; he need not also be responsible for accounting for the moment-to-moment existence of tendencies.

Any molar theory can be neutral with respect to its molecular underpinnings. However, if it is useful in organizing data and fruitful of researchable hypotheses, in other words if it is successful, a molar theory will generate a demand for molecular analysis. Such an analysis will turn to a new set of postulates, concepts, and mechanisms which may not resemble closely those in the molar theory. A little later in this chapter we will use the fractional anticipatory goal response mechanism, the r_g-s_g, as an example of the way in which the molar concept of persisting tendency can be provided with a molecular base. Before turning to that, it will be helpful to survey briefly some of the instances in the literature where statements relevant to the concept of persisting tendency can be found.

a. Background. Among the early theories in which ideas about persisting tendencies appear were those of Freud (1949) who referred to persisting wishes and of Lewin (1938) who appealed to persisting states of tension. More recently and in quite a different domain, Hebb (1949) conceived of a central nervous system replete with cell assemblies and phase sequences that had the property of reverberation which could maintain nervous system activity over time. Atkinson (1964) reviews these and other contributions to the topic as a background for his own development of the concept of inertial tendency.

Other writers also have put forth theoretical suggestions that embody the central idea of a persisting tendency. Maltzman (1952), in a paper that contains many points that are important for a theory of action, proposes a variable he calls "process need" that carries several of the properties and explanatory responsibilities ascribed to persisting tendency. Process needs do not remain stable within trials but vary as a function of stimulation and consummatory activity. Maltzman looks to data demonstrating the effects on performance of prefeeding and shifts in amount of reward for evidence supporting the process need. Interpretation of these findings requires that the process need persist over some period of time and Maltzman (1952, p. 42) is explicit on this point when he hypothesizes that "the process need will decay as a function of time following commerce with a goal object." To hypothesize that the process need decays is also to hypothesize that it perseverates.

A much more recent contribution by Whalen, who presents a theory of sexual motivation, is constructed on the premise that the effects of stimulation continue through time. In the context of discussing the effects of applying a single sexual stimulus to individuals of different degrees of arousability, Whalen (1966, p. 153) writes "Each stimulus produces an immediate increment in arousal which reaches a peak and then decays in time. If a second stimulus is applied before the effects of the first stimulus have completely decayed, sexual arousal will progressively increase. Arousal would accumulate more rapidly for the high-arousable individual than for the low-arousable, both because each stimulus would add relatively more excitation and because the decay of arousal would require more time." It is not difficult to see the correspondence between arousal and arousability and persisting tendency and instigating force.

The possibility that the fractional anticipatory goal response, r_g, might persist over time was entertained by Amsel, Ernhart, and Galbrecht (1961) and Bower (1962). Amsel *et al.* varied the length of a runway as a method for manipulating the strength of r_g under the assumption that the strength of r_g is some function of the duration of goal-antedating stimuli which presumably elicit r_g. Bower appealed specifically to a persisting r_g in giving an alternative account of the frustration effect found in double runway studies (e.g., Amsel & Roussel, 1952) when he proposed (Bower, 1962, p. 585), "... when the r_g is aroused in R_1 and then not satisfied by reward in G_1, this r_g and its consequent excitement persist for some amount of time. If during this time the animal is permitted to perform a second response, the persisting r_g and its excitement add in to increase the net incentive motivation for this second response."

b. A Molecular Basis in the r_g-s_g *Mechanism.* With this as a backdrop we now return to consider a molecular basis for the molar concept of persisting tendency. Hull gives us the lead we need. In a classic paper dealing with the r_g-s_g mechanism, Hull (1931) postulated four sources of stimulus events to be considered in an analysis of molar behavior: the external physical environment, the internal physiological environment defined by conditions of deprivation, and the proprioceptive feedback from movement and consummatory or goal responses. The stimuli coordinated to these sources can be symbolized as s_E, s_D, s_p, and s_g. Two kinds of responses, movement and consummatory, are also postulated; they can be represented as r_m and r_g and their overt manifestations as R_M and R_G. In repeated sequences of goal-directed movements all four stimulus types can become associated with both kinds of responses. A diagram illustrating this is presented in Fig. 12.

Elements inside the rectangle correspond to unobservable stimulus and response events in the organism and those outside to events observable in the external world. Input to the nervous system originates with the external physical environment and with conditions of deprivation. With repetition s_E and s_D have the opportunity to become associated with r_m and r_g as do the stimuli, s_p and s_g, all of which is shown by the arrows of Fig. 12.

The concept of persisting tendency is captured very effectively in the diagram. It can be identified with the unit composed of the elements r_m, s_p, r_g, and s_g and their interrelations as indicated by the solid lines and arrows. The lines stand for the stimulus feedback from responses and the arrows for the associations from stimuli to responses. Once begun, activity in the r_m, r_g unit continues by virtue of the interrelations among the elements. This, of course, can be viewed as the molecular basis for the postulated property of persistence of tendencies.

The r_m, r_g unit includes a representation of the two attributes required for the definition of a tendency, the movement response and the consummatory activity. Up to this point in the chapter, it has not been necessary to place more than one subscript on a tendency. We could refer to T_A and T_B as separate tendencies and not be concerned with further descriptive details about A and B. In general, however, tendencies

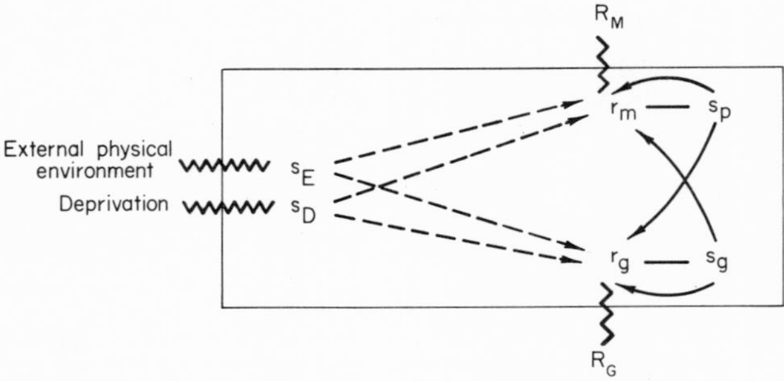

FIG. 12. Diagrammatic representation of persisting tendency based on the r_g-s_g mechanism.

require a subscript to identify the consummatory activity involved and at least one subscript to identify the movement response. For example, $T_{R,E}$ might stand for the tendency to run and eat and $T_{P,D}$ for the tendency to bar press and drink. Then $T_{P,E}$ would stand for the tendency to bar press and eat, $T_{R,D}$ for the tendency to run and drink, $T_{R,P,E}$ for the tendency to run and bar press and eat, etc. The r_m, r_g unit in the diagram is a molecular representation of the unitary character of a tendency.

The mechanism diagrammed in Fig. 12 shares another important and interesting property with the theory of tendencies as presented in this chapter. Tendencies were postulated to remain at a given level of strength unless influenced by instigating or consummatory forces. Instigating forces originate in the environment and consummatory forces in the expression of a tendency in activity. The effect of an instigating force on the strength of a tendency is also represented in the diagram of Fig. 12. Note that the r_m, r_g unit has the potential to be active to varying degrees and that s_E and s_D can provide booster inputs to the unit. In other words, the external physical environment and conditions of deprivation can increase the level of activity in the unit by virtue of associations from s_E and s_D to r_m and r_g. This capacity for the r_m, r_g unit to be increased in strength by stimulation captures the meaning of instigating force.

Reducing concepts used at one level of explanation to those used at a more molecular level is important and perhaps somewhat reassuring. It is only worthwhile, however, if the molar theory is scientifically interesting and fruitful and if the molecular theory is a useful one. There is considerable evidence as to the utility of S-R theory generally and of the "calculus of r_g theory" (Lachman, 1960) specifically in giving quite molecular accounts of certain behavior. The molar theory of tendencies seems promising; its worth will be determined from its future encounters with data, however, not by its reducibility.

VI. Concluding Remarks

A. Coding Activities

The flux of molar behavior is a sequence of activities. If such a statement is to provide a useful takeoff point for a theory of behavior, several problems must be solved, but perhaps the most critical is the identification of activities. This is the problem of coding behavior but it is not "merely" the problem of coding behavior. Discovering meaningful units of activity is not a trivial task nor is it necessarily a simple one.

We mentioned early in this chapter that rats were selected as *S*s in our experiments primarily because they could be expected to display their tendencies in observable activity whereas more complex organisms, especially human beings, would be more likely to engage in extensive covert activities. Coding covert activities is obviously an exceedingly difficult task and one which probably cannot be done properly until we have a much more adequate theory to carry us back from the activities we can observe to those we cannot. Even in our main shift in activity experiment with rats, however, we ran into coding difficulties. The method in that experiment was designed to yield a situation in which the rats could be observed to shift directly from one easily identifiable activity to another and in that way to provide a realization of the most simple shift in activity. It will be helpful to this discussion of coding to review briefly the way in which the description of the initial activity was changed and the data that led to that change.

In the beginning the ongoing activity was defined in a gross geographical way. That is, *S*s were described as engaging in the initial activity so long as they were in the food chamber. This is a perfectly clear and easy way to define an activity and on the basis of this definition the data designated "total time spent in the food chamber" were obtained. These data show effects attributable to both the food deprivation and exploratory chamber manipulations and appear suitable for more extensive analyses in which the various models for shift in activity could be used.

The results of these analyses, however, would be misleading because the total time spent in the food chamber is not a measure of a single, homogeneous activity. What is even more important are the grounds on which the heterogeneity can be established. The second time measure taken in the food chamber, namely, the time *S* spent in the immediate vicinity of the food trough (called the food-oriented time) does not bear the same relationship to the experimental manipulations as does the total time spent measure. The food-oriented time was affected significantly by the degree of food deprivation but not by the complexity of the exploratory chamber. Correspondingly, the residual time measure (called the nonfood-oriented time) was affected significantly by the complexity of the exploratory chamber but not by the degree of food deprivation. Thus, heterogeneity of initial activity can be established on the theoretical grounds that the time measures associated with the activities are not sensitive to experimental manipulations in the same way.

Contrast this criterion for heterogeneous activities with one based on direct observation where judges code activities in terms of perceptual units that they can agree upon. In the latter case categories for activities are decided upon according to how the flux of behavior looks. The beginning, middle, and end of an activity can be agreed upon by their appearances. Units of activity arrived at in this way should not be expected necessarily to match with those defined in terms of relationships with experimental manipulations.

Let us take this discussion one step more and explore the question of the molarity of a unit of activity. The activity of eating is a convenient example. When should "eating" be coded? According to tendency theory, we want to do so whenever an activity is an expression of the eating tendency; that is, when engaging in the activity results in the application of a consummatory force to the eating tendency. Would we want to go so far as to say "eating" has begun as soon as the instrumental acts that eventuate in the intake of food begin? It seems that we might. This suggests the possibility that a rat running down an alley to food might be expressing the eating tendency with its running. The tendency to run and eat is symbolized by $T_{R,E}$ and it is $T_{R,E}$ that is being expressed in the running. It is interesting, and perhaps important to the tendency theory, that in the second experiment preliminary to the main shift in activity experiment (see Section III,A,2) *Ss* consumed fewer pellets before shifting to the exploratory activity when they ran into the goal box of the alley than when they were placed into it. This finding could be anticipated on the basis of tendency theory by assuming that the eating tendency was subjected to a consummatory force originating in the expression of the tendency to run and eat.

To return to the question of the molarity of a unit of activity, we see that a unit of activity is as molar as the tendency that is being expressed by that activity. With this view of the problem of coding activities, it is possible that tendencies are elaborated to include a variety of components that are nonobvious from the standpoint of direct observation.

B. Dynamics of the S-R Interval

Analysis of shift in activity is an important part of the development of behavior theory. Knowledge of the processes that take place in the interval between the onset of a stimulus and the occurrence of an activity is fundamental to an understanding of shift in activity. The discrete random process and the continuous deterministic process models presented in this chapter are examples of theoretical attacks in this area. More theory and much more experimentation are needed.

One of the questions that took on special significance in the analysis of shift in activity was the fate of the tendency for an activity that was supplanted by another activity. Does a tendency persist beyond the point when it is being supported by stimulation? At a molar level there seem to be sharp differences between stimulus-bound theories in which stimuli are viewed as the "causes" of responses and tendency theory in which stimuli effect changes in the strength of tendencies but tendencies are responsible for the existence of activities. The distinction between the types of theories is lost at the molecular level, however, where an S-R connectionistic mechanism is available to both. The distinctions at the molar level remain as interesting researchable problems despite the convergence at the molecular level.

References

Allison, J. Strength of preference for food, magnitude of food reward, and performance in instrumental conditioning. *Journal of Comparative and Physiological Psychology*, 1964, **57**, 217–223.

Amsel, A., Ernhart, C. B., & Galbrecht, C. R. Magnitude of frustration effect and strength of antedating goal factors. *Psychological Reports*, 1961, **8**, 183–186.

Amsel, A., & Roussel, J. Motivational properties of frustration: I. Effect on a running response of the addition of frustration to the motivational complex. *Journal of Experimental Psychology*, 1952, **43**, 363–368.

Atkinson, J. W. *An introduction to motivation.* Princeton, N.J.: Van Nostrand, 1964.

Atkinson, J. W. Change of activity: A new focus for the theory of motivation. In T. Mischel (Ed.) *Human action: Recent trends in scientific and philosophical psychology.* New York: Academic Press (in press).

Atkinson, J. W., & Birch, D. *The dynamics of action*. Manuscript in preparation (Mimeo), 1967.

Atkinson, J. W., & Cartwright, D. Some neglected variables in contemporary conceptions of decision and performance. *Psychological Reports*, 1964, **14**, 575–590.

Barker, R. G. *The stream of behavior*. New York: Appleton, 1963.

Barker, R. G., & Wright, H. F. *Midwest and its children*. New York: Harper & Row, 1954.

Birch, D. Selective learning, comments on Professor Noble's paper. In E. A. Bilodeau (Ed.), *Acquisition of skill*. New York: Academic Press, 1966. Pp. 99–107. (a)

Birch, D. Verbal control of nonverbal behavior. *Journal of Experimental Child Psychology*, 1966, **4**, 266–275. (b)

Birch, D., Burnstein, E., & Clark, R. A. Response strength as a function of hours of food deprivation under a controlled maintenance schedule. *Journal of Comparative and Physiological Psychology*, 1958, **51**, 350–354.

Birch, D., & Veroff, J. *Motivation: A study of action*. Belmont, Calif.: Brooks/Cole, 1966.

Bower, G. H. The influence of graded reductions in reward and prior frustrating events upon the magnitude of the frustration effect. *Journal of Comparative and Physiological Psychology*, 1962, **55**, 582–587.

Brown, J. S., & Belloni, M. Performance as a function of deprivation time following periodic feeding in an isolated environment. *Journal of Comparative and Physiological Psychology*, 1963, **56**, 105–110.

Cotton, J. W. Running time as a function of amount of food deprivation. *Journal of Experimental Psychology*, 1953, **46**, 188–198.

Estes, W. K. Toward a statistical theory of learning. *Psychological Review*, 1950, **57**, 94–107.

Estes, W. K. Stimulus-response theory of drive. In M. R. Jones (Ed.), *Nebraska symposium on motivation*. Lincoln, Nebr.: University of Nebraska Press, 1958.

Estes, W. K. The statistical approach to learning theory. In S. Koch (Ed.), *Psychology: A study of a science*, Vol. 2. New York: McGraw-Hill, 1959. Pp. 380–491.

Feller, W. *An introduction to probability theory and its applications*. Vol. 1. New York: Wiley, 1957.

Freud, S. *Collected papers*. London: The Hogarth Press and the Institute of Psychoanalysis; New York: Basic Books, 1949.

Hebb, D. O. *The organization of behavior*. New York: Wiley, 1949.

Hull, C. L. Goal attraction and directing ideas conceived as habit phenomena. *Psychological Review*, 1931, **38**, 487–506.

Hull, C. L. *Principles of behavior*. New York: Appleton, 1943.

Jensen, G. D. Preference for bar pressing over "freeloading" as a function of number of rewarded presses. *Journal of Experimental Psychology*, 1963, **65**, 451–454.

La Berge, D. A recruitment theory of simple behavior. *Psychometrika*, 1962, **27**, 375–396.

Lachman, R. The model in theory construction. *Psychological Review*, 1960, **67**, 113–129.

Lewin, K. *The conceptual representation and the measurement of psychological forces*. Durham, N.C.: Duke University Press, 1938.

Lough, T. S. An equilibrium model of a relationship between feelings and behavior. Unpublished doctoral dissertation, University of Michigan, 1960.

McGill, W. J. Stochastic latency mechanisms. In R. D. Luce, R. R. Bush, and E. Galanter (Eds.), *Handbook of mathematical psychology*, Vol. I. New York: Wiley, 1963. Pp. 309–360.

Maltzman, I. The process need. *Psychological Review*, 1952, **59**, 50–58.

Muenzinger, K. F. Vicarious trial and error at a point of choice: I. A general survey of its relation to learning efficiency. *Journal of Genetic Psychology*, 1938, **53**, 75–86.

Richter, C. P. A behavioristic study of the activity of the rat. *Comparative Psychology Monographs*, 1922, **1**, No. 2.

Spence, K. W. The differential response in animals to stimuli varying within a single dimension. *Psychological Review*, 1937, **44**, 430–444.

Spence, K. W. The relation of response latency and speed to the intervening variables and N in S-R theory. *Psychological Review*, 1954, **61**, 209–216.

Spence, K. W. Conceptual models of spatial and non-spatial selective learning. In K. W. Spence (Ed.), *Behavior theory and learning*. Englewood Cliffs, N.J.: Prentice-Hall, 1960. Pp. 366–392.

Stellar, E., & Hill, J. H. The rat's rate of drinking as a function of water deprivation. *Journal of Comparative and Physiological Psychology*, 1952, **45**, 96–102.

Timberlake, W., & Birch, D. Complexity, novelty, and food deprivation as determinants of the speed of a shift from one behavior to another. *Journal of Comparative and Physiological Psychology*, 1967, **63**, 545–548.

Tolman, E. C. Prediction of vicarious trial and error by means of the schematic sow bug. *Psychological Review*, 1939, **46**, 318–336.

Whalen, R. E. Sexual motivation. *Psychological Review*, 1966, **73**, 151–163.

HUMAN MEMORY: A PROPOSED SYSTEM AND ITS CONTROL PROCESSES[1]

R. C. Atkinson and R. M. Shiffrin

STANFORD UNIVERSITY
STANFORD, CALIFORNIA

[1] This research was supported by the National Aeronautics and Space Administration, Grant No. NGR-05-020-036. The authors are indebted to W. K. Estes and G. H. Bower who provided many valuable suggestions and comments at various stages of the work. Special credit is due J. W. Brelsford who was instrumental in carrying out the research discussed in Section IV and whose overall contributions are too numerous to report in detail. We should also like to thank those co-workers who carried out a number of the experiments discussed in the latter half of the paper; rather than list them here, each will be acknowledged at the appropriate place.

I. Introduction

This paper is divided into two major portions; the first outlines a general theoretical framework in which to view human memory, and the second describes the results of a number of experiments designed to test specific models that can be derived from the overall theory.

The general theoretical framework, set forth in Sections II and III, categorizes the memory system along two major dimensions. One categorization distinguishes permanent, structural features of the system from control processes that can be readily modified or reprogrammed at the will of the subject. Because we feel that this distinction helps clarify a number of results, we will take time to elaborate it at the outset. The permanent features of memory, which will be referred to as the memory structure, include both the physical system and the built-in processes that are unvarying and fixed from one situation to another. Control processes, on the other hand, are selected, constructed, and used at the option of the subject and may vary dramatically from one task to another even though superficially the tasks may appear very similar. The use of a particular control process in a given situation will depend upon such factors as the nature of the instructions, the meaningfulness of the material, and the individual subject's history.

A computer analogy might help illustrate the distinction between memory structure and control processes. If the memory system is viewed as a computer under the direction of a programmer at a remote console, then both the computer hardware and those programs built into the system that cannot be modified by the programmer are analogous to our structural features; those programs and instruction sequences which the programmer can write at his console and which determine the operation of the computer, are analogous to our control processes. In the sense that the computer's method of processing a given batch of data depends on the operating program, so the way a stimulus input is processed depends on the particular control processes the subject brings into play. The structural components include the basic memory stores; examples of control processes are coding procedures, rehearsal operations, and search strategies.

Our second categorization divides memory into three structural components: the sensory register, the short-term store, and the long-term store. Incoming sensory information first enters the sensory register, where it resides for a very brief period of time, then decays and is lost. The short-term store is the subject's working memory; it receives selected inputs from the sensory register and also from long-term store. Information in the short-term store decays completely and is lost within a period of about 30 seconds, but a control process called rehearsal can maintain a limited amount of information in this store as long as the subject desires. The long-term store is a fairly permanent repository for information, information which is transferred from the short-term store. Note that "transfer" is not meant to imply that information is removed from one store and placed in the next; we use transfer to mean the copying of selected information from one store into the next without removing this information from the original store.

In presenting our theoretical framework we will consider first the structural features of the system (Section II) and then some of the more generally used control processes (Section III). In both of these sections the discussion is organized first around the sensory register, then the short-term store, and finally the long-term store. Thus, the outline of Sections II and III can be represented as follows:

	Sensory register	Short-term store	Long-term store
Structure	Sec. II,A	Sec. II,B	Sec. II,C
Control processes	Sec. III,A	Sec. III,B	Sec. III,C

These first sections of the paper do not present a finished theory; instead they set forth a general framework within which specific models can be formulated. We attempt to demonstrate that a large number of results may be handled parsimoniously within this framework, even without coming to final decisions at many of the choice points that occur. At some of the choice points several hypotheses will be presented, and the evidence that is available to help make the choice will be reviewed. The primary goal of Sections II and III is to justify our theoretical framework and to demonstrate that it is a useful way of viewing a wide variety of memory phenomena.

The remaining sections of the paper present a number of precise models that satisfy the conditions imposed by our general theoretical framework. These sections also present data from a series of experiments designed to evaluate the models. Section IV is concerned with an analysis of short-term memory; the model used to analyze the data emphasizes a control process based in the short-term store which we designate a rehearsal buffer. Section V presents several experiments that shed some light upon processes in the long-term store, especially subject-controlled search processes. Some of the experiments in Sections IV and V have been reported by us and our co-workers in previous publications, but the earlier treatments were primarily mathematical whereas the present emphasis is upon discussion and overall synthesis.

If the reader is willing to accept our overall framework on a provisional basis and wishes to proceed at once to the specific models and experiments, then he may begin with Section IV and as a prerequisite need only read that portion of Section III,B concerned with the rehearsal buffer.

II. Structural Features of the Memory System

This section of the paper will describe the permanent, structural features of the memory system. The basic structural division is into the three components diagrammed in Fig. 1: the sensory register, the short-term store, and the long-term store.

When a stimulus is presented there is an immediate registration of that stimulus within the appropriate sensory dimensions. The form of this registration is fairly well understood in the case of the visual system (Sperling, 1960); in fact, the particular features of visual registration (including a several hundred millisecond decay of an initially accurate visual image) allow us positively to identify this system as a distinct component of memory. It is obvious that incoming information in other sense modalities also receives an initial registration, but it is not clear whether these other registrations have an appreciable decay period or any other features which would enable us to refer to them as components of memory.

The second basic component of our system is the short-term store. This store may be regarded as the subject's "working memory." Information entering the short-term store is assumed to decay and disappear completely, but the time required for the information to be lost is considerably longer than for the sensory register. The character of the information in the short-term store does not depend necessarily upon the form of the sensory input. For example, a word presented visually may be encoded from the visual sensory register into an auditory short-term store. Since the auditory short-term system will play a major role in subsequent discussions, we shall use the abbreviation a-v-l to stand for auditory-verbal-linguistic store. The triple term is used because, as we shall see, it is not easy to separate these three functions.

The exact rate of decay of information in the short-term store is difficult to estimate because it is greatly influenced by subject-controlled processes. In the a-v-l mode, for example, the subject can invoke rehearsal mechanisms that maintain the information in STS and thereby complicate the problem of measuring the structural characteristics of the decay process. However, the available evidence suggests that information represented in the a-v-l mode decays and is lost within a period of about 15–30 seconds. Storage of information in other modalities is less well understood and, for reasons to be discussed later, it is difficult to assign values to their decay rates.

The last major component of our system is the long-term store. This store differs from the preceding ones in that information stored here does not decay and become lost in the same manner. All information eventually is completely lost from the sensory register and the short-term store,

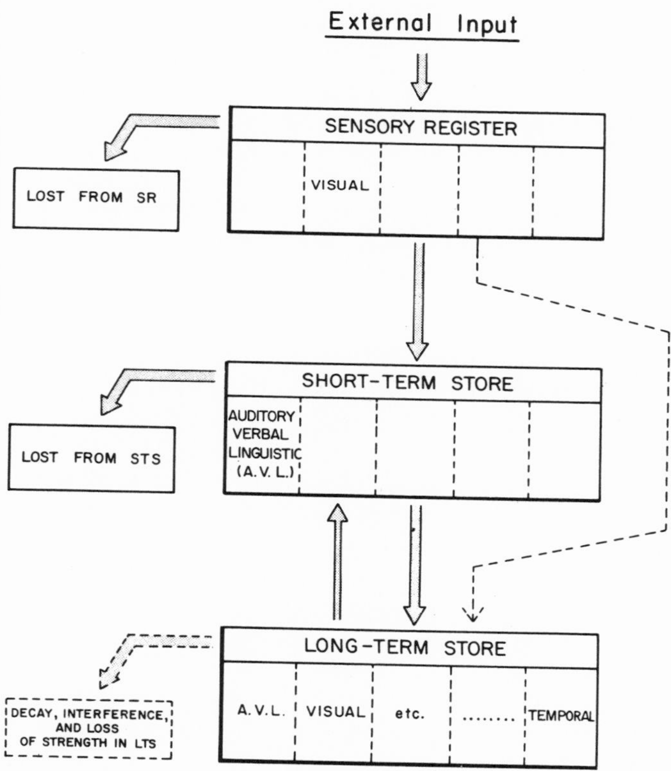

FIG. 1. Structure of the memory system.

whereas information in the long-term store is relatively permanent (although it may be modified or rendered temporarily irretrievable as the result of other incoming information). Most experiments in the literature dealing with long-term store have been concerned with storage in the a-v-l mode, but it is clear that there is long-term memory in each of the other sensory modalities, as demonstrated by an ability to recognize stimuli presented to these senses. There may even be information in the long-term store which is not classifiable into any of the sensory modalities, the prime example being temporal memory.

The flow of information among the three systems is to a large degree under the control of the subject. Note that by information flow and transfer between stores we refer to the same process: the copying of selected information from one store into the next. This copying takes place without the transferred information being removed from its original store. The information remains in the store from which it is transferred and decays according to the decay characteristics of that store. In considering information flow in the system, we start with its initial input into the sensory register. The next step is a subject-controlled scan of the information in the register; as a result of this scan and an associated search of long-term store, selected information is introduced into short-term store. We assume that transfer to the long-term store takes place throughout the period that information resides in the short-term store, although the amount and form of the transferred information is markedly influenced by control processes. The possibility that there may be direct transfer to the long-term store from the sensory register is represented by the dashed line in Fig. 1; we do not know whether such transfer occurs. Finally, there is transfer from the long-term store to the short-term store, mostly under the control of the subject; such transfer occurs, for example, in problem solving, hypothesis testing, and "thinking" in general.

This brief encapsulation of the system raises more questions than it answers. Not yet mentioned are such features as the cause of the decay in each memory store and the form of the transfer functions between the stores. In an attempt to specify these aspects of the system, we now turn to a more detailed outline, including a review of some relevant literature.

A. Sensory Register

The prime example of a sensory register is the short-term visual image investigated by Sperling (1960, 1963), Averbach and Coriell (1961), Estes and Taylor (1964, 1966), and others. As reported by Sperling (1967), if an array of letters is presented tachistoscopically and the subject is instructed to write out as many letters as possible, usually about six letters are reported. Further, a 30-second delay between presentation and report does not cause a decrement in performance. This fact (plus the facts that confusions tend to be based on auditory rather than visual similarities, and that subjects report rehearsing and subvocalizing the letters) indicates that the process being examined is in the a-v-l short-term store; i.e., subjects scan the visual image and transfer a number of letters to the a-v-l short-term store for rehearsal and output.

In order to study the registered visual image itself, partial-report procedures (Averbach & Coriell, 1961; Averbach & Sperling, 1961; Sperling, 1960, 1963) and forced-choice detection procedures (Estes, 1965; Estes & Taylor, 1964, 1966; Estes & Wessel, 1966) have been employed. The partial-report method typically involves presenting a display (usually a 3×4 matrix of letters and numbers) tachistoscopically for a very brief period. After the presentation the subject is given a signal that tells him which row to report. If the signal is given almost immediately after stimulus offset, the requested information is reported with good precision, otherwise considerable loss occurs. Thus we infer that a highly accurate visual image lasts for a short period of time and then decays. It has also been established that succeeding visual stimulation can modify or possibly even erase prior stimulation. By using a number of different methods, the decay period of the image has been estimated to take several hundred milliseconds, or a little more, depending on experimental conditions; that is, information cannot be recovered from this store after a period of several hundred milliseconds.

Using the detection method, in which the subject must report which of two critical letters was presented in a display, Estes and Taylor (1964, 1966) and Estes and Wessel (1966) have examined some models for the scanning process. Although no completely satisfactory models have yet been proposed, it seems reasonably certain that the letters are scanned serially (which letters are scanned seems to be a momentary decision of the subject), and a figure of about 10 msec to scan one letter seems generally satisfactory.

Thus it appears fairly well established that a visual stimulus leaves a more or less photographic trace which decays during a period of several hundred milliseconds and is subject to masking and replacement by succeeding stimulation. Not known at present is the form of the decay, that is, whether letters in a display decay together or individually, probabilistically or temporally, all-or-none, or continuously. The reader may ask whether these results are specific to extremely brief visual presentations; although presentations of long duration complicate analysis (because of eye movements and physical scanning of the stimulus), there is no reason to believe that the basic fact of a highly veridical image quickly decaying after stimulus offset does not hold also for longer visual presentations. It is interesting that the stimulation seems to be transferred from the visual image to the a-v-l short-term store, rather than to a visual short-term store. The fact that a written report was requested may provide the explanation, or it may be that the visual short-term store lacks rehearsal capacity.

There is not much one can say about registers in sensory modalities other than the visual. A fair amount of work has been carried out on the auditory system without isolating a registration mechanism comparable to the visual one. On the other hand, the widely differing structures of the different sensory systems makes it questionable whether we should expect similar systems for registration.

Before leaving the sensory register, it is worth adding a few comments about the transfer to higher order systems. In the case of the transfer from the visual image to the a-v-l short-term store, it seems likely that a selective scan is made at the discretion of the subject.[2] As each element in the register is scanned, a matching program of some sort is carried out against information in long-term store and the verbal "name" of the element is recovered from long-term memory and fed into the short-term store. Other information might also be recovered in the long-term search; for example, if the scanned element was a pineapple, the word, its associates, the taste, smell, and feel of a pineapple might all be recovered and transferred to various short-term stores. This communication between the sensory register and long-term store does not, however, permit us to infer that information is transferred directly to long-term store from the register. Another interesting theoretical question is whether the search into long-term store is necessary to transfer information from the sensory register to the short-term store within a modality. We see no a priori theoretical reason to exclude nonmediated transfer. (For example, why should a scan or match be necessary to transfer a spoken word to the a-v-l short-term store?) For lack of evidence, we leave these matters unspecified.

B. Short-Term Store

The first point to be examined in this section is the validity of the division of memory into short- and long-term stores. Workers of a traditional bent have argued against dichotomizing memory (e.g., Melton, 1963; Postman, 1964). However, we feel there is much evidence indicating the parsimony and usefulness of such a division. The argument is often given that one memory is somehow "simpler" than two; but quite the opposite is usually the case. A good example may be found in a comparison of the model for free recall presented in this paper and the model proposed by Postman and Phillips (1965). Any single-process system making a fair attempt to explain the mass of data currently available must, of necessity, be sufficiently complex that the term *single process* becomes a misnomer. We do not wish, however, to engage in the controversy here. We ask the reader to accept our model provisionally until its power to deal with data becomes clear. Still, some justification

[2] Sperling (1960) has presented evidence relating the type of scan used to the subject's performance level.

of our decision would seem indicated at this point. For this reason, we turn to what is perhaps the single most convincing demonstration of a dichotomy in the memory system: the effects of hippocampal lesions reported by Milner (1959, 1966, 1968). In her words:

"Bilateral surgical lesions in the hippocampal region, on the mesial aspect of the temporal lobes, produce a remarkably severe and persistent memory disorder in human patients, the pattern of breakdown providing valuable clues to the cerebral organization of memory. Patients with these lesions show no loss of preoperatively acquired skills, and intelligence as measured by formal tests is unimpaired, but, with the possible exception of acquiring motor skill, they seem largely incapable of adding new information to the long-term store. This is true whether acquisition is measured by free recall, recognition, or learning with savings. Nevertheless, the immediate registration of new input (as measured, for example, by digit span and dichotic listening tests) appears to take place normally and material which can be encompassed by verbal rehearsal is held for many minutes without further loss than that entailed in the initial verbalization. Interruption of rehearsal, regardless of the nature of the distracting task, produces immediate forgetting of what went before, and some quite simple material which cannot be categorized in verbal terms decays in 30 seconds or so, even without an interpolated distraction. Material already in long-term store is unaffected by the lesion, except for a certain amount of retrograde amnesia for preoperative events" (Milner, 1966).

Apparently, a short-term store remains to the patients, but the lesions have produced a breakdown either in the ability to store new information in long-term store or to retrieve new information from it. These patients appear to be incapable of retaining new material on a long-term basis.[3]

As with most clinical research, however, there are several problems that should be considered. First, the patients were in a general sense abnormal to begin with; second, once the memory defect had been discovered, the operations were discontinued, leaving only a few subjects for observation; third, the results of the lesions seem to be somewhat variable, depending for one thing upon the size of the lesion, the larger lesions giving rise to the full syndrome. Thus there are only a few patients who exhibit the deficit described above in full detail. As startling as these patients are, there might be a temptation to discount them as anomalies but for the following additional findings. Patients who had

[3] A related defect, called Korsakoff's syndrome, has been known for many years. Patients suffering from this abnormal condition are unable to retain new events for longer than a few seconds or minutes (e.g., they cannot recall the meal they have just eaten or recognize the face of the doctor who treated them a few minutes earlier), but their memory for events and people prior to their illness remains largely unimpaired and they can perform adequately on tests of immediate memory span. Recent evidence suggests that Korsakoff's syndrome is related to damage of brain tissue, frequently as the result of chronic alcoholism, in the hippocampal region and the mammillary body (Barbizet, 1963).

known damage to the hippocampal area in one hemisphere were tested for memory deficit after an intracarotid injection of sodium amytal temporarily inactivated the other hemisphere. Controls were patients without known damage, and patients who received injections inactivating their damaged side. A number of memory tests were used as a criterion for memory deficit; the easiest consisted of presenting four pictures, distracting the patient, and then presenting nine pictures containing the original four. If the patient cannot identify the critical four pictures then evidence of memory deficit is assumed. The results showed that in almost all cases memory deficit occurs only after bilateral damage; if side A is damaged and side B inactivated, memory deficit appears, but if the inactivated side is the damaged side, no deficit occurs. These results suggest that the patients described above by Milner were not anomalous cases and their memory deficits therefore give strong support to the hypothesis of distinct short- and long-term memory stores.

1. *Mechanisms Involved in Short-Term Store*

We now turn to a discussion of some of the mechanisms involved in the short-term store. The purpose of this section is not to review the extensive literature on short-term memory, but rather to describe a few experiments which have been important in providing a basis for our model. The first study in this category is that of Peterson and Peterson (1959). In their experiment subjects attempted to recall a single trigram of three consonants after intervals of 3, 6, 9, 12, 15, and 18 seconds. The trigram, presented auditorily, was followed immediately by a number, and the subject was instructed to count backward by three's from that number until he received a cue to recall the trigram. The probability of a correct answer was nearly perfect at 3 seconds, then dropped off rapidly and seemed to reach an asymptote of about .08 at 15–18 seconds. Under the assumption that the arithmetic task played the role of preventing rehearsal and had no direct interfering effect, it may be concluded that a consonant trigram decays from short-term store within a period of about 15 seconds. In terms of the model, the following events are assumed to occur in this situation: the consonant trigram enters the visual register and is at once transferred to the a-v-l short-term store where an attempt is made to code or otherwise "memorize" the item. Such attempts terminate when attention is given to the task of counting backward. In this initial period a trace of some sort is built up in long-term store and it is this long-term trace which accounts for the .08 probability correct at long intervals. Although discussion of the long-term system will come later, one point should be noted in this context; namely, that the long-term trace should be more powerful the more repetitions of the trigram before arithmetic, or the longer the time before arithmetic. These effects were found by Hellyer (1962); that is, the model predicts the probability correct curve will reach an asymptote that reflects long-term strength, and in the aforementioned experiment, the more repetitions before arithmetic, the higher the asymptote.

It should be noted that these findings tie in nicely with the results from a similar experiment that Milner (1968) carried out on her patients. Stimuli that could not be easily coded verbally were used; for example, clicks, light flashes, and nonsense figures. Five values were assigned to each stimulus; a test consisted of presenting a particular value of one stimulus, followed by a distracting task, followed by another value of the stimulus. The subject was required to state whether the two stimuli were the same or different. The patient with the most complete memory deficit was performing at a chance level after 60 seconds, whether or not a distracting task was given. In terms of the model, the reduction to chance level is due to the lack of a long-term store. That the reduction occurred even without a distracting task indicates that the patient could not readily verbalize the stimuli, and that rehearsal in modes other than the verbal one was either not possible or of no value. From this view, the better asymptotic performance demonstrated by normal subjects on the same tasks (with or without distraction) would be attributed to a long-term trace. At the moment, however, the conclusion that rehearsal is lacking in nonverbal modes can only be considered a highly tentative hypothesis.

We next ask whether or not there are short-term stores other than in the a-v-l mode, and if so, whether they have a comparable structure. A natural approach to this problem would use stimuli in different sense modalities and compare the decay curves found with or without a distracting task. If there was reason to believe that the subjects were not verbally encoding the stimuli, and if a relatively fast decay curve was found, then there would be evidence for a short-term memory in that modality. Furthermore, any difference between the control group and the group with a distracting task should indicate the existence of a rehearsal mechanism. Posner (1966) has undertaken several experiments of this sort. In one experiment the subject saw the position of a circle on a 180-mm line and later had to reproduce it; in another the subject moved a lever in a covered box a certain distance with only kinesthetic feedback and later tried to reproduce it. In both cases, testing was performed at 0, 5, 10, and 20 seconds; the interval was filled with either rest, or one of three intervening tasks of varying difficulty. These tasks, in order of increasing difficulty, consisted of reading numbers, adding numbers, and classifying numbers into categories. For the kinesthetic task there was a decline in performance over 30 seconds, but with no obvious differences among the different intervening conditions. This could be taken as evidence for a short-term kinesthetic memory without a rehearsal capability. For the visual task, on the other hand, there was a decline in performance over the 30 seconds only for the two most difficult intervening tasks; performance was essentially constant over time for the other conditions. One possibility, difficult to rule out, is that the subjects' performance was based on a verbal encoding of the visual stimulus. Posner tends to doubt this possibility for reasons that include the accuracy of the performance. Another possibility is that there is a short-term visual memory with a rehearsal component; this hypothesis seems somewhat at variance with the results from Milner's patient who performed at chance level in the experiment cited above. Inasmuch as the data reported by Posner (1966) seem to be rather variable, it would probably be best to hold off a decision on the question of rehearsal capability until further evidence is in.

2. *Characteristics of the a-v-l Short-Term Store*

We restrict ourselves in the remainder of this section to a discussion of the characteristics of the a-v-l short-term store. Work by Conrad (1964) is particularly interesting in this regard. He showed that confusions among visually presented letters in a short-term memory task are correlated with the confusions that subjects make when the same letters are read aloud in a noise background; that is, the letters most confused are those sounding alike. This might suggest an auditory short-term store, essentially the auditory portion of what has been called to this point an a-v-l store. In fact, it is very difficult to separate the verbal and linguistic aspects from the auditory ones. Hintzman (1965, 1967) has argued that the confusions are based upon similar kinesthetic feedback patterns during subvocal rehearsal. When subjects were given white noise on certain trials, several could be heard rehearsing the items aloud, suggesting subvocal rehearsal as the usual process. In addition, Hintzman found that confusions were based upon both the voicing qualities of the letters and the place of articulation. The place-of-articulation errors indicate confusion in kinesthetic feedback, rather than in hearing. Nevertheless, the errors found cannot be definitely assigned to a verbal rather than an auditory cause until the range of auditory confusions is examined more thoroughly. This discussion should make it clear that it is difficult to distinguish between the verbal, auditory, and linguistic aspects of short-term memory; for the purposes of this paper, then, we group the three together into one short-term memory, which we have called the a-v-l short-term store. This store will henceforth be labeled STS. (Restricting the term STS to the a-v-l mode does not imply that there are not other short-term memories with similar properties.)

The notation system should be made clear at this point. As just noted, STS refers to the auditory-verbal-linguistic short-term store. LTS will refer to the comparable memory in long-term store. It is important not to confuse our theoretical constructs STS and LTS (or the more general terms short-term store and long-term store) with the terms short-term memory (STM) and long-term memory (LTM) used in much of the psychological literature. These latter terms have come to take on an operational definition in the literature; STM refers to the memory examined in experiments with short durations or single trials, and LTM to the memory examined in long-duration experiments, typically list learning, or multiple-list learning experiments. According to our general theory, both STS and LTS are active in both STM and LTM experiments. It is important to keep these terms clear lest confusion results. For example, the Keppel and Underwood (1962) finding that performance in the Peterson situation is better on the first trials of a session has been appropriately interpreted as evidence for proactive interference in short-term memory (STM). The model we propose, however, attributes the effect to changes in the long-term store over the session, hence placing the cause in LTS and not STS.

At this point a finished model would set forth the structural characteristics of STS. Unfortunately, despite a large and growing body of experiments concerned with short-term memory, our knowledge about its structure is very limited. Control processes and structural features are so complexly interrelated that it is difficult to isolate those aspects of the data that are due solely to the structure of the memory system. Consequently, this paper presumes only a minimal structure for STS; we assume a trace in STS with auditory or verbal components which decays fairly rapidly in the absence of rehearsal, perhaps within 30 seconds. A few of the more promising possibilities concerning the precise nature of the trace will be considered next. Because most workers in this area make no particular distinction between traces in the two systems, the comments to follow are relevant to the memory trace in the long-term as well as the short-term store.

Bower (1967a) has made a significant exploration of the nature of the trace. In his paper, he has demonstrated the usefulness of models based on the assumption that the memory trace consists of a number of pieces of information (possibly redundant, correlated, or in error, as the case may be), and that the information ensemble may be construed as a multicomponent vector. While Bower makes a strong case for such a viewpoint, the details are too lengthy to review here. A somewhat different approach has been proposed by Wickelgren and Norman (1966) who view the trace as a unidimensional strength measure varying over time. They demonstrate that such a model fits the results of certain types of recognition-memory experiments if the appropriate decay and retrieval assumptions are made. A third approach is based upon a phenomenon reported by Murdock (1966), which has been given a theoretical analysis by Bernbach (1967). Using methods derived from the theory of signal detectability, Bernbach found that there was an all-or-none aspect to the confidence ratings that subjects gave regarding the correctness of their response. The confidence ratings indicated that an answer was either "correct" or "in error" as far as the subject could tell; if intermediate trace strengths existed, the subject was not able to distinguish between them. The locus of this all-or-none feature, however, may lie in the retrieval process rather than in the trace; that is, even if trace strengths vary, the result of a retrieval attempt might always be one of two distinct outcomes: a success or a failure. Thus, one cannot rule out models that assume varying trace strengths. Our preference is to consider the trace as a multicomponent array of information (which we shall often represent in experimental models by a unidimensional strength measure), and reserve judgment on the locus of the all-or-none aspect revealed by an analysis of confidence ratings.

There are two experimental procedures which might be expected to shed some light on the decay characteristics of STS and both depend upon controlling rehearsal; one is similar to the Peterson paradigm in which rehearsal is controlled by an intervening activity and the other involves a very rapid presentation of items followed by an immediate test. An example of the former procedure is Posner's (1966) experiment in which the difficulty of the intervening activity was varied. He found that as the difficulty of an intervening task increased, accuracy of recall decreased.

Although this result might be regarded as evidence that decay from STS is affected by the kind of intervening activity, an alternative hypothesis would ascribe the result to a reduction in rehearsal with more difficult intervening tasks. It would be desirable to measure STS decay when rehearsal is completely eliminated, but it has proved difficult to establish how much rehearsal takes place during various intervening tasks.

Similar problems arise when attempts are made to control rehearsal by increasing presentation rates. Even at the fastest conceivable presentation rates subjects can rehearse during presentation if they attend to only a portion of the incoming items. In general, experiments manipulating presentation rate have not proved of value in determining decay characteristics for STS, primarily because of the control processes the subject brings into play. Thus Waugh and Norman (1965) found no difference between 1-second and 4-second rates in their probe digit experiment; Conrad and Hille (1958) found improvement with faster rates; and Buschke and Lim (1967) found increases in the amount of primacy in their missing-span serial position curves as input rate increased from one item per second to four items per second. Complex results of this sort make it difficult to determine the structural decay characteristics of STS. Eventually, models that include the control processes involved in these situations should help clarify the STS structure.

3. *Transfer from STS to LTS*

The amount and form of information transferred from STS to LTS is primarily a function of control processes. We will assume, however, that transfer itself is an unvarying feature of the system; throughout the period that information resides in the short-term store, transfer takes place to long-term store. Support for such an assumption is given by studies on incidental learning which indicate that learning takes place even when the subject is not trying to store material in the long-term store. Better examples may be the experiments reported by Hebb (1961) and Melton (1963). In these experiments subjects had to repeat sequences of digits. If a particular sequence was presented every several trials, it was gradually learned. It may be assumed that subjects in this situation attempt to perform solely by rehearsal of the sequence within STS; nevertheless, transfer to LTS clearly takes place. This Hebb-Melton procedure is currently being used to explore transfer characteristics in some detail. R. L. Cohen and Johansson (1967), for example, have found that an overt response to the repeated sequence was necessary for improvement in performance to occur in this situation; thus information transfer is accentuated by overt responses and appears to be quite weak if no response is demanded.

The form of the STS-LTS transfer may be probabilistic, continuous, or some combination; neither the literature nor our own data provide a firm basis for making a decision. Often the form of the information to be remembered and the type of test used may dictate a particular transfer process, as for example in Bower's (1961) research on an all-or-none paired-associate learning model, but the issue is nevertheless far from settled. In fact, the changes in the transfer process induced by the subject effectively alter the transfer function form experiment to experiment, making a search for a universal, unchanging process unproductive.

C. Long-Term Store

Because it is easiest to test for recall in the a-v-l mode, this part of long-term store has been the most extensively studied. It is clear, however, that long-term memory exists in each of the sensory modalities; this is shown by subjects' recognition capability for smells, taste, and so on. Other long-term information may be stored which is not necessarily related to any of the sensory modalities. Yntema and Trask (1963), for example, have proposed that temporal memory is stored in the form of "time-tags." Once again, however, lack of data forces us to restrict our attention primarily to the a-v-l mode, which we have designated LTS.

First a number of possible formulations of the LTS trace will be considered. The simplest hypothesis is to assume that the trace is all-or-none; if a trace is placed in memory, then a correct retrieval and response will occur. Second-guessing experiments provide evidence concerning an hypothesis of this sort.

Binford and Gettys (1965) presented the subject with a number of alternatives, one of which was the correct answer. If his first response is incorrect, he picks again from the remaining alternatives. The results indicate that second guesses are correct well above the chance level to be expected if the subject were guessing randomly from the remaining alternatives. This result rules out the simple trace model described above because an all-or-none trace would predict second guesses to be at the chance level. Actually, the above model was a model of both the form of the trace and the type of retrieval. We can expand the retrieval hypothesis and still leave open the possibility of an all-or-none trace. For example, in searching for a correct all-or-none trace in LTS, the subject might find a similar but different trace and mistakenly terminate the search and generate an answer; upon being told that the answer is wrong the subject renews the search and may find the correct trace the next time. Given this hypothesis, it would be instructive to know whether the results differ if the subject must rank the response alternatives without being given feedback after each choice. In this case all the alternatives would be ranked on the basis of the same search of LTS; if the response ranked second was still above chance, then it would become difficult to defend an all-or-none trace.

A second source of information about the nature of the trace comes from the tip-of-the-tongue phenomenon examined by Hart (1965), R. Brown and McNeill (1966), and Freedman and Landauer (1966). This phenomenon refers to a person's ability to predict accurately that he will be able to recognize a correct answer even though he cannot recall it at the moment. He feels as if the correct answer were on the "tip of the tongue." Experiments have shown that if subjects who cannot recall an answer are asked to estimate whether they will be able to choose the correct answer from a set of alternatives, they often show good accuracy in predicting their success in recognition. One explanation might be that the subject recalls some information, but not enough to generate an answer and feels that this partial information is likely to be sufficient to choose among a set of alternatives. Indeed, Brown and McNeill found that the initial sound of the word to be retrieved was often correctly recalled in cases where a correct identification was later made. On the other hand, the subject often is absolutely certain upon seeing the correct response that it is indeed correct. This might indicate that some new, relevant information has become available after recognition. In any case, a simple trace model can probably not handle these results. A class of models for the trace which can explain the tip-of-the-tongue phenomenon are the multiple-copy models suggested by Atkinson and Shiffrin (1965). In these schemes there are many traces or copies of information laid in long-term store, each of which may be either partial or complete. In a particular search of LTS perhaps only a small number or just one of these copies is retrieved, none complete enough to generate the correct answer; upon recognition, however, access is gained to the other copies, presumably through some associative process. Some of these other copies contain enough information to make the subject certain of his choice. These multiple-copy memory models are described more fully in Atkinson and Shiffrin (1965).

The decay and/or interference characteristics of LTS have been studied more intensively over the past 50 years than any other aspect of memory. Partly for this reason a considerable body of theory has been advanced known as interference theory.[4] We tend to regard this theory as descriptive rather than explanatory; this statement is not meant to detract from the value of the theory as a whole, but to indicate that a search for mechanisms at a deeper level might prove to be of value. Thus, for example, if the interfering effect of a previously learned list upon recall of a second list increases over time until the second list is retested, it is not enough to accept "proactive interference increasing over time" as an explanation of the effect; rather one should look for the underlying search, storage, and retrieval mechanisms responsible.

We are going to use a very restricted definition of interference in the rest of this paper; interference will be considered a structural feature of memory not under the control of the subject. It will refer to such possibilities as disruption and loss of information. On the other hand, there are search mechanisms which generate effects like those of structural interference, but which are control processes. Interference theory, of course, includes both types of possibilities, but we prefer to break down interference effects into those which are structurally based, and those under the control of the subject. Therefore the term *interference* is used henceforth to designate a structural feature of the long-term system.

[4] For an overview of interference theory see Postman (1961).

It is important to realize that often it is possible to explain a given phenomenon with either interference or search notions. Although both factors will usually be present, the experimental situation sometimes indicates which is more important. For example, as we shall see in Section V, the decrease in the percentage of words recalled in a free verbal-recall experiment with increases in list length could be due either to interference between items or to a search of decreasing effectiveness as the number of items increase. The typical free recall situation, however, forces the subject to engage in a search of memory at test and indicates to us that the search process is the major factor. Finally, note that the interference effect itself may take many forms and arise in a number of ways. Information within a trace may be destroyed, replaced, or lessened in value by subsequent information. Alternatively, information may never be destroyed but may become irretrievable, temporarily or permanently.

In this section an attempt has been made to establish a reasonable basis for at least three systems—the sensory register, the short-term store, and the long-term store; to indicate the transfer characteristics between the various stores; and to consider possible decay and interference functions within each store.

III. Control Processes in Memory

The term *control process* refers to those processes that are not permanent features of memory, but are instead transient phenomena under the control of the subject; their appearance depends on such factors as instructional set, the experimental task, and the past history of the subject. A simple example of a control process can be demonstrated in a paired-associate learning task involving a list of stimuli each paired with either an A or B response (Bower, 1961). The subject may try to learn each stimulus-response pair as a separate, integral unit or he may adopt the more efficient strategy of answering B to any item not remembered and attempting to remember only the stimuli paired with the A response. This latter scheme will yield a radically different pattern of performance than the former; it exemplifies one rather limited control process. The various rehearsal strategies, on the other hand, are examples of control processes with almost universal applicability.

Since subject-controlled memory processes include any schemes, coding techniques, or mnemonics used by the subject in his effort to remember, their variety is virtually unlimited and classification becomes difficult. Such classification as is possible arises because these processes, while under the voluntary control of the subject, are nevertheless dependent upon the permanent memory structures described in the previous section. This section therefore will follow the format of Section II, organizing the control processes into those primarily associated with the sensory register, STS, and LTS. Apart from this, the presentation will be somewhat fragmentary, drawing upon examples from many disparate experiments in an attempt to emphasize the variety, pervasiveness, and importance of the subject-controlled processes.

A. Control Processes in the Sensory Register

Because a large amount of information enters the sensory register and then decays very quickly, the primary function of control processes at this level is the selection of particular portions of this information for transfer to the short-term store. The first decision the subject must make concerns which sensory register to attend to. Thus, in experiments with simultaneous inputs from several sensory channels, the subject can readily report information from a given sense modality if so instructed in advance, but his accuracy is greatly reduced if instructions are delayed until after presentation. A related attention process is the transfer to STS of a selected portion of a large information display within a sensory modality. An example to keep in mind here is the scanning process in the visual registration system. Letters in a tachistoscopically presented display may be scanned at a rate of about 10 msec a letter, the form of the scan being under the control of the subject. Sperling (1960) found the following result. When the signal identifying which row to report from a matrix of letters was delayed for an interval of time following stimulus offset, the subjects developed two observing strategies. One strategy consisted of obeying the experimenter's instructions to pay equal attention to all rows; this strategy resulted in evenly distributed errors and quite poor performance at long delays. The other strategy consisted of anticipating which row would be tested and attending to only that row; in this case the error variance is increased but performance is better at longer delay intervals than for the other strategy. The subjects were aware of and reported using these strategies. For example, one experienced subject reported switching from the first to the second strategy in an effort to maximize performance when the delay between presentation and report rose above .15 seconds. The graph of his probability of a correct response plotted against delay interval, while generally decreasing with delay, showed a dip at about .15 seconds, indicating that he did not switch strategies soon enough for optimal performance.

The decisions as to which sensory register to attend to, and where and what to scan within the system, are not the only choices that must be made at this level. There are a number of strategies available to the subject for matching information in the register against the long-term store and thereby identifying the input. In an experiment by Estes and Taylor (1966) for example, the subject had to decide whether an F or B was embedded in a matrix display of letters. One strategy would have the subject scan the letters in order, generating the "name" of each letter and checking to see whether it is a B or an F. If the scan ends before all letters are processed, and no B or F has been found, the subject would presumably guess according to some bias. Another strategy might have the subject do a features match on each letter against B and then F, moving on as soon as a difference is found; in this strategy it would not be necessary to scan all features of each letter (i.e., it would not be necessary to generate the name of each letter). A third strategy might have the subject compare with only one of the crucial letters, guessing the other if a match is not found by the time the scan terminates.

B. Control Processes in Short-Term Store

1. *Storage, Search, and Retrieval Strategies*

Search processes in STS, while not as elaborate as those in LTS because of the smaller amount of information in STS through which the search must take place, are nevertheless important. Since information in STS in excess of the rehearsal capability is decaying at a rapid rate, a search for a particular datum must be performed quickly and efficiently. One indirect method of examining the search process consists of comparing the results of recognition and recall experiments in which STS plays the major role. Presumably there is a search component in the recall situation that is absent in the recognition situation. It is difficult to come to strong conclusions on this basis, but recognition studies such as Wickelgren and Norman (1966) have usually given rise to less complicated models than comparable recall experiments, indicating that the search component in STS might be playing a large role.

One result indicating that the STS search occurs along ordered dimensions is based upon binaural stimulus presentation (Broadbent, 1954, 1956, 1958). A pair of items is presented, one to each ear simultaneously. Three such pairs are given, one every half second. Subjects perform best if asked to report the items first from one ear and then the other, rather than, say, in pairs. While Broadbent interprets these results in terms of a postulated time needed to switch attention from one ear to the other (a control process in itself), other interpretations are possible. In particular, part of the information stored with each item might include which ear was used for input. This information might then provide a simple dimension along which to search STS and report during recall. Another related possibility would have the subject group the items along this dimension during presentation. In any case we would expect similar results if another dimension other than "sides" (which ear) were provided. Yntema and Trask (1963) used three word-number pairs presented sequentially, one every half second; one member of a pair was presented to one ear and the other member to the other ear. There were three conditions: the first in which three words were presented consecutively on one side (and therefore the three numbers on the other), the second in which two words and one number were presented consecutively on one side, the third in which a number separated the two words on one side. Three test conditions were used: the subject was asked to report words, the numbers (types); or to report one ear followed by the other (sides); or the simultaneous pairs in order (pairs). The results are easy to describe. In terms of probability correct, presentation condition one was best, condition two next, and condition three worst. For the test conditions, "types" yielded the highest probability of correct response, followed by "sides" and then "pairs." "Sides" being better than "pairs" was one of the results found by Broadbent, but "types" being even better than "sides" suggests that the organization along available dimensions, with the concomitant increase of efficiency in the search process, is the dominant factor in the situation.

One difficulty in studying the search process in STS is the fact that the subject will perform perfectly if the number of items presented is within his rehearsal span. Sternberg (1966) has overcome this difficulty by examining the latency of responses within the rehearsal span. His typical experiment consists of presenting from one to six digits to the subject at the rate of 1.2 seconds each. Following a 2-second delay, a single digit is presented and the subjects must respond "yes" or "no" depending on whether or not the test digit was a member of the set just presented. Following this response the subject is required to recall the complete set in order. Since the subjects were 98.7% correct on the recognition test and 98.6% correct on the recall test, it may be assumed that the task was within their rehearsal span. Interesting results were found in the latencies of the recognition responses: there was a linear increase in latency as the set size increased from one to six digits. The fact that there was no difference in latencies for "yes" versus "no" responses indicates that the search process in this situation is exhaustive and does not terminate the moment a match is found. Sternberg concludes that the subject engages in an exhaustive serial comparison process which evaluates elements at the rate of 25 to 30 per second. The high processing rate makes it seem likely that the rehearsal the subjects report is not an integral part of the scanning process, but instead maintains the image in STS so that it may be scanned at the time of the test. This conclusion depends upon accepting as a reasonable rehearsal rate for digits the values reported by Landauer (1962) which were never higher than six per second.

Buschke's (1963) missing-span method provides additional insight into search and retrieval processes in STS. The missing-span procedure consists of presenting in a random order all but one of a previously specified set of digits; the subject is then asked to report the missing digit. This technique eliminates the output interference associated with the usual digit-span studies in which the entire presented set must be reported. Buschke found that subjects had superior performance on a missing-span task as compared with an identical digit-span task in which all of the presented items were to be reported in any order. A natural hypothesis would explain the difference in performance as being caused by output interference; that is, the multiple recalls in the digit-span procedure produce interference not seen in the single test procedure of the missing span. An alternative explanation would hold that different storage and search strategies were being employed in the two situations. Madsen and Drucker (1966) examined this question by comparing test instructions given just prior to or immediately following each presentation sequence; the instructions specify whether the subject is to report the set of presented digits or simply to report the missing digit. Output interference would imply that the difference between missing-span and digit-span would hold up in both cases. The results showed that the missing-span procedure with prior instructions was superior to both missing-span and digit-span with instructions following presentation; the latter two conditions produced equal results and were superior to digit-span with prior instructions. It seems clear, then, that two storage and search strategies are being used: a missing-span type, and a digit-span type. Prior instructions (specifying the form of the subject's report) lead the subject to use one or the other of these strategies, but instructions following presentation are associated with a mixture of the two strategies. It appeared in this case that the strategies differed in terms of the type of storage during presentation; the digit-span group with prior instructions tended to report their digits in their presentation order, while the digit-span group with instructions after presentation more often reported the digits in their numerical order. This indicates that the missing-span strategy involved checking off the numbers as they were presented against a fixed, numerically ordered list, while the digit-span strategy involved rehearsing the items in their presented order. It is interesting to note that if the subjects had been aware of the superiority of the missing-span strategy, they could have used it in the digit-span task also, since the two types of tests called for the same information.

It should be noted that retrieval from STS depends upon a number of factors, some under the control of the subject and some depending upon the decay characteristics of STS. If the decay is partial in some sense, so that the trace contains only part of the information necessary for direct output, then the problem arises of how the partial information should be used to generate a response. In this case, it would be expected that the subject would then engage in a search of LTS in an effort to match or recognize the partial information. On the other hand, even though traces may decay in a partial manner, the rehearsal capability can hold a select set of items in a state of immediate recall availability and thereby impart to these items what is essentially an all-or-none status. It is to this rehearsal process that we now turn.

2. *Rehearsal Processes*

Rehearsal is one of the most important factors in experiments on human memory. This is particularly true in the laboratory because the concentrated, often meaningless, memory tasks used increase the relative efficacy of rehearsal as compared with the longer term coding and associative processes. Rehearsal may be less pervasive in everyday memory, but nevertheless has many uses, as Broadbent (1958) and others have pointed out. Such examples as remembering a telephone number or table-tennis score serve to illustrate the primary purpose of rehearsal, the lengthening of the time period information stays in the short-term store. A second purpose of rehearsal is illustrated by the fact that even if one wishes to remember a telephone number permanently, one will often rehearse the number several times. This rehearsal serves the purpose of increasing the strength built up in a long-term store, both by increasing the length of stay in STS (during which time a trace is built up in LTS) and by giving coding and other storage processes time to operate. Indeed, almost any kind of operation on an array of information (such as coding) can be viewed as a form of rehearsal, but this paper reserves the term only for the duration-lengthening repetition process.

In terms of STS structure, we can imagine that each rehearsal regenerates the STS trace and thereby prolongs the decay. This does not imply that the entire information ensemble available in STS immediately after presentation is regenerated and maintained at each rehearsal. Only that information selected by the subject, often a small proportion of the initial ensemble, is maintained. If the word "cow" is presented, for example, the sound of the word cow will enter STS; in addition, associates of cow, like milk, may be retrieved from LTS and also entered in STS; furthermore, an image of a cow may be entered into a short-term visual store. In succeeding rehearsals, however, the subject may rehearse only the word "cow" and the initial associates will decay and be lost. The process may be similar to the loss of meaningfulness that occurs when a word is repeated over and over (Lambert & Jakobovitz, 1960).

An interesting question concerns the maximum number of items that can be maintained via rehearsal. This number will depend upon the rate of STS decay and the form of the trace regenerated in STS by rehearsal. With almost any reasonable assumptions about either of these processes, however, an ordered rehearsal will allow the greatest number of items to be maintained. To give a simple example, suppose that individual items take 1.1 seconds to decay and may be restarted if rehearsal begins before decay is complete. Suppose further that each rehearsal takes .25 seconds. It is then clear that five items may be maintained indefinitely if they are rehearsed in a fixed order over and over. On the other hand, a rehearsal scheme in which items are chosen for rehearsal on a random basis will quickly result in one or more items decaying and becoming lost. It would be expected, therefore, that in situations where subjects are relying primarily upon their rehearsal capability in STS, rehearsal will take place in an ordered fashion. One such situation, from which we can derive an estimate of rehearsal capability, is the digit-span task. A series of numbers is read to the subject who is then required to recall them, usually in the forward or backward order. Because the subject has a long-term store which sometimes can be used to supplement the short-term rehearsal memory, the length of a series which can be correctly recalled may exceed the rehearsal capacity. A lower limit on this capacity can be found by identifying the series length at which a subject never errs; this series length is usually in the range of five to eight numbers.[5]

The above estimates of rehearsal capability are obtained in a discrete-trial situation where the requirement is to remember every item of a small input. A very similar rehearsal strategy can be employed, however, in situations such as free recall where a much greater number of items is input than rehearsal can possibly encompass. One strategy in this case would be to replace one of the items currently being rehearsed by each new item input. In this case every item would receive at least some rehearsal. Because of input and reorganization factors, which undoubtedly consume some time, the rehearsal capacity would probably be reduced. It should be clear that under this scheme a constant number of items will be undergoing rehearsal at any one moment. As an analogy, one might think of a bin always containing exactly n items; each new item enters the bin and knocks out an item already there. This process has been called in earlier reports a "rehearsal buffer," or simply a "buffer," and we will use this terminology here (Atkinson & Shiffrin, 1965).

[5] Wickelgren (1965) has examined rehearsal in the digit-span task in greater detail and found that rehearsal capacity is a function of the groupings engaged in by the subject; in particular, rehearsal in distinct groups of three was superior to rehearsal in four's and five's.

In our view, the maintenance and use of the buffer is a process entirely under the control of the subject. Presumably a buffer is set up and used in an attempt to maximize performance in certain situations. In setting up a maximal-sized buffer, however, the subject is devoting all his effort to rehearsal and not engaging in other processes such as coding and hypothesis testing. In situations, therefore, where coding, long-term search, hypothesis testing, and other mechanisms appreciably improve performance, it is likely that a trade-off will occur in which the buffer size will be reduced and rehearsal may even become somewhat random while coding and other strategies increase.

At this point we want to discuss various buffer operations in greater detail. Figure 2 illustrates a fixed-size buffer and its relation to the rest

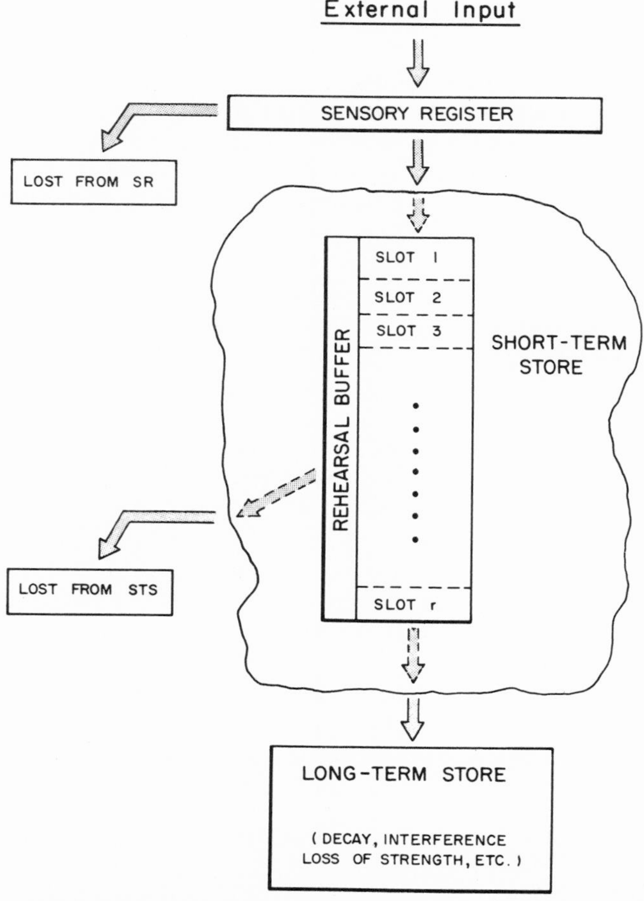

FIG. 2. The rehearsal buffer and its relation to the memory system.

of the memory system. The content of the buffer is constructed from items that have entered STS, items which have been input from the sensory register or from LTS. The arrow going toward LTS indicates that some long-term trace is being built up during an item's stay in the buffer. The other arrow from the buffer indicates that the input of a new item into the buffer causes an item currently in the buffer to be bumped out; this item then decays from STS and is lost (except for any trace which has accumulated in LTS during its stay). An item dropped from the buffer is likely to decay more quickly in STS than a newly presented item which has just entered STS. There are several reasons for this. For one thing, the item is probably already in some state of partial decay when dropped; in addition, the information making up an item in the buffer is likely to be only a partial copy of the ensemble present immediately following stimulus input.

There are two additional processes not shown in Fig. 2 that the subject can use on appropriate occasions. First, the subject may decide not to enter every item into the buffer; the reasons are manifold. For example, the items may be presented at a very fast rate so that input and reorganization time encroach too far upon rehearsal time. Another possibility is that some combinations of items are particularly easy to rehearse, making the subject loath to break up the combination. In fact, the work involved in introducing a new item into the buffer and deleting an old one may alone give the subject incentive to keep the buffer unchanged. Judging from these remarks, the choice of which items to enter into the buffer is based on momentary characteristics of the current string of input items and may appear at times to be essentially random.

The second process not diagrammed in Fig. 2 is the choice of which item to eliminate from the buffer when a new item is entered. There are several possibilities. The choice could be random; it could be based upon the state of decay of the current items; it could depend upon the ease of rehearsing the various items; most important, it could be based upon the length of time the various items have resided in the buffer. It is not unreasonable that the subject knows which items he has been rehearsing the longest, as he might if rehearsal takes place in a fixed order. It is for this reason that the slots or positions of the buffer have been numbered consecutively in Fig. 2; that is, to indicate that the subject might have some notion of the relative recency of the various items in the buffer.

The experimental justification for these various buffer mechanisms will be presented in Section IV. It should be emphasized that the subject will use a fixed-size buffer of the sort described here only in select situations, primarily those in which he feels that trading off rehearsal time for coding and other longer term control processes would not be fruitful. To the extent that long-term storage operations prove to be successful as compared with rehearsal, the structure of the rehearsal mechanism will tend to become impoverished. One other point concerning the buffer should be noted. While this paper consistently considers a fixed-size short-term buffer as a rehearsal strategy of the subject, it is possible to apply a fixed-size model of a similar kind to the structure of the short-term system as a whole, that is, to consider a short-term buffer as a permanent feature of memory. Waugh and Norman (1965), for example, have done this in their paper on primary memory. The data on the structure of STS is currently so nebulous that such an hypothesis can be neither firmly supported nor rejected.

3. *Coding Processes and Transfer between Short- and Long-Term Store*

It should be evident that there is a close relationship between the short- and long-term store. In general, information entering STS comes directly from LTS and only indirectly from the sensory register. For example, a visually presented word cannot be entered into STS as an auditory-verbal unit until a long-term search and match has identified the verbal representation of the visual image. For words, letters, and highly familar stimuli, this long-term search and match process may be executed very quickly, but one can imagine unfamiliar stimuli, such as, say, a nonsense scribble, where considerable search might be necessary before a suitable verbal representation is found to enter into STS. In such cases, the subject might enter the visual image directly into his short-term visual memory and not attempt a verbal coding operation.

Transfer from STS to LTS may be considered a permanent feature of memory; any information in STS is transferred to LTS to some degree throughout its stay in the short-term store. The important aspect of this transfer, however, is the wide variance in the amount and form of the transferred information that may be induced by control processes. When the subject is concentrating upon rehearsal, the information transferred would be in a relatively weak state and easily subject to interference. On the other hand, the subject may divert his effort from rehearsal to various coding operations which will increase the strength of the stored information. In answer to the question of what is a coding process, we can most generally state that a coding process is a select alteration and/or addition to the information in the short-term store as the result of a search of the long-term store. This change may take a number of forms, often using strong preexisting associations already in long-term store. A number of these coding possibilities will be considered later.

Experiments may be roughly classified in terms of the control operations the subject will be led to use. Concept formation problems or tasks where there is a clear solution will lead the subject to strategy selection and hypothesis-testing procedures (Restle, 1964). Experiments which do not involve problem solving, where there are a large number of easily coded items, and where there is a long period between presentation and test, will prompt the subject to expend his efforts on long-term coding operations. Finally, experiments in which memory is required, but long-term memory is not efficacious, will lead the subject to adopt rehearsal strategies that maintain the information the limited period needed for the task. Several examples of the latter experiment will be examined in this paper; they are characterized by the fact that the responses assigned to particular stimuli are continually changing, so that coding of a specific stimulus-response pair will prove harmful to succeeding pairs using the same stimulus. There are experiments, of course, for which it will not be possible to decide on a priori grounds which control processes are being used. In these cases the usual identification procedures must be used, including model fits and careful questioning of the subjects.

There are other short-term processes that do not fit easily into the above classification. They include grouping, organizing, and chunking strategies. One form that organizing may take is the selection of a subset of presented items for special attention, coding and/or rehearsal. This selection process is clearly illustrated in a series of studies on magnitude of reward by Harley (1965a, 1965b). Items in a paired-associate list were given two monetary incentives, one high and one low. In one experiment the subjects learned two paired-associate lists, one consisting of all high incentive items, the other consisting of all low incentive items; there were no differences in the learning rates for these lists. In a second experiment, subjects learned a list which included both high and low incentive items; in this case learning was faster for the high than the low incentive items. However, the overall rate of learning for the mixed list was about the same as for the two previous lists. It seems clear that when the high and low incentive items are mixed, the subject selectively attends to, codes, and rehearses those items with the higher payoffs. A second kind of organizing that occurs is the grouping of items into small sets, often with the object of memorizing the set as a whole, rather than as individual items. Typically in this case the grouped items will have some common factor. A good example may be found in the series of studies by Battig (1966) and his colleagues. He found a tendency to group items according to difficulty and according to degree of prior learning; this tendency was found even in paired-associate tasks where an extensive effort had been made to eliminate any basis for such grouping. A third type of information organization is found in the "chunking" process suggested by Miller (1956). In his view there is some optimal size that a set of information should have in order to best facilitate remembering. The incoming information is therefore organized into chunks of the desired magnitude.

C. Control Processes in Long-Term Store

Control processes to be considered in this section fall roughly into two categories: those concerned with transfer between short-term and long-term store and those concerned with search for and retrieval of information from LTS.

1. *Storage in Long-Term Store*

It was stated earlier that some information is transferred to LTS throughout an item's stay in STS, but that its amount and form is determined by control processes. This proposition will now be examined in greater detail. First of all, it would be helpful to consider a few simple examples where long-term storage is differentially affected by the coding strategy adopted. One example is found in a study on mediators performed by Montague, Adams, and Kiess (1966). Pairs of nonsense syllables were presented to the subject who had to write down any natural language mediator (word, phrase, or sentence associated with a pair) which occurred to him. At test 24 hours later the subject attempted to give the response member of each pair and the natural language mediator (NLM) that had been used in acquisition. Proportion correct for items on which the NLM was retained was 70%, while the proportion correct was negligible for items where the NLM was forgotten or significantly changed. Taken in conjunction with earlier studies showing that a group using NLMs was superior to a group learning by rote (Runquist & Farley, 1964), this result indicates a strong dependence of recall upon natural language mediators. A somewhat different encoding technique has been examined by Clark and Bower (personal communication). Subjects were required to learn several lists of paired-associate items, in which each item was a pair of familiar words. Two groups of subjects were given identical instructions, except for an extra section read to the experimental group explaining that the best method of learning the pairs was to form an elaborate visual image containing the objects designated by the two words. This experimental group was then given a few examples of the technique. There was a marked difference in performance between the groups on both immediate and delayed tests, the experimental group outperforming the control group by better than 40% in terms of probability correct. In fact, postexperimental questioning of the subjects revealed that the occasional high performers in the control group were often using the experimental technique even in the absence of instructions to do so. This technique of associating through the use of visual images is a very old one; it has been described in considerable detail, for example, by Cicero in *De Oratore* when he discusses memory as one of the five parts of rhetoric, and is clearly very effective.

We now consider the question of how these encoding techniques improve performance. The answer depends to a degree upon the fine structure of long-term store, and therefore cannot be stated precisely. Nevertheless, a number of possibilities should be mentioned. First, the encoding may make use of strong preexisting associations, eliminating the necessity of making new ones. Thus in mediating a word pair in a paired-associate task, word A might elicit word A' which in turn elicits the response. This merely moves the question back a level: how does the subject know which associates are the correct ones? It may be that the appropriate associations are identified by temporal position; that is, the subject may search through the associations looking for one which has been elicited recently. Alternatively, information could be stored with the appropriate association identifying it as having been used in the current paired-associates task. Second, the encoding might greatly decrease the effective area of memory which must be searched at the time of test. A response word not encoded must be in the set of all English words, or perhaps in the set of all words presented "recently," while a code may allow a smaller search through the associates of one or two items. One could use further search-limiting techniques such as restricting the mediator to the same first letter as the stimulus. A third possibility, related to the second, is that encoding might give some order to an otherwise random search. Fourth, encoding might greatly increase the amount of information stored. Finally, and perhaps most important, the encoding might protect a fledgling association from interference by succeeding items. Thus if one encodes a particular pair through an image of, say, a specific room in one's home, it is unlikely that future inputs will have any relation to that image; hence they will not interfere with it. In most cases coding probably works well for all of the above reasons.

There is another possible set of effects of the coding process which should be mentioned here. As background, we need to consider the results of several recent experiments which examine the effect of spacing between study and test in paired-associate learning (Bjork, 1966; Young, 1966). The result of primary interest to us is the decrease in probability correct as the number of other paired-associate items presented between study and test increases. This decrease seems to reach asymptote only after a fairly large number (e.g., 20) of intervening items. There are several possible explanations for this "short-term" effect. Although the effect probably occurs over too great an interval to consider direct decay from STS as an explanation, any of several rehearsal strategies could give rise to an appropriate-looking curve. Since a paired-associate task usually requires coding, a fixed-size rehearsal buffer may not be a reasonable hypothesis, unless the buffer size is fairly small; on the other hand, a variable rehearsal set with semirandomly spaced rehearsals may be both reasonable and accurate. If, on the other hand, one decides that almost no continuing rehearsal occurs in this task, what other hypotheses are available? One could appeal to retroactive interference but this does little more than name the phenomenon. Greeno (1967) has proposed a coding model which can explain the effect. In his view, the subject may select one of several possible codes at the time of study. In particular, he might select a "permanent" code, which will not be disturbed by any other items or codes in the experiment; if this occurs, the item is said to be learned. On the other hand, a "transitory" code might be selected, one which is disturbed or eliminated as succeeding items are presented. This transitory code will last for a probabilistically determined number of trials before becoming useless or lost. The important point to note here is the fact that a decreasing "short-term" effect can occur as a result of solely long-term operations. In experiments emphasizing long-term coding, therefore, the decision concerning which decay process, or combination of decay processes, is operative will not be easy to make in an a priori manner; rather the decision would have to be based upon such a posteriori grounds as goodness-of-fit results for a particular model and introspective reports from the subject.

2. *Long-Term Search Processes*

One of the most fascinating features of memory is the long-term search process. We have all, at one time or another, been asked for information which we once knew, but which is momentarily unavailable, and we are aware of the ensuing period (often lasting for hours) during which memory was searched, occasionally resulting in the correct answer. Nevertheless, there has been a marked lack of experimental work dealing with this rather common phenomenon. For this reason, our discussion of search processes will be primarily theoretical, but the absence of a large experimental literature should not lead us to underestimate the importance of the search mechanism.

The primary component of the search process is locating the sought-for trace (or one of the traces) in long-term store. This process is seen in operation via several examples. The occasionally very long latencies prior to a correct response for well-known information indicates a non-perfect search. A subject reporting that he will think "of it the moment he thinks about something else" indicates a prior fixation on an unsuccessful search procedure. Similarly, the tip-of-the-tongue phenomenon mentioned earlier indicates a failure to find an otherwise very strong trace. We have also observed the following while quizzing a graduate student on the names of state capitals. The student gave up trying to remember the capital of the state of Washington after pondering for a long time. Later this student quickly identified the capital of Oregon as Salem and then said at once that the capital of Washington was Olympia. When asked how he suddenly remembered, he replied that he had learned the two capitals together. Presumably this information would have been available during the first search if the student had known where to look: namely in conjunction with the capital of Oregon. Such descriptive examples are numerous and serve to indicate that a search can sometimes fail to uncover a very strong trace. One of the decisions the subject must make is when to terminate an unsuccessful search. An important determiner of the length of search is the amount of order imposed during the search; if one is asked to name all the states and does so strictly geographically, one is likely to do better than someone who spews out names in a haphazard fashion. The person naming states in a haphazard fashion will presently encounter in his search for new names those which he has already given; if this occurs repeatedly, the search will be terminated as being unfruitful. The problem of terminating the search is especially acute in the case of recalling a set of items without a good natural ordering. Such a case is found in free-verbal-recall experiments in which a list of words is presented to the subject who must then recall as many as possible. The subject presumably searches along some sort of temporal dimension, a dimension which lets the subject know when he finds a word whether or not it was on the list presented most recently. The temporal ordering is by no means perfect, however, and the search must therefore be carried out with a degree of randomness. This procedure may lead to missing an item which has a fairly strong trace. It has been found in free-verbal-recall experiments, for example, that repeated recall tests on a given list sometimes result in the inclusion on the second test of items left out on the first test. In our own experiments we have even observed intrusions from an earlier list that had not been recalled during the test of that list.

It would be illustrative at this point to consider an experiment carried out by Norma Graham at Stanford University. Subjects were asked to name the capitals of the states. If a correct answer was not given within 5 seconds following presentation of the state name, the subjects were then given a hint and allowed 30 seconds more to search their memory. The hint consisted of either 1, 2, 4, 12, or 24 consecutive letters of the alphabet, one of which was the first letter in the name of the state capital. The probability correct dropped steadily as the hint size increased from 1 to 24 letters. The average response latencies for correct answers, however, showed a different effect; the 1-letter hint was associated with the fastest response time, the 2-letter hint was slower, the 4-letter hint was slower yet, but the 12- and 24-letter hints were faster than the 4-letter hint. One simple hypothesis that can explain why latencies were slower after the 4-letter hint than after the 12- and 24-letter hints depends upon differing search processes. Suppose the subject in the absence of a hint engages in "normal" search, or N search. When given the first letter, however, we will assume the subject switches to a first letter search, or L search, consisting of a deeper exploration of memory based upon the first letter. This L search might consist of forming possible sounds beginning with the appropriate letter, and matching them against possible city names. When the size of the hint increases, the subject must apply the L search to each of the letters in turn, obviously a time-consuming procedure. In fact, for 12- or 24-letter hints the probability is high that the subject would use up the entire 30-second search period without carrying out an L search on the correct first letter. Clearly a stage is reached, in terms of hint size, where the subject will switch from an L search to N search in order to maximize performance. In the present experiment it seems clear that the switch in strategy occurred between the 4- and 12-letter hints.

In the above experiment there were two search-stopping events, one subject-controlled and the other determined by the 30-second time limit. It is instructive to consider some of the possible subject-controlled stopping rules. One possibility is simply an internal time limit, beyond which the subject decides further search is useless. Related to this would be an event-counter stopping rule that would halt the subject when a fixed number of prespecified events had occurred. The events could be total number of distinct "searches," total number of incorrect traces found, and so on. A third possibility is dependent on a consecutive-events counter. For example, search could be stopped whenever x consecutive searches recovered traces that had been found in previous searches.

It was noted earlier that searches may vary in their apparent orderliness. Since long-term memory is extremely large, any truly random search would invariably be doomed to failure. The search must always be made along some dimension, or on the basis of some available cues. Nevertheless, searches do vary in their degree of order; a letter-by-letter search is highly structured, whereas a free associative search that proceeds from point to point in a seemingly arbitrary manner will be considerably less restrained, even to the point where the same ground may be covered many times. One other possible feature of the search process is not as desirable as the ones previously mentioned. The search itself might prove destructive to the sought-after trace. That is, just as new information transferred to the long-term store might interfere with previous material stored there, the generation of traces during the search might prove to have a similar interfering effect.

A somewhat different perspective on search procedures is obtained by considering the types of experimental tests that typically are used. Sometimes the very nature of the task presumes a specific search procedure. An example is found in the free-verbal-recall task in which the subject must identify a subset of a larger well-learned group of words. A search of smaller scope is made in a paired-associate task; when the set of possible responses is large, the search for the answer is similar to that made in free recall, with a search component and a recognition component to identify the recovered trace as the appropriate one. When the set of responses in a paired-associate task is quite small, the task becomes one of recognition alone: the subject can generate each possible response in order and perform a recognition test on each. The recognition test presumably probes the trace for information identifying it as being from the correct list and being associated with the correct stimulus.

It was said that the primary component of the search process is locating the desired memory trace in LTS. The secondary component is the recovery of the trace once found. It has been more or less assumed for simplicity in the above discussions that the trace is all-or-none. This may not be the case, and the result of a search might be the recovery of a partial trace. Retrieval would then depend either upon correctly guessing the missing information or performing a further search to match the partial trace with known responses. It is possible, therefore, to divide the recovery processes into a search component and retrieval component, both of which must be successfully concluded in order to output the correct response. The two components undoubtedly are correlated in the sense that stronger, more complete traces will both be easier to find and easier to retrieve, having been found.

One final problem of some importance should be mentioned at this time. The effects of trace interference may be quite difficult to separate from those of search failure. Trace interference here refers either to loss of information in the trace due to succeeding inputs or to confusions caused by competition among multiple traces at the moment of test. Search failure refers to an inability to find the trace at all. Thus a decrease in the probability of a correct response as the number of items intervening between study and test increases could be due to trace interference generated by those items. It could also be due to an increased likelihood of failing to find the trace because of the increasing number of items that have to be searched in memory. One way these processes might be separated experimentally would be in a comparison of recognition and recall measures, assuming that a failure to find the trace is less likely in the case of recognition than in the case of recall. At the present, research along these lines has not given us a definitive answer to this question.

IV. Experiments Concerned with Short-Term Processes

Sections II and III of this paper have outlined a theoretical framework for human memory. As we have seen, the framework is extremely general, and there are many alternative choices that can be made in formulating models for particular experimental situations. The many choice points make it impossible for us to examine each process experimentally. Instead we shall devote our attention to a number of processes universally agreed to occur in experiments on memory, namely rehearsal and search processes. In Section V the LTS search processes will be examined in detail; in the present section the major emphasis will be on STS mechanisms, particularly the control process designated as the rehearsal buffer. The sensory registration system is not an important factor in these models; the experiments are designed so that all items enter the sensory register and then are transferred to STS. The long-term store will be presented in the models of this section but only in the simplest possible manner. We now turn to a series of experiments designed to establish in some detail the workings of the buffer mechanism.

A. A Continuous Paired-Associate Memory Task (Experiment 1)

This study is the prototype for a series of experiments reported in this section designed specifically to study buffer processes. The buffer is a fixed-size rehearsal scheme in STS; conditions which prompt the subject to make use of a buffer include difficulty in using long-term store, a large number of short study-test intervals, and a presentation rate slow enough that cognitive manipulations in STS are not excessively rushed. The task that was developed to establish these conditions is described below.[6]

The subject was required to keep track of constantly changing responses associated with a fixed set of stimuli.[7] The stimuli were 2-digit numbers chosen from the set 00–99; the responses were letters of the alphabet. At the start of a particular subject-session a set of s stimuli was chosen randomly from the numbers 00 to 99; these stimuli were not changed over the course of that day's session. To begin the session each stimulus was paired with a letter chosen randomly from the alphabet. Following this initial period, a continuous sequence of trials made up the rest of the session, each trial consisting of a test phase followed by a

[6] The reader may consult Atkinson, Brelsford, and Shiffrin (1967) for details of the experimental procedure and theoretical analyses that are not covered in the present discussion. Also presented there is an account of the mathematics of the model.

[7] The task is similar to those used by Yntema and Mueser (1960, 1962), Brelsford *et al.* (1966), and Katz (1966).

study phase. During the test phase, one of the s stimuli was randomly selected and presented alone for test. The subject was required to respond with the most recent response paired with that stimulus. No feedback was given to the subject. Following his response the study portion of the trial began. During the study portion the stimulus just presented for test was paired with a new response selected randomly from the alphabet; the only restriction was that the previous response (the correct response during the immediately preceding test phase) was not used during the study phase of the same trial. The subject was instructed to forget the previous pairing and try to remember the new pairing currently being presented for study. Following the study period, a stimulus was again selected randomly from the set of s stimuli and the test portion of the next trial began.

The result of this procedure is as follows: a particular stimulus-response pair is presented for study, followed by a randomly determined number of trials involving other stimuli, and then tested. Having been tested, the pair is broken up and the stimulus is paired with a different response; in other words, no stimulus-response pair is presented for study twice in succession. It is easy to imagine the effects of this procedure on the subject's long-term memory processes. If any particular pair is strongly stored in long-term memory, it will interfere with subsequent pairings involving that same stimulus. In addition, the nature of the stimuli and responses used makes coding a difficult task. For these reasons, the subject soon learns that the usual long-term storage operations, such as coding, are not particularly useful; in fact, the subject is forced to rely heavily on his short-term store and his rehearsal capacity. The experimental procedure also was designed so that it would be possible to carry out extensive parametric analyses on data from individual subjects. This was accomplished by running each subject for 12 or more days and collecting the data on a system under the control of a time-sharing computer, a procedure which made the precise sequence of events during each session available for analysis.

1. *Method*

The subjects were nine students from Stanford University who received $2 per experimental session. This experiment, and most of the others reported in this paper, was conducted in the Computer-Based Learning Laboratory at Stanford University. The control functions were performed by computer programs run on a modified PDP-1 computer manufactured by the Digital Equipment Corp., and under control of a time-sharing system. The subject was seated at a cathode-ray-tube display terminal; there were six terminals, each located in a separate 7×8 foot sound-shielded room. Stimuli were displayed on the face of the cathode ray tube (CRT); responses were made on an electric typewriter keyboard located immediately below the lower edge of the CRT.

For each session the subject was assigned to one of the three experimental conditions. The three conditions were defined in terms of s, the size of the set of stimuli to be remembered, which took on the values 4, 6, or 8. An attempt was made to assign subjects to each condition once in consecutive three-session blocks. Every session began with a series of study trials: one study trial for each stimulus to be used in the session. On a study trial the word "study" appeared on the upper face of the CRT. Beneath the word "study" one of the stimuli (a 2-digit number) appeared along with a randomly selected letter from the alphabet. Subjects were instructed to try to remember the stimulus-response pairs. Each of these initial study trials lasted for 3 seconds with a 3-second intertrial interval. As soon as there had been an initial study trial for each stimulus to be used in the session, the session proper began.

Each subsequent trial involved a fixed series of events. (1) The word "test" appeared on the upper face of the CRT. Beneath the word "test" a randomly selected member of the stimulus set appeared. Subjects were instructed that when the word "test" and a stimulus appeared on the CRT, they were to respond with the last response that had been associated with that simulus, guessing if necessary. This test portion of a trial lasted for 3 seconds. (2) The CRT was blacked out for 2 seconds. (3) The word "study" appeared on the upper face of the CRT for 3 seconds. Below the word "study" a stimulus-response pair appeared. The stimulus was the same one used in the preceding test portion of the trial. The response was randomly selected from the letters of the alphabet, with the stipulation that it be different from the immediately preceding response assigned to that stimulus. (4) There was a 3-second intertrial interval before the next trial. Thus a complete trial (test plus study) took 11 seconds. A subject was run for 220 such trials during each experimental session.

2. *Theoretical Analysis*

In order that the reader may visualize the sequence of events which occurs in this situation, a sample sequence of 18 trials is illustrated in Fig. 3. Within the boxes are the displays seen on the CRT screen. In this session the stimulus set includes the four stimuli 20, 31, 42, and 53 (i.e., $s = 4$). On trial n, item 31-Q is presented for study. On trial $n+1$, 42 is tested and 42-B presented for study. Then on trial $n+2$, 31 is tested; the correct answer is Q as is seen by referring to trial n. After the subject answers he is given 31-S to study. He is instructed to forget the previous pair, 31-Q, and remember only the new pair, 31-S. The response letter S was selected randomly from the alphabet, with the restriction that the previous response, Q, could not be used. A previously used response may through chance, however, be chosen again later in the session; for example, on trial $n+7$, 31-Q is again presented for study. It is also possible that two or more stimuli might be paired with the same response concurrently; as an example, on trial $n+15$, 20 is paired with C and on trial $n+16$, 42 also is paired with C. The stimulus presented on each trial is chosen randomly; for this reason the number of trials intervening

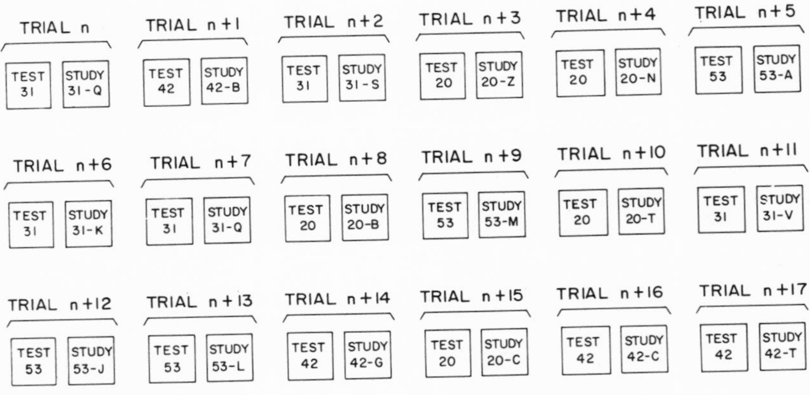

FIG. 3. A sample sequence of trials for Experiment 1.

between study and test is a random variable distributed geometrically. In the analysis of the results, a very important variable is the number of trials intervening between study and test on a particular stimulus-response pair; this variable is called the *lag*. Thus 20 is tested on trial $n+4$ at a lag of 0 because it was studied on trial $n+3$. On the other hand, 42 is tested on trial $n+14$ at a lag of 12, because it was last studied on trial $n+1$.

Consider now the processes the subject will tend to adopt in this situation. The obvious difficulties involved in the use of LTS force the subject to rely heavily upon rehearsal mechanisms in STS for optimal performance.[8] A strategy making effective use of STS is an ordered rehearsal scheme of fixed size called the buffer in Section III,B. The fixed-size requirement may not be necessary for maximal utilization of

[8] The usual examples given for the usefulness of a distinct short-term store do not stress the positive benefits of a memory decaying quickly and completely. Without such a memory, many minor tasks such as adding a long column of numbers might become far more difficult. The current experiment, in which associative bonds are frequently broken and re-formed, is an example of a class of operations for which a short-term store is almost essential.

STS, but is indicated by the following considerations. Keeping the size of the rehearsal set constant gives the subject a great deal of control over the situation; each rehearsal cycle will take about the same amount of time, and it is easier to reorganize the buffer when a new item is introduced. Furthermore, an attempt to stretch the rehearsal capacity to its limit may result in confusion which causes the entire rehearsal set to be disrupted; the confusion results from the variable time that must be allowed for operations such as responding at the keyboard and processing the new incoming items. The hypothesis of an ordered fixed-size buffer is given support by the subjects' reports and the authors' observations while acting as subjects. The reader is not asked, however, to take our word on this matter; the analysis of the results will provide the strongest support for the hypothesis.

It must be decided next just what is being rehearsed. The obvious candidate, and the one reported by subjects, is the stimulus-response pair to be remembered. That is, the unit of rehearsal is the two-digit stimulus number plus the associated response letter. Under certain conditions, however, the subject may adopt a more optimal strategy in which only the responses are rehearsed. This strategy will clearly be more effective because many more items may be encompassed with the same rehearsal effort. The strategy depends upon ordering the stimuli (usually in numerical order in the present case) and rehearsing the responses in an order corresponding to the stimulus order; in this way the subject may keep track of which response goes with which stimulus. For a number of reasons, the scheme is most effective when the size of the stimulus set is small; for a large set the subject may have difficulty ordering the stimuli, and difficulty reorganizing the rehearsal as each new item is presented. When the number of stimulus-response pairs to be remembered is large, the subject may alter this scheme in order to make it feasible. The alteration might consist of rehearsing only the responses associated with a portion of the ordered stimuli. In a previous experiment (Brelsford *et al.*, 1966) with a similar design, several subjects reported using such a strategy when the stimulus set size was four, and an examination of their results showed better performance than the other subjects. Subject reports lead us to believe that this strategy is used infrequently in the present experiment; consequently, our model assumes that the unit of rehearsal is the stimulus-response pair, henceforth called an "item."

Figure 2 outlines the structure of the model to be applied to the data. Despite the emphasis on rehearsal, a small amount of long-term storage occurs during the period that an item resides in the buffer. The information stored in LTS is comparatively weak and decays rapidly as succeeding items are presented. In accord with the argument that the long-term process is uncomplicated, we assume here that information stored in LTS increases linearly with the time an item resides in the buffer. Once an item leaves the buffer, the LTS trace is assumed to decrease as each succeeding item is presented for study.

Every item is assumed to enter first the sensory register and then STS. At that point the subject must decide whether or not to place the new item in the rehearsal buffer. There are a number of reasons why every incoming item may not be placed in the buffer. For one thing, the effort involved in reorganizing the buffer on every trial may not always appear worthwhile, especially when the gains from doing so are not immediately evident; for another, the buffer at some particular time may consist of a combination of items especially easy to rehearse and the subject may not wish to destroy the combination. In order to be more specific about which items enter the buffer and which do not, two kinds of items must be distinguished. An O item is an incoming stimulus-response pair whose stimulus is currently in the buffer. Thus if 52-L is currently in the buffer, 52 is tested, and 52-G is presented for study, then 52-G is said to be an O item. Whenever an O item is presented it is automatically entered into the buffer; this entry, of course, involves replacing the old response by the appropriate new response. Indeed, if an O item did not enter the buffer, the subject would be forced to rehearse the now incorrect previous response, or to leave a useless blank spot in the buffer; for these reasons, the assumption that O items are always entered into the buffer seems reasonable. The other kind of item that may be presented is an N item. An N item is a stimulus-response pair whose stimulus currently is not in the buffer. Whenever an N item is entered into the buffer, one item currently in the buffer must be removed to make room the new item (i.e., the buffer is assumed to be of fixed size, r, meaning that the number of items being rehearsed at any one time is constant). The assumption is made that an N item enters into the buffer with probability α; whenever an N item is entered, one of the items currently in the buffer is randomly selected and removed to make room for it.

The model used to describe the present experiment is now almost complete. A factor still not specified is the response rule. At the moment of test any item which is in the buffer is responded to correctly. If the stimulus tested is not in the buffer, a search is carried out in LTS with the hope of finding the trace. The probability of retrieving the correct response from LTS depends upon the current trace strength, which in turn, depends on the amount of information transferred to LTS. Specifically we assume that information is transferred to LTS at a constant rate θ during the entire period an item resides in the buffer; θ is the transfer rate per trial. Thus, if an item remains in the rehearsal buffer for exactly j trials, then that item accumulated an amount of information equal to $j\theta$. We also assume that each trial following the trial on which an item is knocked out of the buffer causes the information stored in LTS for that item to decrease by a constant proportion τ. Thus, if an item were knocked out of the buffer at trial j, and i trials intervened between the original study and test on that item, then the amount of information in LTS at the time of the test would be $j\theta\tau^{i-j}$. We now want to specify the probability of a correct retrieval of an item from LTS. If the amount of information in LTS at the moment of test is zero, then the probability of a correct retrieval should be at the guessing level. As the amount of information increases, the probability of a correct retrieval should increase toward unity. We define ρ_{ij} as the probability of a correct response from LTS for an item that was tested at lag i, and resided in the buffer for exactly j trials. Considering the above specifications on the retrieval process,

$$\rho_{ij} = 1 - (1-g)\exp[-j\theta(\tau^{i-j})]$$

where g is the guessing probability, which is 1/26 since there were 26 response alternatives.[9]

The basic dependent variable in the present experiment is the probability of a correct response at the time of a test, given lag i. In order to derive this probability we need to know the length of time that an item resides in the memory buffer. Therefore, define $\beta_j =$ probability that an item resides in the buffer for exactly j trials, given that it is tested at a lag greater than j. The probability of a correct response to an item tested at lag i can now be written in terms of the β_j's. Let "C_i" represent the occurrence of a correct response to an item tested at lag i. Then

$$\Pr(C_i) = \left[1 - \sum_{k=0}^{i} \beta_k\right] + \left[\sum_{k=0}^{i} \beta_k \rho_{ik}\right]$$

The first bracketed term is the probability that the item is in the buffer at the time of the test. The second bracket contains a sum of probabilities, each term representing the probability of a correct retrieval

[9] Lest the use of an exponential function seem entirely arbitrary, it should be noted that this function bears a close relation to the familiar linear model of learning theory. If we ignore for the moment the decay feature, then

$$\rho_{ij} = 1 - (1-g)\exp(-j\theta).$$

It is easily seen that this is the linear model expression for the probability of a correct response after j reinforcements with parameter $e^{-\theta}$. Thus, the retrieval function ρ_{ij} can be viewed as a linear model with time in the buffer as the independent variable. To be sure, the decay process complicates matters, but the reason for choosing the exponential function becomes somewhat less arbitrary. A decay process is needed so that the probability of a correct retrieval from LTS will approach chance as the lag tends toward infinity.

from LTS of an item which remained in the buffer for exactly k trials and was then lost.[10] There are four parameters in the model: r, the buffer size which must be an integer; α, the probability of entering an N item into the buffer; θ, the transfer rate of information to LTS; and τ, the decay rate of information from LTS after an item has left the buffer.

One final process must be considered before the model is complete. This process is the recovery of information from STS which is not in the buffer. It will be assumed that the decay of an item which has entered and then left the buffer is very rapid, so rapid that an item which has left the buffer cannot be recovered from STS on the succeeding test.[11] The only time in which a recovery is made from STS, apart from the buffer, occurs if an item is tested immediately following its study (i.e., at a lag of 0). In this case there is virtually no time between study and test and it is assumed therefore that the recovery probability is one, regardless of whether the item was entered into the buffer or not. In other words, the probability correct is one when the lag is zero.

3. *Data Analysis*

Figure 4 presents the probability of a correct response as a function of lag for each of the three stimulus set sizes examined. It can be seen that the smaller the stimulus set size, the better the overall performance. It is important to note that the theory predicts such a difference on the following basis: the larger the size of the stimulus set, the more often an N item will be presented; and the more often N items will be presented, the more often items in the buffer will be knocked out. Recall that only N items can knock items from the buffer; O items merely replace themselves.

It can be seen that performance is almost perfect for lag 0 in all three conditions. This was expected because lag 0 means that the item was tested immediately following its study, and was therefore available in STS. The curves drop sharply at first and slowly thereafter, but have not yet reached the chance level at lag 17, the largest lag plotted. The chance level should be 1/26 since there were 26 response alternatives.

The four parameters of the model were estimated by fitting the model to the lag curves in Fig. 4 using a minimum chi-square as a best fit

[10] One factor which the model as outlined ignores is the probability of recovering from LTS an old, incorrect trace. In the interest of simplicity this process has not been introduced into the model, although it could be appended with no major changes.

[11] Clearly this assumption depends on the time intervals involved. In the present experiment the trials were quite slow; in experiments where a faster presentation rate is used, the model probably would need to be modified slightly to allow a nonzero probability of recovery of an item from STS on the test following its removal from the buffer.

criterion.[12] The solid lines in Fig. 5 give the best fit of the model, which occurred when the parameter values were: $r = 2$, $\alpha = .39$, $\theta = .40$, and $\tau = .93$. It can be seen that the observed data and the predictions from the model are in close agreement. It should be emphasized that the three curves are fit simultaneously using the same parameter values, and the differences between the curves depend only on the value of s (the stimulus

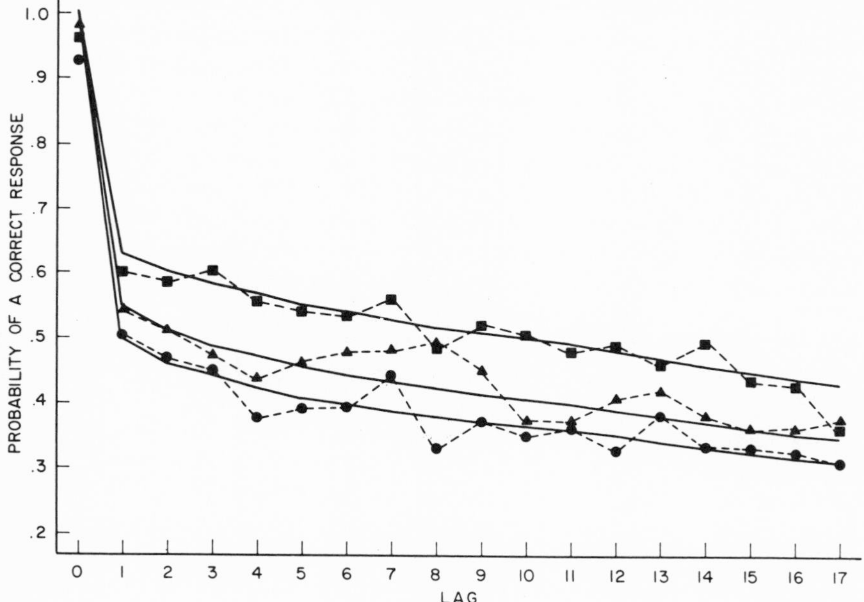

FIG. 4. Observed and theoretical probabilities of a correct response as a function of lag (Experiment 1). --■-- $s = 4$; --▲-- $s = 6$; --●-- $s = 8$;—theory.

set size) which, of course, is determined by the experimenter. The predicted probabilities of a correct response weighted and summed over all lag positions are .562, .469, and .426 for s equal to 4, 6, and 8, respectively; the observed values are .548, .472, and .421.

The estimated value of r might seem surprising at first glance; two items appear to be a rather small buffer capacity. But there are a number of considerations that render this estimate reasonable. It seems clear that the capacity estimated in a task where the subject is constantly interrupted for tests must be lower than the capacity estimated, for example, in a typical digit-span task. This is so because part of the attention time that would be otherwise allotted to rehearsal must be used to search memory in order to respond to the continuous sequence

[12] See Atkinson, Brelsford, and Shiffrin (1967) for details of the estimation procedure and a statistical evaluation of the goodness-of-fit.

of tests. Considering that two items in this situation consist of four numbers and two letters, an estimate of r equal to two is not particularly surprising. The estimated value of α indicates that only 39% of the N items actually enter the buffer (remember that O items always enter the buffer). This low value may indicate that a good deal of mental effort is involved in keeping an item in the buffer via rehearsal, leading to a reluctance to discard an item from the buffer that has not yet been tested. A similar reluctance to discard items would be found if certain

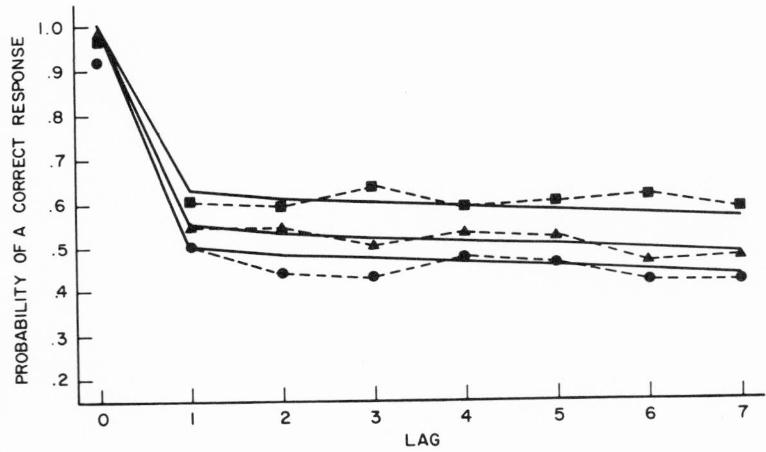

FIG. 5. Observed and theoretical probabilities of a correct response as a function of lag when every intervening item uses the same stimulus (Experiment 1). --■-- $s = 4$; --▲-- $s = 6$; --●-- $s = 8$;—theory.

combinations of items were particularly easy to rehearse. Finally, note that the theory predicts that, if there were no long-term storage, the subject's overall probability of a correct response would be independent of α. Thus it might be expected that α would be higher the greater the effectiveness of long-term storage. In accord with this reasoning, the low value of α found would result from the weak long-term storage associated with the present situation.

In addition to the lag curves in Fig. 4, there are a number of other predictions that can be examined. One aspect of the theory maintains that O items always enter the buffer and replace themselves, while N items enter the buffer with probability α and knock an item out of the buffer whenever they do so. The effects of different stimulus-set sizes displayed in Fig. 5 are due to this assumption. The assumption, however, may be examined in other ways; if it is true, then an item's probability of being correct will be affected by the specific items that intervene between its initial study and its later test. If every intervening trial uses the same stimulus, then the probability of knocking the item of interest from the buffer is minimized. This is so because once any intervening item enters the buffer, every succeeding intervening item is an O item (since it uses the same stimulus), and hence also enters the buffer. Indeed, if α were one, then every intervening item after the first would be an O

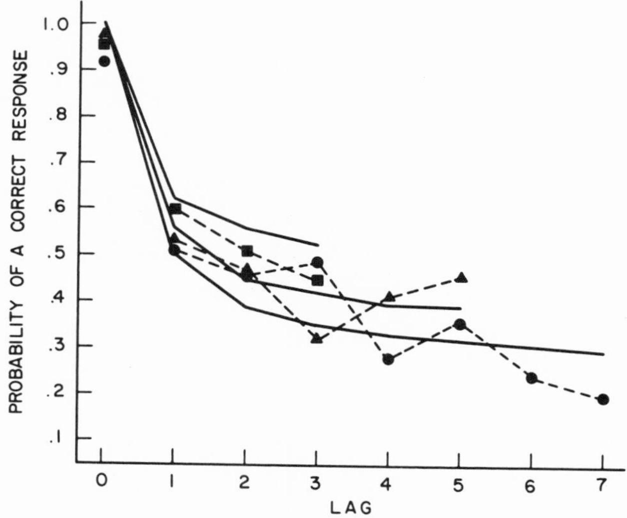

FIG. 6. Observed and theoretical probabilities of a correct response as a function of lag when every intervening item uses a different stimulus (Experiment 1). --■-- $s = 4$; --▲-- $s = 6$; --●-- $s = 8$;—theory.

item, and hence only the first intervening item would have a chance of knocking the item of interest from the buffer; if $\alpha = 1$ and there were no long-term decay, then the lag curve for this condition would be flat from lag 1 onward. In this case, however, α is not equal to one and there is long-term decay; hence the lag curve will decrease somewhat when the intervening items all have the same stimulus, but not to the extent found in Fig. 4. This lag curve, called the "all-same" curve, is shown in Fig. 5; it plots the probability of a correct response as a function of lag, when all the intervening trials between study and test involve the same stimulus. The parameters previously estimated were used to generate predictions for these curves and they are displayed as solid lines. It seems clear that the predictions are highly accurate.

A converse result, called the "all-different" lag curve, is shown in Fig. 6. In this condition, every intervening item has a different stimulus, and therefore the probability of knocking the item of interest from the buffer is maximized. The lag curves for this condition, therefore, should drop faster than the unconditional lag curves of Fig. 4. Predictions were again generated using the previous parameter values and are represented by the solid lines in Fig. 6. Relatively few observations were available in this condition; considering the instability of the data the predictions seem reasonable.

The procedure used in this experiment is an excellent example of what has been traditionally called a negative transfer paradigm. The problems inherent in such a paradigm were mentioned earlier as contributing to the subjects' heavy reliance upon the short-term store. To the extent that there is any use of LTS, however, we would expect intrusion errors from previously correct responses. The model could be extended in several obvious ways to predict the occurrence of such intrusions. For example, the subject could, upon failing to recover the most recent trace from LTS, continue his search and find the remains of the previous, now incorrect, trace. In order to examine intrusion errors, the proportion of errors which were the correct response for the previous presentation of the stimulus in question were calculated for each lag and each condition. The proportions were quite stable over lags with mean values of .065, .068, and .073 for the 4, 6, and 8 stimulus conditions, respectively. If the previously correct response to an item is generated randomly for any given error, these values should not differ significantly from $1/25 = .04$. In both the $s = 4$ and $s = 6$ conditions seven of the nine subjects had mean values above chance; in the $s = 8$ condition eight of the nine subjects were above chance. Intrusion errors may therefore be considered a reliable phenomenon in this situation; on the other hand, the relatively low frequency with which they occur indicates a rather weak and quickly decaying long-term trace.

A second error category of interest includes those responses that are members of the current set of responses to be remembered but are not the correct responses. This set, of course, includes the set of responses in the buffer at any one time; if the subject tends to give as a guess a response currently in the buffer (and therefore highly available), then the probability of giving as an error a response in the current to-be-remembered set will be higher than chance. Since responses may be assigned to more than one stimulus simultaneously, the number of responses in the to-be-remembered set is bound by, but may be less than, the size of the stimulus set, s. Thus, on the basis of chance the error probabilities would be bounded below.12, .20, and .28 for $s = 4$, 6, and 8, respectively. The actual values found were .23, .28, and .35, respectively. This finding suggests that when the subject cannot retrieve the response from his buffer or LTS and is forced to guess, he has a somewhat greater than chance likelihood of giving a response currently in the rehearsal set but assigned to another stimulus. It is not surprising that a subject will give as a guess one of the responses in his buffer since they are immediately available.

Other analyses have been performed on the data of this experiment, but the results will not be presented until a second experiment has been described. Before considering the second experiment, however, a few words should be said about individual differences. One of the reasons for running a single subject for many sessions was the expectation that the model could be applied to each subject's data separately. Such analyses have been made and are reported elsewhere (Atkinson, Brelsford & Shiffrin, 1967). The results are too complex to go into here, but they establish that individual subjects by and large conform to the predictions of the model quite well. Since our aim in this paper is to present a nontechnical discussion of the model, to simplify matters we will make most of our analyses on group data.

B. The "All-Different" Stimulus Procedure (Experiment 2)

In the preceding experiment, the number of stimuli used in a given experimental session and the size of the to-be-remembered set were identical. These two factors, however, can be made independent. Specifically, a set of all-different stimuli could be used while keeping the size of the to-be-remembered set constant. The name, all-different, for this experiment results from the use of all-different stimuli, i.e., once a given stimulus-response pair is presented for test, that stimulus is not used again. In other respects the experiment is identical to Experiment 1.

One reason for carrying out an experiment of this type is to gain some information about the replacement hypothesis for O items. In Experiment 1 we assumed that a new item with a stimulus the same as an item currently in the buffer automatically replaced that item in the buffer; that is, the response switched from old to new. In the all-different experiment subjects are instructed, as in Experiment 1, to forget each item once it has been tested. If an item currently in the buffer is tested (say, 52-G) and a new item is then presented for study (say, 65-Q), we might ask whether the tested item will be automatically replaced by the new item (whether 65-Q will replace 52-G in the buffer). This replacement strategy is clearly optimal for it does no good to retain an item in the buffer that already has been tested. Nevertheless, if the reorganization of the buffer is difficult and time consuming, then the replacement of a tested item currently in the buffer might not be carried out. One simple assumption along these lines would postulate that every item has an independent probability α of entering the buffer.

The all-different experiment was identical to Experiment 1 in all respects except the following. In Experiment 1 the s stimuli were the same throughout an experimental session, with only the associated responses being changed on each trial, whereas in the all-different experiment 100 stimuli were available for use in each session. In fact, every stimulus was effectively new since the stimulus for each study trial was selected randomly from the set of all 100 stimuli under the restriction that no stimulus could be used if it had been tested or studied in the previous 50 trials. There were still three experimental conditions with s equal to 4, 6, or 8 denoting the number of items that the subject was required to try to remember at any point in time. Thus a session began with either 4, 6, or 8 study trials on different randomly selected stimuli, each of which was paired with a randomly selected response (from the 26 letters). On each trial a stimulus in the current to-be-remembered set was presented for test. After the subject made his response he was instructed to forget the item he had just been tested on, since he would not be tested on it again. Following the test a new stimulus was selected (one that had not appeared for at least 50 trials) and randomly paired with a response for the subject to study. Thus the number of items to be remembered at any one time stays constant throughout the session. However, the procedure is quite different from Experiment 1 where the study stimulus was always the one just tested.

Denote an item presented for study on a trial as an O item (old item) if the item just tested was in the buffer. Denote an item presented for study as an N item (new item) if the item just tested was not in the buffer. This terminology conforms precisely to that used to describe Experiment 1. If an O item is presented there will be at least one spot in the buffer occupied by a useless item (the one just tested). If an N item is presented, the buffer will be filled with information of the same value as that before the test. If we assume that an N item has probability α of entering the buffer, and that an O item will always enter the buffer and knock out the item just made useless, then the model for Experiment 1 will apply here with no change whatsoever. In this case we again expect that the lag curves for $s = 4$, 6, and 8 would be separated. In fact, given the same parameter values, exactly the same curves would be predicted for the all-different experiment as for Experiment 1.

As noted earlier, however, there is some doubt that the assumptions regarding N items and O items will still hold for the all-different experiment. In Experiment 1 the stimulus just tested was re-paired with a new response, virtually forcing the subject to replace the old response with a new one if the item was in the buffer. Put another way, if an item is in the buffer when tested, only a minor change need be made in the buffer to enter the succeeding study item: a single response is replaced by another. In the all-different experiment, however, a greater change needs to be made in order to enter an O item; both a stimulus and a response member have to be replaced. Thus an alternative hypothesis might maintain that every entering item (whether an N item or an O item) has the same probability α of entering the buffer, and will knock out any item currently in the buffer with equal likelihood. In this case we predict no differences among the lag curves for the $s = 4$, 6, and 8 conditions.

1. *Results*

The observed lag curves for Experiment 2 are displayed in Fig. 7. It should be emphasized that, except for the procedural changes described

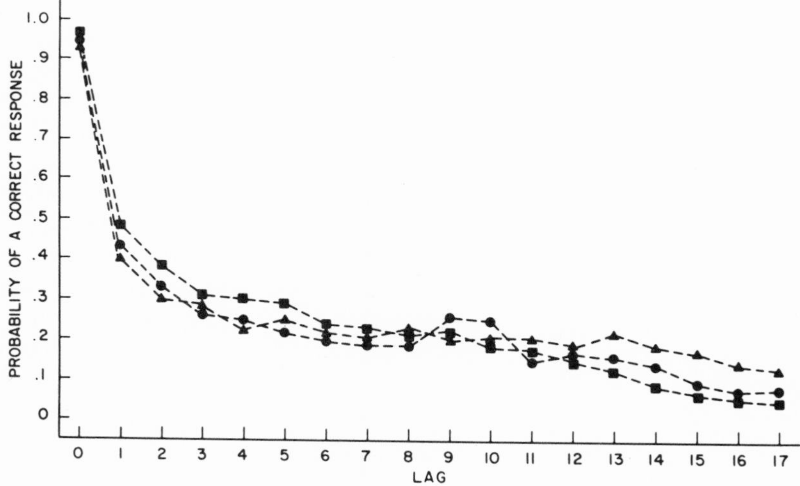

FIG. 7. Observed and theoretical probabilities of a correct response as a function of lag (Experiment 2). --■-- $s = 4$; --▲-- $s = 6$; --●-- $s = 8$.

above and the fact that a new sample of subjects was used, the experimental conditions and operations were identical in Experiments 1 and 2. The important point about this data is that the lag curves for the three conditions appear to overlap.[13] For this reason we lump the three curves to form the single lag curve displayed in Fig. 8.

Because the three curves overlap, it is apparent that the theory used in Experiment 1 needs modification. The hypothesis suggested above

[13] To determine whether the three curves in Fig. 7 differ reliably, the proportions correct for each subject and condition were calculated and then ranked. An analysis of variance for correlated means did not yield significant effects ($F = 2.67$, $df = 2/16$, $p > .05$).

will be used: every item enters the buffer with probability α. If an item enters the buffer it knocks out an item already there on a random basis. This model implies that useless items are being rehearsed on occasion, and subjects reported doing just that despite instructions to forget each item once tested.

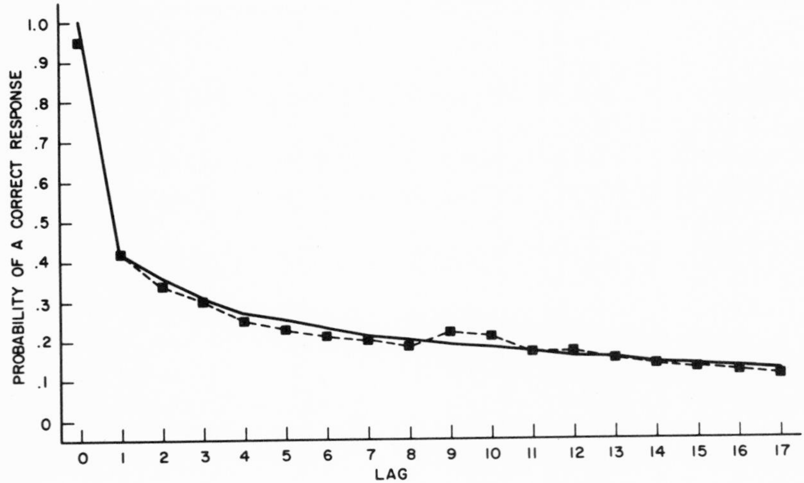

Fig. 8. Observed and theoretical probabilities of a correct response as a function of lag. Data from the $s = 4$, 6, and 8 conditions have been pooled (Experiment 2). --■-- Data;—theory.

The curve in Fig. 8 was fit using a minimum χ^2 procedure; the parameter estimates were $r = 2$, $\alpha = .52$, $\theta = .17$, and $\tau = .90$. It can be seen that the fit is excellent. Except for r, the parameters differ somewhat from those found in Experiment 1, primarily in a slower transfer rate, θ. In Experiment 1 the estimate of θ was .40. This reduction in long-term storage is not too surprising since the subjects were on occasion rehearsing useless information. It could have been argued in advance of the data that the change away from a strong "negative-transfer" paradigm in Experiment 2 would lead to increased use of LTS; that this did not occur is indicated not only by the low θ value, but also by the low probability of a correct response at long lags. One outcome of this result is the possibility that the all-different procedure would give superior long-term memory in situations where subjects could be induced to attempt coding or other long-term storage strategies. It seems apparent that LTS was comparatively usless in the present situation.

2. *Some Statistics Comparing Experiments 1 and 2*

In terms of the model, the only difference between Experiments 1 and 2 lies in the replacement assumption governing the buffer. In Experiment 1, an item in the buffer when tested is automatically replaced by the immediately succeeding study item; if the tested item is not in the buffer, the succeeding study item enters the buffer with probability α, randomly displacing an item already there. In Experiment 2, every study item, independent of the contents of the buffer, enters the buffer with probability α, randomly displacing an item already there. While these assumptions are given credence by the predictions of the various lag curves of Figs. 4 and 8, there are other statistics that can be examined to evaluate their adequacy. These statistics depend upon the fact that items vary in their probability of entering the buffer. Since items which enter the buffer will have a higher probability correct than items which do not, it is relatively easy to check the veracity of the replacement assumptions in the two experiments.

In Experiment 1, the probability that an item will be in the buffer at test is higher the greater the number of consecutive preceding trials that involve the same stimulus. Thus if the study of 42-B is preceded, for example, by six consecutive trials using stimulus 42, there is a very high probability that 42-B will enter the buffer. This occurs because there is a high probability that the stimulus 42 already will be in the buffer when 42-B is presented, and if so, then 42-B will automatically enter the buffer. In any series of consecutive trials all with the same stimulus, once any item in the series enters the buffer, every succeeding item will enter the buffer. Hence, the longer the series of items with the same stimulus, the higher the probability that that stimulus will be in the buffer. Figure 9 graphs the probability of a correct response to the last stimulus-response pair studied in a series of consecutive trials involving the same stimulus; the probability correct is lumped over all possible lags at which that stimulus-response pair is subsequently tested. This probability is graphed as a function of the length of the consecutive run of trials with the same stimulus and is the line labeled Experiment 1. These curves are combined over the three experimental conditions (i.e., $s = 4$, 6, 8). We see that the probability of a correct response to the last item studied in a series of trials all involving the same stimulus increases as the length of that series increases, as predicted by the theory.

In Experiment 2 stimuli are not repeated, so the above statistic cannot be examined. A comparable statistic exists, however, if we consider a sequence of items all of which are tested at zero lag (i.e., tested immediately after presentation). One could hypothesize that the effect displayed in Fig. 9 for Experiment 1 was due to a consecutive sequence of zero-lag tests, or due to factors related to the sequence of correct answers (at zero-lag an item is always correct). These same arguments would apply, however, to the sequence of zero-lag items in Experiment 2. In Fig. 9, the line labeled Experiment 2 represents a probability measure comparable to the one displayed for Experiment 1. Specifically, it is the probability of a correct response on the eventual test of the last S-R pair studied in a consecutive sequence of trials all involving S-R pairs tested at lag zero, as a function of the length of the

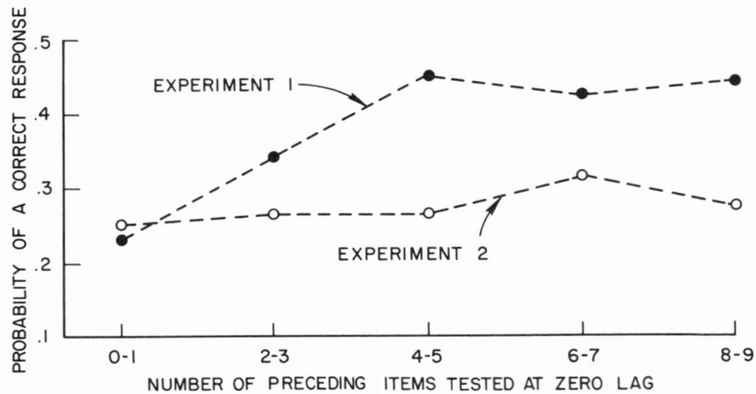

FIG. 9. Probability of a correct response as a function of the number of consecutive preceding items tested at zero lag (Experiment 1 and Experiment 2).

sequence. The model for Experiment 2 with its scheme for entering items in the buffer predicts that this curve should be flat; the data seem to bear out this prediction.

The close correspondence between the predicted and observed results in Experiments 1 and 2 provides strong support for the theory. The assumptions justified most strongly appear to be the fixed-size rehearsal buffer containing number-letter pairs as units, and the replacement assumptions governing O and N items. It is difficult to imagine a consistent system without these assumptions that would give rise to similar effects. Some of the predictions supported by the data are not at all intuitive. For example, the phenomenon displayed in Fig. 9 seems to be contrary to predictions based upon considerations of negative transfer. Negative transfer would seem to predict that a sequence of items having the same stimulus but different responses would lead to large amounts of interference and hence reduce the probability correct of the last item in the sequence; however, just the opposite effect was found. Furthermore, the lack of an effect in Experiment 2 seems to rule out explanations based on successive correct responses or successive zero-lag tests. Intuition notwithstanding, this effect was predicted by the model.

C. A Continuous Paired-Associate Memory Task with Multiple Reinforcements (Experiment 3)

In contrast to a typical short-term memory task, the subjects' strategy in paired-associate learning shifts from a reliance on rehearsal processes to a heavy emphasis on coding schemes and related processes that facilitate long-term storage. There are many factors, however, that contribute to such a shift, and the fact that items are reinforced more than once in a paired-associate learning task is only one of these. In the present experiment, all factors are kept the same as in Experiment 1, except for the number of reinforcements. It is not surprising, then, that subjects use essentially the same rehearsal strategy found in Experiment 1. It is therefore of considerable interest to examine the effects associated with repeated reinforcements of the same item.

In Experiment 3 only one stimulus set size, $s = 8$, was used. Each session began with eight study trials on which the eight stimuli were each randomly paired with a response. The stimuli and responses were two-digit numbers and letters, respectively. After the initial study trials, the session involved a series of consecutive trials each consisting of a test phase followed by a study phase. On each trial a stimulus was randomly selected for testing and the same stimulus was then presented for study on the latter portion of the trial. Whereas in Experiment 1, during the study phase of a trial, the stimulus was always re-paired with a new response, in the present experiment the stimulus was sometimes left paired with the old response. To be precise, when a particular S-R pair was presented for study the first time, a decision was made as to how many reinforcements (study periods) it would be given; it was given either 1, 2, 3, or 4 reinforcements with probabilities .30, .20, .40, and .10 respectively. When a particular S-R pair had received its assigned number of reinforcements, its stimulus was then re-paired with a new response on the next study trial, and this new item was assigned a number of reinforcements using the probability distribution specified above. In order to clarify the procedure, a sample sequence from trials n to $n + 19$ is shown in Fig. 10. On trial $n + 2$ stimulus 22 is given a new response, L, and assigned three reinforcements, the first occurring on trial $n + 2$. The second reinforcement occurs on trial $n + 3$ after a lag of zero. After a lag of 6, the third reinforcement is presented on trial $n + 10$. After a lag of 8, stimulus 22 is re-paired with a new response on trial $n + 19$. Stimulus 33 is sampled for test on trial $n + 6$ and during the study phase is assigned the new response, B, which is to receive two reinforcements, the second on trial $n + 9$. Stimulus 44 is tested on trial $n + 4$, assigned the new response X which is to receive only one reinforcement; thus when 44 is presented again on trial $n + 16$ it is assigned another response which by chance also is to receive only one reinforcement, for on the next trial 44 is studied with response Q. The subject is instructed, as in Experiments 1 and 2, to respond on the test phase of each trial with the letter that was *last* studied with the stimulus being tested.

The same display devices, control equipment, and timing relations used in Experiment 1 were used in this study. There were 20 subjects, each run for 10 or more sessions; a session consisted of 220 trials. Details of the experimental procedure, and a more extensive account of the data

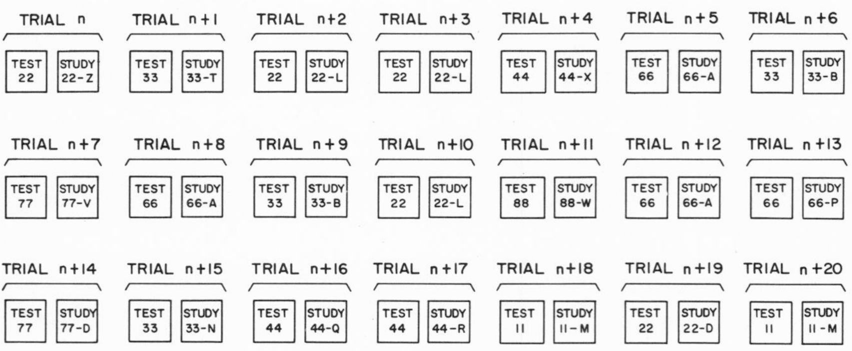

FIG. 10. A sample sequence of trials for Experiment 3.

analysis, including a fit of the model to response protocols of individual subjects, can be found in Brelsford, Shiffrin, and Atkinson (1968).

The model for Experiment 1 may be used without change in the present situation. There is some question, however, whether it is reasonable to do so. The assumptions concerning LTS storage and decay may be applied to items which are given multiple reinforcements: information is transferred to LTS at a rate θ whenever the item resides in the buffer, and decays from LTS by the proportion τ on each trial that the item is not present in the buffer. The assumption regarding O items also may be applied: since the stimulus already is in the buffer, the new response replaces the old one, thereby entering the item in the buffer (if, as is the case in this experiment, the old response is given yet another study, then nothing changes in the buffer). N items, however, are not so easily dealt with. N items, remember, are items whose stimuli are not currently represented in the buffer. In Experiment 1, the stimulus of every N item also was being paired with a new response. In the current experiment this is not always the case; some N items, although not in the buffer, will be receiving their second, third, or fourth reinforcement when presented for study. That is, some N items in this experiment will already have a substantial amount of information stored on them in LTS. It seems reasonable that subjects may not rehearse an item which has just been retrieved correctly from LTS. The assumption regarding N items is therefore modified for purposes of the present experiment as follows. If a stimulus is tested and is not in the buffer, then a search of LTS is made. If the response is correctly retrieved from LTS, and if that stimulus-response pair is repeated for study, then that item will not be entered into the buffer (since the subject "knows" it already). If a new item is presented for study (i.e., the response to that stimulus is changed), or if the correct response is not retrieved from LTS (even though the subject may have made the correct response by guessing), then the study item enters the buffer with probability α. This slight adjustment of the replacement assumption allows for the fact that some items presented for study may already be known and will not enter the rehearsal buffer. This version of the model is the one used later to generate predictions for the data.

1. *Results*

Figure 11 presents the probability of a correct response as a function of lag for items tested after their first, second, and third reinforcements. The number of observations is weighted not only toward the short lags,

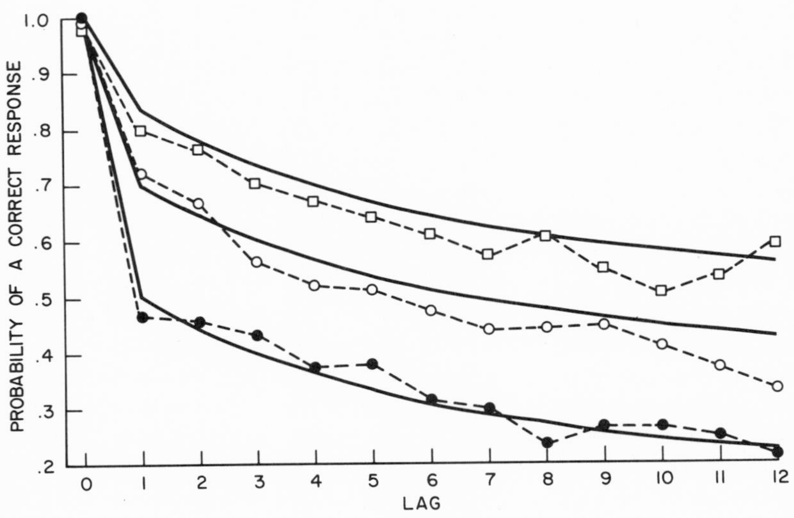

FIG. 11. Observed and theoretical probabilities of a correct response as a function of lag for items tested following their first, second, or third reinforcement (Experiment 3). --□-- Three reinforcements; --○-- two reinforcements; --●-- one reinforcement;— theory.

but also toward the smaller numbers of reinforcements. This occurs because the one-reinforcement lag curve contains not only the data from the items given just one reinforcement, but also the data from the first reinforcement of items given two, three, and four reinforcements. Similarly, the lag curve following two reinforcements contains the data from the second reinforcement of items given two, three, and four reinforcements, and the three-reinforcement curve contains data from the third reinforcement of items given three and four reinforcements. The lag curves in Fig. 11 are comparable to those presented elsewhere in this paper. What is graphed is the probability of a correct response to an item that received its jth reinforcement, and was then tested after a lag of n trials. The graph presents data for n ranging from 0 to 15 and for j equal to 1, 2, and 3. Inspecting the figure, we see that an item which received its first reinforcement and was then tested at a lag of 8 trials gave a correct response about 23% of the time; an item that received its second reinforcement and was then tested at lag 8 had about 44% correct responses; and an item that received its third reinforcement and was then tested at lag 8 had about 61% correct.

The curves in Fig. 11 exhibit a consistent pattern. The probability correct decreases regularly with lag, starting at a higher value on lag 1 the greater the number of prior reinforcements. Although these curves are quite regular, there are a number of dependencies masked by them. For example, the probability of a correct response to an item that received its second reinforcement and was then tested at some later trial will depend on the number of trials that intervened between the first and second reinforcements. To clarify this point consider the following diagram

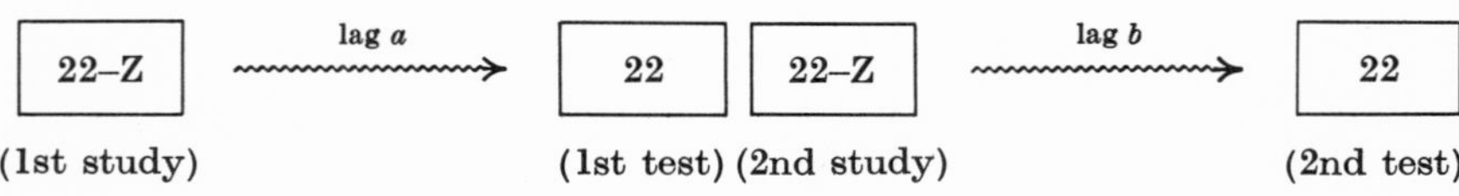

Item 22-Z is given its first reinforcement, tested at lag a and given a second reinforcement, and then given a second test at lag b. For a fixed lag b, the probability of a correct response on the second test will depend on lag a. In terms of the model it is easy to see why this is so. The probability correct for an item on the second test will depend upon the amount of information about it in LTS. If lag a is extremely short, then there will have been very little time for LTS strength to build up. Conversely, a very long lag a will result in any LTS strength decaying and disappearing. Hence the probability of a correct response on the second test will be maximal at some intermediate value of lag a; namely, at a lag which will give time for LTS strength to build up, but not so much time that excessive decay will occur. For this reason a plot of probability correct on the second test as a function of the lag between the first and second reinforcement should exhibit an inverted U-shape. Figure 12 is such a plot. The probability correct on the second test is graphed as a function of lag *a*. Four curves are shown for different values of lag *b*. The

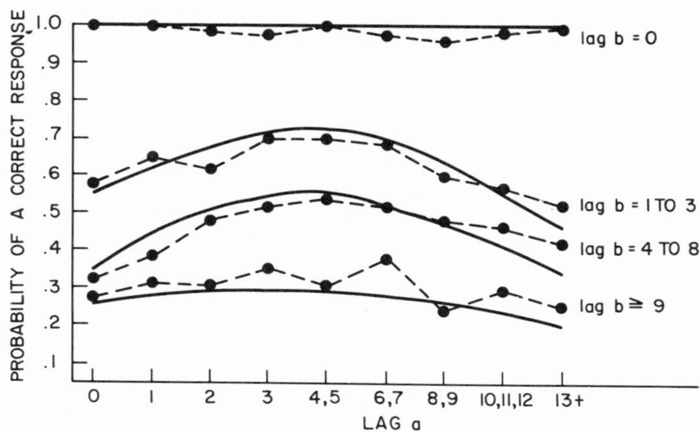

FIG. 12. Observed and theoretical probabilities of a correct response as a function of lag *a* (the spacing between the first and second reinforcement) (Experiment 3).

four curves have not been lumped over all values of lag *b* because we wish to indicate how the U-shaped effect changes with changes in lag *b*. Clearly, when lag *b* is zero, the probability correct is one and there is no U-shaped effect. Conversely, when lag *b* is very large, the probability correct will tend toward chance regardless of lag *a*, and again the U-shaped effect will disappear. The functions shown in Fig. 12 give support to the assumption that information is being transferred to LTS during the entire period an item resides in the buffer. If information is transferred, for example, only when an item first enters the buffer, then our model will not predict the rise in the functions of Fig. 12 for lag *a* going from zero to about five. The rise is due to the additional information transferred to LTS as lag *a* increases.

2. *Theoretical Analysis*

A brief review of the model is in order. O items (whose stimulus is currently in the buffer) always enter the buffer. N items (whose stimulus is not currently in the buffer) enter the buffer with probability α if they are also new items (i.e., receiving their first reinforcement). However, N items do not enter the buffer if they are repeat items and were correctly retreived from LTS on the immediately preceding test; if they are repeat items and a retrieval was not made, then they enter the buffer with probability α. An O item entering the buffer occupies the position of the item already there with the same stimulus; an entering N item randomly replaces one of the items currently in the buffer. During the period an item resides in the buffer, information is transferred to LTS at a rate θ per trial. This information decays by a proportion τ on each trial after an item has left the buffer.[14] The subject is always correct at a lag of zero, or if the item is currently in the buffer. If the item is not in the buffer a search of LTS is made, and the correct response is retrieved with a probability that is an exponential function of the amount of information currently in LTS (i.e., the same function specified for Experiments 1 and 2). If the subject fails to retrieve from LTS, then he guesses. There are four parameters for this model: r, the buffer size; α, the buffer entry probability; θ, the transfer rate of information to LTS; and τ, the parameter characterizing the LTS decay rate once an item has left the buffer.

Estimates of r, α, θ, and τ were made using the data presented in Figs. 11 and 12. We shall not go into the estimation procedures here, for they are fairly complex; in essence they involve a modified minimum χ^2 procedure where the theoretical values are based on Monte Carlo runs. The parameter estimates that gave the best fit to the data displayed in Figs. 11 and 12 were as follows: $r = 3$; $\alpha = .65$; $\theta = 1.24$; and $\tau = .82$. Once these estimates had been obtained they were then used to generate a large-scale Monte Carlo run of 12,500 trials. The Monte Carlo procedure involved generating pseudo-data following precisely the rules specified by the model and consulting a random number generator whenever an event occurred in the model that was probabilistically determined. Thus the pseudo-data from a Monte Carlo run is an example of how real data would look if the model was correct, and the parameters had the values used in the Monte Carlo computation. In all subsequent discussions of Experiment 3, the predicted values are based on the output of the Monte Carlo run. The run was very long so that in all cases the theoretical curves are quite smooth, and we doubt if they reflect fluctuations due to sampling error. A detailed account of the estimation and prediction procedures for this experiment is given in Brelsford, Shiffrin, and Atkinson (1968).

The predictions from the theory are shown as the smooth curves in

[14] In this experiment an item receiving x reinforcements may enter the buffer as many as x times. When the item is in the buffer the θ-process is activated, and when not in the buffer the τ-process takes over.

Figs. 11 and 12. It should be evident that the predicted values are quite close to the observed ones. Note also that the seven curves in the two figures are fit simultaneously with the same four parameter values; the fact that the spacing of the curves is accurately predicted is particularly interesting.

We now examine a number of statistics that were not used in making parameter estimates. First consider the all-same and all-different curves shown in Fig. 13; these are the same functions displayed in Figs. 5 and 6

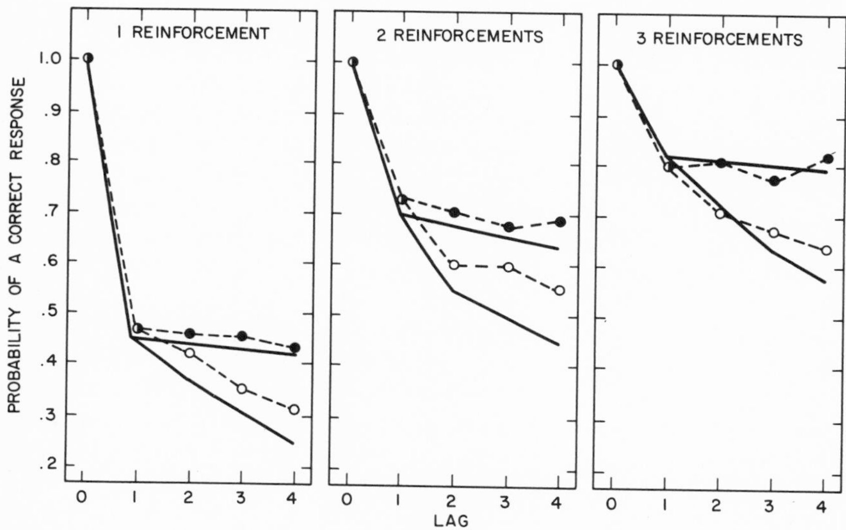

FIG. 13. Observed and theoretical probabilities of a correct response as a function of lag for the "all-same" and "all-different" conditions (Experiment 3). --●-- all-same; --○-- all-different;—theory.

for Experiment 1. For the all-same curve, we compute the probability of a correct response as a function of the lag, when all the intervening items between study and test involve the same stimulus. There are three such curves, depending on whether the study was the first, second, or third reinforcement of the particular S-R pair. The model predicts that once the intervening stimulus enters the buffer, there will be no further chance of any other item being knocked out of the buffer. Hence these curves should drop at a much slower rate than the unconditional lag curves in Fig. 11. The all-different curve plots the probability of a correct response as a function of lag, when the intervening items between study and test all involve different stimuli. Again there are three curves depending on whether the study was the first, second, or third reinforcement of the S-R pair. The all-different sequence maximizes the expected number of intervening N items and therefore the curve should have a much faster drop than the unconditional lag curves in Fig. 11. The predictions are shown in the figure as solid lines. The correspondence between predicted and observed values is reasonably good. It is particularly impressive when it is noted that the parameter values used in making the predictions were estimated from the previous data.

We next examine the data displayed in Fig. 14. Consider a sequence of consecutive trials all involving the same stimulus, but where the

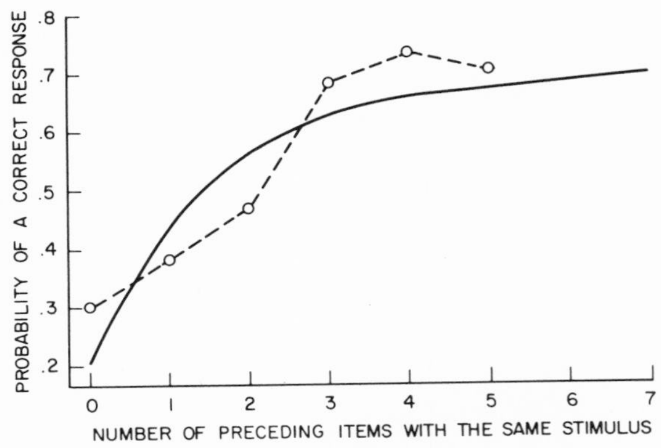

FIG. 14. Observed and theoretical probabilities of a correct response as a function of the number of consecutive preceding items using the same stimulus (Experiment 3).

response paired with the stimulus on the study phase of the last trial in the sequence is different from the response on the immediately preceding trial. Then, the theory predicts that the longer this sequence of consecutive trials, the higher will be the probability of a correct response when the last item studied in the sequence is eventually tested. This is so because the probability of the last item entering the buffer increases as the length of the sequence increases: once any item in the sequence enters the buffer, every succeeding one will. The data is shown in Fig. 14. What is graphed is the length of the sequence of trials all involving the same stimulus versus the probability of a correct response when the last item studied in the sequence is eventually tested. In this graph we have lumped over all lags at which the eventual test of the last item is made. The predictions generated from the previously estimated parameter values are shown as the smooth line. The predicted values, though not perfect, are surprisingly close to the observed proportions correct. It is worth reemphasizing that considerations of negative transfer make this result somewhat unexpected (see p. 140).

We next examine another prediction of the theory that ran counter to our initial intuitions. To make matters clear, consider the following diagram:

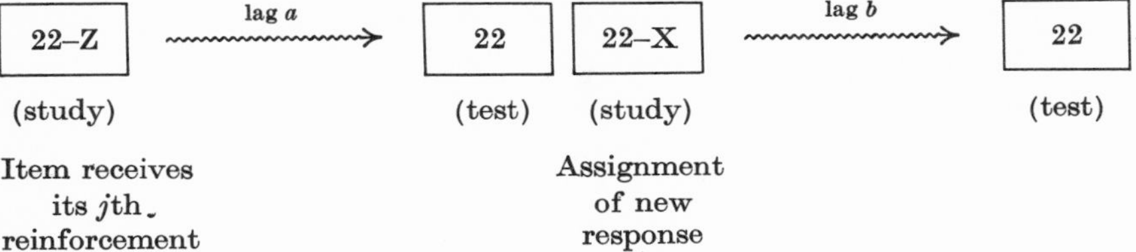

Item 22-Z is studied for the jth time and then tested at lag a; on this trial 22 is paired with a new response X, and tested next at lag b. According to the theory, the shorter lag a, the better performance should be when the item is tested after lag b. This prediction is based on the fact that the more recently a stimulus had appeared, the more likely that it was still in the buffer when the next item using it was presented for study; if the stimulus was in the buffer, then the item using it would automatically enter the buffer. In the present analysis, we examine this effect for three conditions: the preceding item using the stimulus in question could have just received its first, second, or third reinforcement. Figure 15 presents the appropriate data. In terms of the above diagram, what is plotted is the value of lag a on the abscissa versus the probability of a correct response lumped over all values of lag b on the ordinate; there is a separate curve for $j = 1$, 2, and 3.

The predicted curves are based upon the previous parameter estimates. The predictions and observations coincide fairly well, but the effect is not as dramatic as one might hope.[15] One problem is that the predicted decrease is not very large. Considerably stronger effects may be expected if each curve is separated into two components: one where the preceding item was correct at test and the other where the preceding item was not correct. In theory the decrease predicted in Fig. 15 is due to a lessened probability of the relevant stimulus being in the buffer as lag a increases. Since an item in the buffer is always responded to correctly, conditionalizing upon correct responses or errors (the center test in the above diagram) should magnify the effect. To be precise, the decrease will be accentuated for the curve conditional upon correct responses, whereas no decrease at all is predicted for the curve conditional upon errors. If an error is made, the relevant stimulus cannot be in the buffer and hence the new item enters the buffer with probability α

[15] A curve comparable to the one displayed in Fig. 15 for the one-reinforcement condition was obtained from the data of Experiment 1. This curve showed a similar but more pronounced drop and was well predicted by the model.

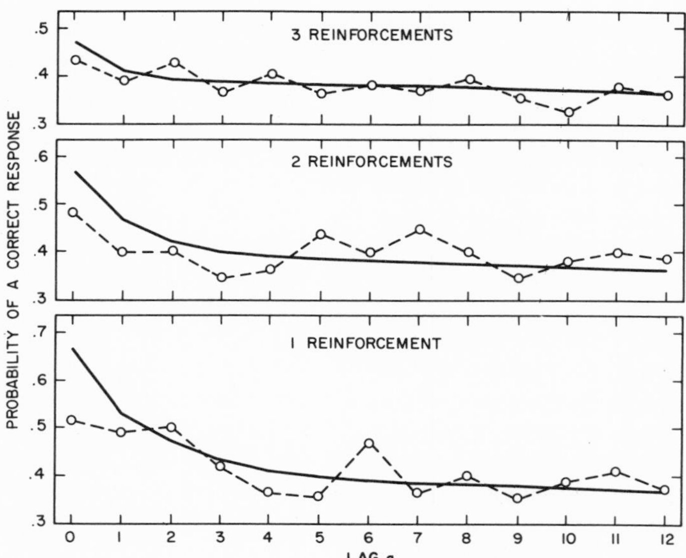

FIG. 15. Observed and theoretical probabilities of a correct response as a function of lag a (the lag of the item preceding the item tested, but using the same stimulus) (Experiment 3). --○-- Data;—theory.

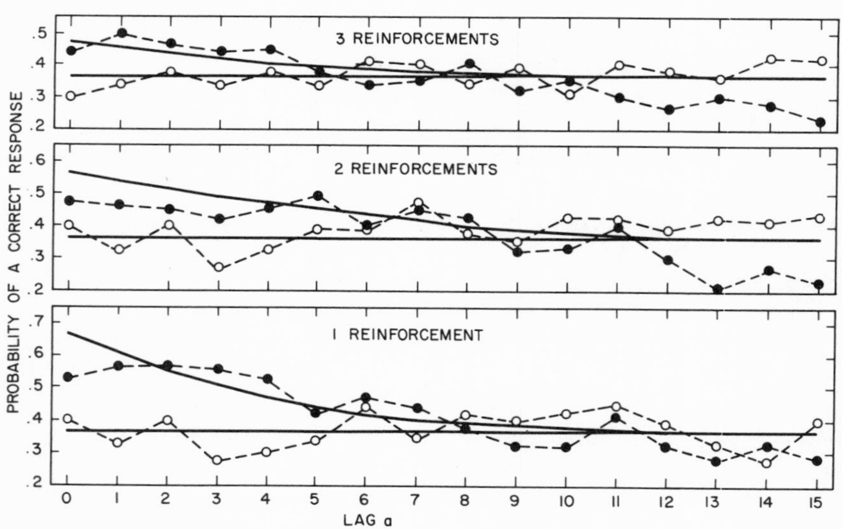

FIG. 16. Observed and theoretical probabilities of a correct response as a function of lag a conditionalized on errors or successes on the test at lag a (Experiment 3). --●-- Correct data; --○-- error data;—theory.

independent of lag a. Figure 16 gives the conditional curves and the predictions. The decreasing effect is fairly evident for the "correct" curves; as predicted, the "error" curves are quite flat over lags.[16] Conceivably one might argue that the effects are due to item selection, correct responses indicating easier stimuli and incorrect responses indicating more difficult ones. This objection, however, seems contraindicated in the present case. It is difficult to imagine how item selection could explain the crossing of the correct and error curves found in each of the three diagrams.[17] Indeed, the model does not explain the crossover —the model predicts that the two curves should meet. The model is in error at this point because it has not been extended to include negative transfer effects, an extension which would not be difficult to implement. An item responded to correctly at a long lag probably has a strong LTS trace; this strong trace would then interfere with the LTS trace of the new item which, of course, uses the same stimulus. All in all, these curves and predictions may be considered to provide fairly strong support for the details of the model, even to the extent of illuminating the one aspect omitted, albeit intentionally, from the assumptions.

The aspect left out is, of course, that of LTS response competition, or negative transfer. The model fails to take account of this effect because it fails to keep track of residual LTS strength remaining as a result of the previous items using the same stimulus. This lack is most clearly indicated by the occurrence of intrusion errors, particularly errors which were correct responses on the preceding occurrence of that stimulus. For example, consider the following sequence:

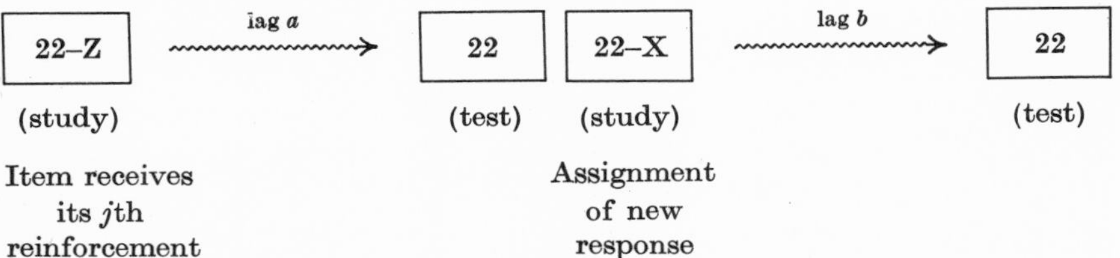

[16] The astute reader will have noticed that the predicted decrease becomes smaller as the number of reinforcements increases. The fact that the data support this prediction is quite interesting, for it sheds light upon the buffer replacement assumptions used in this model. The decreasing effect as reinforcements increase is predicted because the probability of entering the buffer is reduced for an item receiving its third reinforcement; remember, an item recovered from LTS is not entered into the buffer. Thus as reinforcements increase, the probability of being in the buffer decreases, and the normally increased probability of being in the buffer as a result of a short lag a is partially counterbalanced.

[17] Undoubtedly there are some selection effects in the data graphed in Fig. 16, but their magnitude is difficult to determine. Thus, these data should be regarded with some wariness.

Item 22-Z is studied for the jth time and then tested at lag a; on this trial 22 is paired with a new response X and next tested at lag b. By an intrusion error we mean the occurrence of response Z when 22 is tested at the far right of the diagram. The model predicts that these intrusion errors will be at chance level (1/25), independent of lag and number of reinforcements. In fact, these predictions fail. Figure 17 presents the

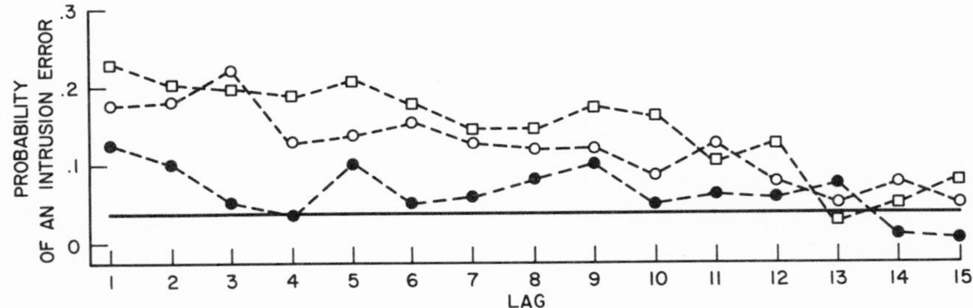

FIG. 17. Probability that the correct response for the preceding item using the same stimulus will be given in error to the present item (Experiment 3). --□-- Three reinforcements; --○-- two reinforcements; --●-- one reinforcement; —chance.

probability of intrusion errors as a function of lag b; where the data have been lumped over all values of lag a, three curves are plotted for $j = 1, 2,$ and 3. This failure of the model is not very distressing because it was expected: the model could be extended in a number of obvious ways to take account of competing LTS traces without appreciably changing any of the predictions so far presented. The extension has not been made because our interest in this study is centered upon short-term effects.

Judging by the agreement between theory and data for each of the effects examined, the accuracy of the model is extremely good. It is interesting to note that the multiple-reinforcement procedure is not sufficient by itself to cause the subjects to switch their strategies from rehearsal to coding. The major emphasis still appears to be on rehearsal manipulations in STS, a not entirely surprising result since the situation is identical to that used in Experiment 1 except for the number of reinforcements given. The comments previously made concerning the difficulty associated with LTS storage in Experiment 1 apply here also. Because the emphasis is upon short-term mechanisms, this experiment is not to be considered in any strong sense as a bridge to the usual paired-associate learning situation. Nevertheless, a number of long-term effects, such as intrusion errors and interference caused by previously learned items on new items with the same stimulus, demonstrate that LTS mechanisms cannot be ignored in the theory. In Section V we consider experiments that are designed to provide a sharper picture of the workings of LTS; experimentally this is accomplished by systematically varying the number of items in LTS through which searches must be made. Before considering this problem, however, there are other features of the STS rehearsal strategy to be explored. We turn next to an experiment in which the probability of entering an item into the buffer is manipulated experimentally.

D. Overt versus Covert Study Procedures (Experiment 4)

The statistics considered in the previous section leave little doubt about the role of O items, N items, and the buffer entry parameter α. But one question we have not considered is whether α is amenable to experimental manipulation; if the process is really under the control of the subject, such manipulation would be expected. We now turn to a study by Brelsford and Atkinson (1968) which was designed to answer this question.

In Experiment 1, the proportions of O items and N items were varied by changing the size of the stimulus set, and the predicted differences were found. Manipulating α, however, is a somewhat more subtle task since it is the subject's strategy that must be affected. One experimental device which seems likely to increase the probability of an item's entering the buffer is to have the subject recite the item aloud as it is presented for study; this will be referred to as the "overt" study procedure. The "covert" study procedure is simply a replication of the procedure used in Experiment 1 where the subject was not required to recite the item aloud when it was presented for study, but simply told to study it.

1. *Method*

The method was identical to that used in Experiment 1 except for the following changes. The size of the stimulus set was fixed at six for all subjects and sessions. Each session consisted of 200 trials divided into four 50-trial blocks alternating between the overt and covert conditions. The initial 50-trial block was randomly chosen to be either an overt or a covert condition. The covert condition was identical in all respects to Experiment 1; when the word "study" and an S-R pair appeared on the CRT (the display screen) the subjects were told to silently study the item being presented. In the overt blocks, instead of the word "study" appearing on the CRT during the study portion of a trial, the word "rehearse" appeared. This was a signal for the subject to recite aloud twice the item then being presented for study. This was the only difference from the procedure used during the covert trials. It was hoped that the act of repeating the items aloud would raise the subject's probability of entering the item into his rehearsal buffer.

2. *Results*

In order to allow for the subject's acclimation to a change in study conditions, the first 15 trials of each 50-trial block are not included in the data analysis. Figure 18 presents the lag curves for the overt and covert conditions. It is evident that performance is superior in the overt condition. Furthermore, the overt lag curve is S-shaped in form, an

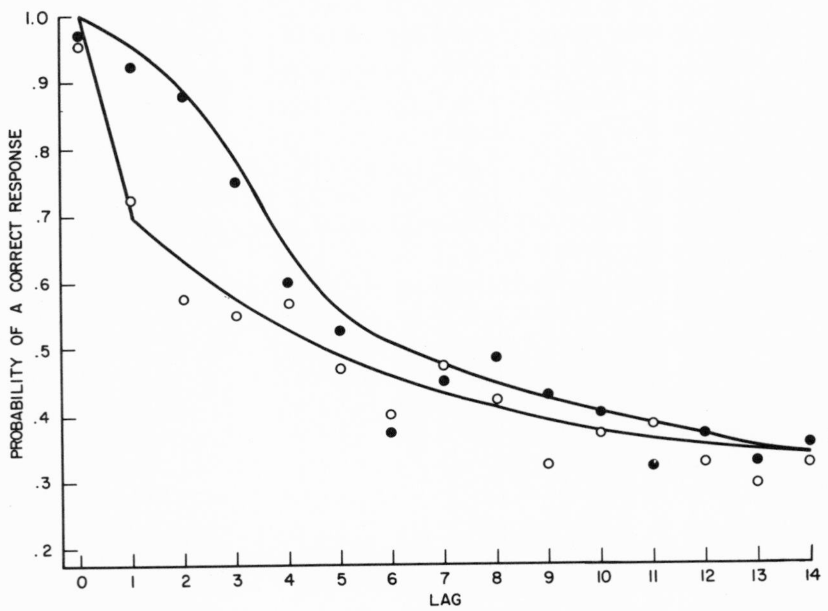

FIG. 18. Observed and theoretical probabilities of a correct response as a function of lag (Experiment 4). ● Overt; ○ covert;—theory.

effect not observed in earlier curves. Since the parameters of the models will be estimated from these curves, the model is presented before considering additional data.

The model for the covert condition is, of course, identical to that used in the analysis of Experiment 1. It has the four parameters r, α, θ, and τ. Since it was hypothesized that α would be raised in the overt condition, we might try estimating α separately for that condition. This version of the model will not fit the overt data, however, because of the pronounced S-shaped form of the lag curve. Although setting α equal to 1.0 will predict better performance in the overt condition, the lag curve will have the form of an exponentially decreasing function, which is clearly not found in the data. In order to account for the S-shaped curve, we need to assume that in the overt condition the subject tends to knock the oldest items out of the buffer first. In the model for the covert case, an entering N item is said to knock out at random any item currently in the buffer. It will be assumed for the overt case that an entering N item tends to replace the oldest item in the buffer; remember O items are items whose stimulus is currently in the buffer and they automatically replace the item with that stimulus. This probability of knocking the oldest items from the buffer first is specified as follows: if there are r items in the buffer and they are numbered so that item 1 is the oldest and item r is the newest, then the probability that an entering N item will knock the jth item from the buffer is

$$\frac{\delta(1-\delta)^{j-1}}{1-(1-\delta)^{r}}.$$

This equation is derived from the following scheme. The oldest item is knocked out with probability δ. If it is not knocked out, then the next oldest is knocked out with probability δ. The process continues cyclically until an item is finally selected to be knocked out. When δ approaches zero, the knockout probabilities are random, as in the covert case. When δ is greater than zero there will be a tendency for the oldest items to be knocked out of the buffer first; in fact if δ equals one, the oldest item will always be the one knocked out. It should be clear that the higher the value of δ, the greater the S-shaped effect predicted for the lag curve.

The model for the curves in Fig. 18 is therefore structured as follows. The parameters r, θ, and τ will be assumed to be the same for the two conditions; the parameters α and δ will be assumed to be affected by the experimental manipulation. To be precise, in the covert case α will be estimated freely and δ will be set equal to zero, which is precisely the model used in Experiment 1. In the overt case, α will be set equal to 1.0, which means that every item enters the buffer, and δ will be estimated freely. The parameter values that provided the best χ^2 fit to the data in Fig. 30 were $r = 3$, $\theta = .97$, $\tau = .90$; for the covert condition the estimate of α was .58 (with δ equal to zero) and for the overt condition the estimate of δ was .63 (with α equal to one). The predictions for this set of parameter values are shown in Fig. 18 as smooth curves. The improvement in performance from the covert to overt conditions is well predicted; actually it is not obvious that variations in either α or δ should affect the overall level of performance. The principal reason for the improvement is due to the value of α; placing every item into the buffer means that an item entering the buffer will be expected to stay there for a shorter period than if some items did not enter the buffer. This shorter period in the buffer, however, is outweighed by the advantages resulting from the entry of every item in the first place. It is not easy to find statistics, other than the gross form of the lag curve, which reflect changes in δ; thus the assumption that the oldest items are lost first is not easy to verify in a direct way. Nevertheless, it is quite common to find experiments that yield S-shaped recency curves and these results can be fit by assuming that the oldest items in the buffer tend to be knocked out first. Other examples will be presented in Section V.

A number of additional aspects of the data will now be examined. First we consider the "all-same" and "all-different" lag curves. Figure 19

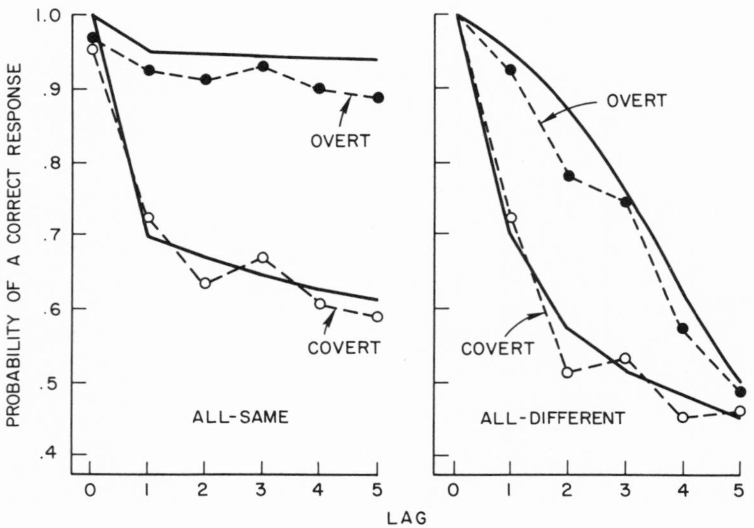

FIG. 19. Observed and theoretical probabilities of a correct response as a function of lag for the "all-same" and "all-different" conditions (Experiment 4).

gives the "all-same" lag curves for the overt and covert conditions. This curve gives the probability of a correct response for an item when all of the intervening items (between its study and test) have the same stimulus. This curve will be quite flat because the items following the first intervening item tend to be O items which will not knock other items from the buffer (for the overt case, *every* item following the first intervening item is an O item, since all items enter the buffer). Figure 19 also presents the "all-different" lag curves. This curve is the probability of making a correct response to a given item when the other items intervening between its study and test all involve different stimuli. The predictions generated by the previous parameter values are given by the smooth curves; they appear to be quite accurate.

We now look for an effect that will be sharply dependent upon the value of α and hence differ for the overt and covert conditions. Such an effect is given in Fig. 20; graphed there is the probability of a correct response as a function of the number of immediately preceding items having the same stimulus as the item in question. This is the same

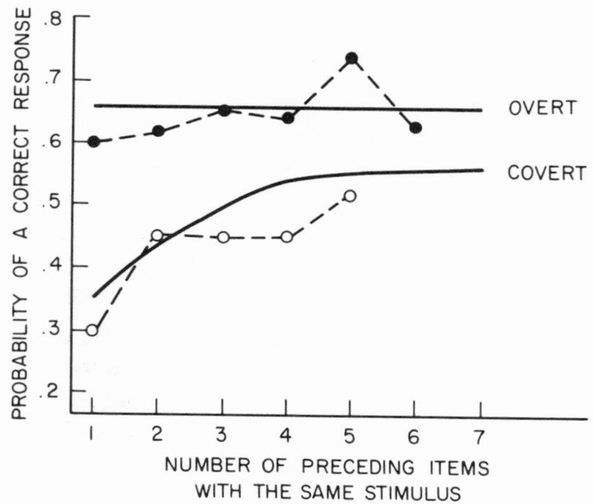

FIG. 20. Observed and theoretical probabilities of a correct response as a function of the number of consecutive preceding items all using the same stimulus (Experiment 4).

statistic that is plotted in Figs. 9 and 14; it is not a lag curve because the probability correct is given as an average over all possible lags at which the item was tested. If α is less than 1, then the length of the preceding sequence of items with the same stimulus will be an important variable; since any item in the sequence which enters the buffer will cause every succeeding item in the sequence to enter the buffer, the probability that the item in question enters the buffer will approach one as the length of the preceding sequence of items all using the same stimulus increases. For α equal to 1 (overt condition), every item enters the buffer and therefore no change would be expected. As indicated in Fig. 20, the data and theory are in good agreement. The slight rise in the data points for the overt condition may indicate that an estimate of α a little below 1.0 would improve the predictions, but the fit as it stands seems adequate.

E. Additional Variables Related to the Rehearsal Buffer (Experiments 5, 6, and 7)

1. *Known Items and the Buffer* (*Experiment 5*)

In this section we shall consider briefly a number of other variables that relate to the rehearsal buffer. The overt manipulation in the preceding section succeeded in raising to near 1.0 the probability of entering an item in the buffer. As an alternative, one would like an experimental manipulation which would cause the entry probability to drop to near zero for some items. W. Thomson at Stanford University has performed an experiment that satisfies this requirement. The experimental manipulation involves interspersing some extremely well-known items among a series of items never seen before. The assumption is that a well-known item will not enter the rehearsal buffer. The experiment was performed using a modification of the "all-different" stimulus procedure employed in Experiment 2. The stimuli were consonant-vowel-consonant trigrams and the responses were the digits 0–9. For each subject two stimuli were chosen at the start of the first session and assigned responses. These S-R pairs never changed throughout the series of sessions. Except for these two items all other items were presented just once. The size of the to-be-remembered set(s) was six which included the two "known" items. The presentation schedule was as follows: on each trial with probability .5 one of the two known items would be presented for test and then given yet another study period; otherwise one of the four items in the current to-be-remembered set would be tested and a new stimulus-response pair then presented for study. Thus, the task was like that used in Experiment 2, except that on half the trials the subject was tested on, and then permitted to study, an S-R pair which was thoroughly known. The data from the first session in which the known items were being learned will not be considered.

The simplest assumption regarding the two known items is that their probability of entering the buffer is zero. This assumption is the one used in the multiple-reinforcement study (Experiment 3); namely, that an item successfully recovered from LTS is not entered into the buffer.[18] In contrast to Experiment 3, in this study it is easy to identify the items that are known since they are experimentally controlled; for this reason we can look at a number of statistics depending upon the likelihood of entering known items into the buffer. The one of particular interest is presented in Fig. 21. Graphed there is the unconditional lag curve, the

[18] Underwood and Ekstrund (1967) have found that insertion of known items from a previously learned list into a succeeding list improves performance on the learning of unknown items on the second list, although list length was a confounded variable.

"all-known-intervening" lag curve and the "all-unknown-intervening" lag curve. By known items we mean the two S-R pairs that repeatedly are being studied and tested; by unknown items we mean those pairs that are studied and tested only once. The unconditional lag curve gives the probability correct for unknown items as a function of lag, independent of the type of items intervening between study and test; of

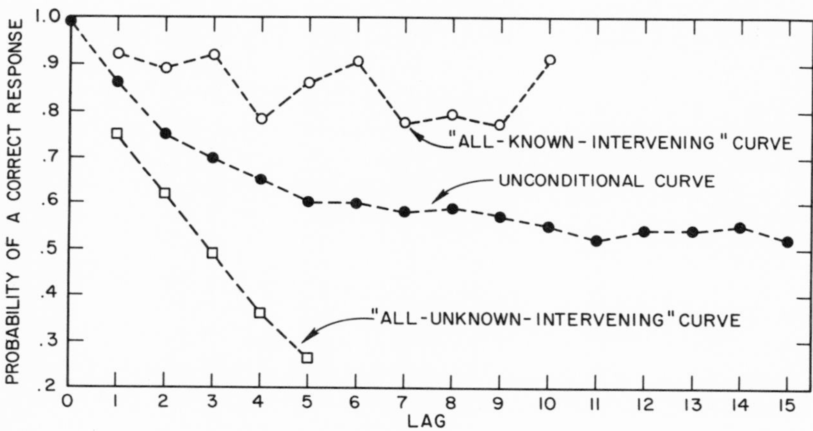

FIG. 21. Observed and theoretical probabilities of a correct response as a function of lag, for the overall condition and for the "all-known-intervening" and "all-unknown-intervening" conditions (Experiment 5).

course, the corresponding curve for known items would be perfect at all lags since subjects never make errors on them. The all-known-intervening curve gives the probability correct as a function of lag, when all of the items intervening between study and test are known items. If none of the known items enter the buffer, this curve should be level from lag 1 on and equal to α, the probability that the item entered the buffer when presented for study. At the opposite extreme is the all-unknown-intervening curve; when all the intervening items are new, the probability of knocking the item of interest from the buffer increases with lag and therefore the curve should decay at a rapid rate. It may be seen that this curve indeed drops at a more rapid rate than the unconditional lag curves. The marked difference between the all-known and all-unknown curves in Fig. 21 leads us to conclude that known and unknown items clearly have different probabilities for entering the rehearsal buffer. If the all-known curve were flat after lag 1, then the probability for entering a known item into the buffer would be zero. Another possibility is that

α is indeed zero for known items, but that the subject occasionally picks an item from LTS for additional rehearsal when a known item is presented.

2. *Response Time Measures* (*Experiment 6*)

We now turn to a consideration of some latency results. Potentially, latencies offer an avenue of analysis that could be more fruitful than the

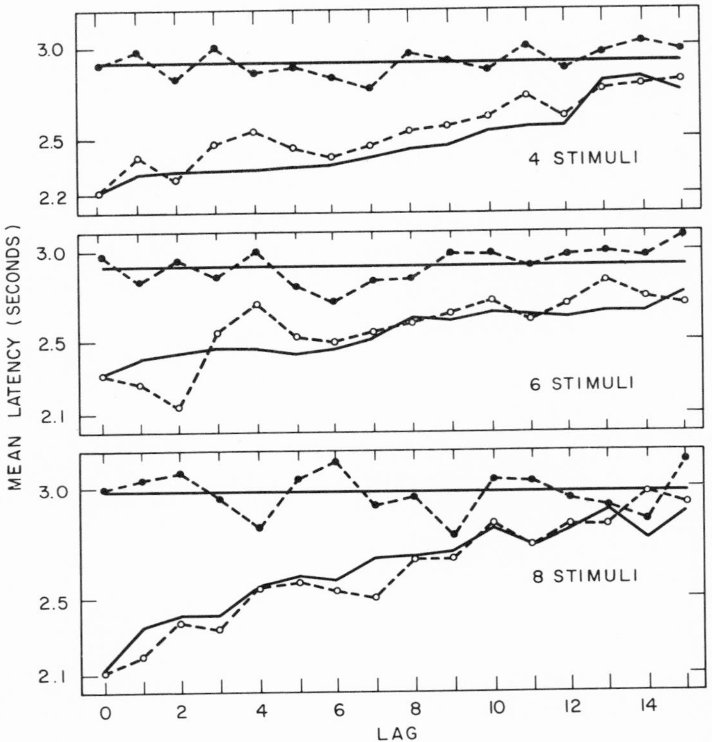

FIG. 22. Observed and theoretical mean latencies as a function of lag for correct and incorrect responses (Experiment 6). --●-- Error latencies; --○-- correct latencies;—predicted latencies.

analysis of choice response data; we say this because the latencies should reflect search and retrieval times from both STS and LTS. A detailed latency analysis is beyond the scope of this paper, but one simple result will be considered. Figure 22 presents the average latencies as a function of lag for correct and incorrect responses in a study by Brelsford *et al.* (1966). This experiment employed the same procedure described earlier in our discussion of Experiment 1 except that only 6 rather than 26 responses were used. As in Experiment 1, this study used three different stimulus-set sizes; i.e., s equalled 4, 6, or 8. For each stimulus set in Fig. 22 it may be seen that the correct and incorrect latency curves converge at long lags. This convergence would be expected since the probability of a correct response is dropping toward chance at long lags. The theoretical curves are based on an extremely simple latency model which assumes that latencies for responses correctly retrieved from either LTS or STS have a fixed mean value λ, whereas a failure to retrieve and a subsequent guess has a fixed mean value of λ'. Thus error responses always have a mean latency λ'; however, a correct response may occur as a result of a retrieval from memory or a correct guess, and consequently its latency is a weighted average of λ and λ'. We can estimate λ' as the average of the points on the latency lag curve for errors, and λ can be set equal to the latency of a correct response at lag zero since all responses are due to retrievals from memory at this lag. In order to predict the remaining latency data, we make use of the observed probability of a correct response as a function of lag; these values are reported in Brelsford *et al.* (1966). If p_i is the observed probability of a correct response at lag i, then

$$p_i = x_i + (1 - x_i)\tfrac{1}{6}$$

where x_i is the probability of retrieving the response from memory and $(1 - x_i)\frac{1}{6}$ is the probability of making a correct response by guessing. Estimating x_i in this way, we predict that the mean latency of a correct response at lag i is simply $x_i\lambda + (1 - x_i)\lambda'$. Using this equation and estimating λ and λ' as indicated above, leads to the theoretical curves displayed in Fig. 22. The error latency curve is predicted to be equal to λ' for all lags, whereas the correct latency curve is λ at lag 0 and approaches λ' over lags as the estimate of x_i goes to zero. This latency model is of course oversimplified, and fails to take into account differences in latencies due to retrieval from STS as compared to retrieval from LTS; the results nevertheless indicate that further analyses along these lines may prove fruitful.

3. *Time Estimation* (*Experiment 7*)

One factor related to our model that has not been discussed is temporal memory. It seems clear that there is some form of long-term temporal memory; in a negative transfer paradigm, for example, there must be some mechanism by which the subject can distinguish between the most recent response paired with a stimulus versus some other response paired with that stimulus at an earlier time. This temporal memory undoubtedly involves the long-term store; somehow when an event is stored in LTS it also must be given a time tag or stored in such a way that the subject can date the event (albeit imperfectly) at the time of retrieval. In addition to long-term temporal storage, there is evidence that a subject's estimate of elapsed time depends upon an item's length of residence in the buffer. An experiment by R. Freund and D. Rundis at Stanford University serves to illustrate the dependence of temporal memory upon the buffer.[19] The study employed essentially

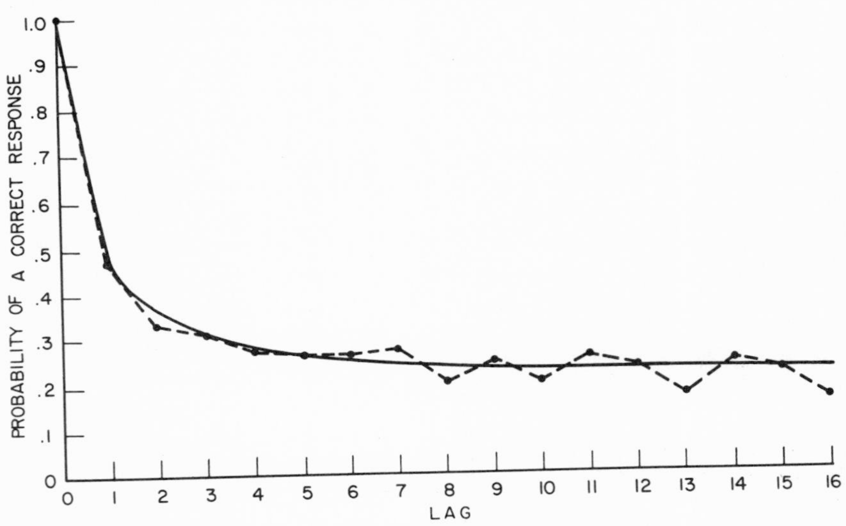

Fig. 23. Observed and theoretical probabilities of a correct response as a function of lag (Experiment 7). --- Observed;—predicted.

the same procedure used in Experiment 2. There was a continuous sequence of test-plus-study trials and the stimuli kept changing throughout each session; each stimulus appeared only once for study and test. The stimuli were consonant-vowel-consonant trigrams and the responses were the 26 letters of the alphabet; the size of the to-be-remembered set of items was fixed at eight. When a stimulus was tested the subject first gave his best guess of the response that had been previously studied with the stimulus and then gave an estimate of the number of trials that intervened between the item's initial study and final test; this estimate could range from 0 to 13; if the subject felt the lag was greater than 13 he responded by pressing a key labeled 14+.

The unconditional lag curve for the probability of a correct response is presented in Fig. 23. The solid line represents the predictions that were

[19] This study employs a time-estimation procedure similar to one developed by L. R. Peterson (personal communication).

generated by the model used to fit Experiment 2. The parameter values providing the best fit to the lag curve were $r = 2$, $\alpha = .57$, $\theta = .13$, $\tau = 1.0$. The data of interest is presented in Fig. 24. The average lag judgment is plotted as a function of the actual lag. The solid dots are the average lag judgments for those items to which a correct response was given; the open circles are the average lag judgments for those items to which an incorrect response was given. If lag judgments were perfect,

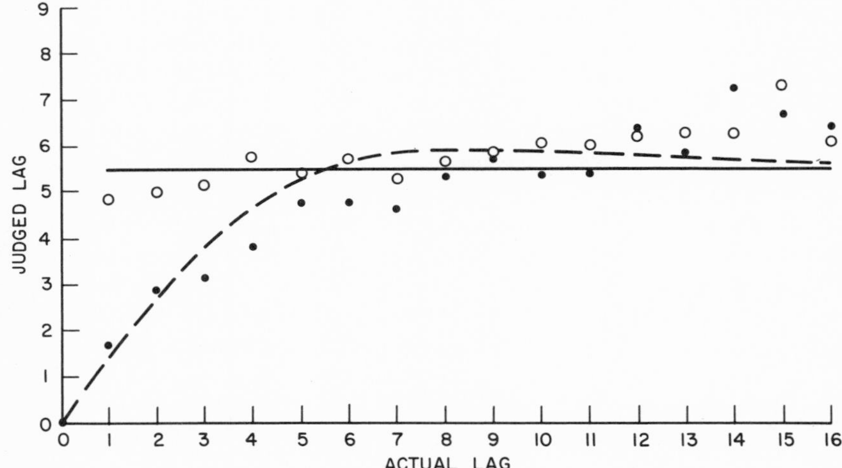

Fig. 24. Observed and theoretical mean lag judgments as a function of the actual lag (Experiment 7). ○ Error data;—error theory; ● correct data; --correct theory.

they would fall on the 45° diagonal; it may be seen that the correct curve is fairly accurate to about lag 5 and then tails off. The lag judgments associated with incorrect responses seem to be virtually unrelated to the actual lag. This indicates that the retrieval of a correct response and temporal estimation are closely related. An extremely simple model for this data assumes that the mean lag judgment for an item in the buffer is the true lag value; any item not in the buffer is given a lag judgment at random from a distribution that is unrelated to the true lag. The predictions using the above parameter estimates are shown in Fig. 24. Freund and Rundis have developed more elaborate models which include both a long- and short-term temporal memory and have obtained quite accurate predictions; but these models will not be examined here. The point we want to make by introducing these data is that temporal memory may be tied to the short-term system even more strongly than to the long-term system.

V. Experiments Concerned with Long-Term Search and Retrieval

The major purpose of this section is to examine a series of experiments concerned with search and retrieval processes in LTS. These experiments differ from those of the preceding section in that the memory tasks are not continuous; rather, they involve a series of discrete trials which are meant to be relatively independent from one to the next. On each trial a new list of items is presented sequentially to the subject for study; following the presentation a test is made on some aspect of the list. Using this procedure, the size of the list, d, can be systematically manipulated. Variations in list size affect the size of the memory set through which the subject must search when tested, and consequently search and retrieval processes can be examined in more detail than was previously possible. The title of this section is not meant to imply, however, that the short-term processes involved in these experiments are different from those appearing in the continuous-presentation situations; in fact, the models used to describe the experiments of this section will be based upon the same STS rehearsal buffer introduced earlier. The difference is one of emphasis; the long-term processes will be elaborated and explored in greater depth in this section. This exploration of long-term models will by no means be exhaustive, and will be less extensive than that carried out for the short-term processes.

Prior to an examination of particular experiments, a few remarks need to be made about the separability of lists. In any experiment in which a series of different lists is presented, we may ask just what information in LTS the subject is searching through at test. The same problem arises, though less seriously, in experiments where the subject is tested on only one list. Clearly the information relevant to the current list of items being tested must be kept separate from the great mass of other information in LTS. This problem is accentuated when individual lists within a session must be kept separated. How this is managed is somewhat of a mystery. One possible explanation would call for a search along a temporal memory dimension: the individual items could be assumed to be temporally ordered, or to have "time tags." It is not enough to propose that search is made through all items indiscriminately and that items recovered from previous lists are recognized as such and not reported; if this were true, the duration and difficulty of the search would increase dramatically over the session. In fact, the usual result is that there is little change in performance over a session except for effects concentrated at the very start. On the other hand, judging from such factors as intrusion errors from previous lists, the subject is not able to restrict his search solely to the current list. In the experiments to follow, we will make the simplifying assumption, without real justification, that the lists are entirely separated in LTS, and that the subject searches only through information relevant to the list currently being tested.

A. A Serial Display Procedure Involving Single Tests (Experiment 8)

This experiment involved a long series of discrete trials. On each trial a new display of items was presented to the subject. A display consisted of a random sequence of playing cards; the cards varied only in the

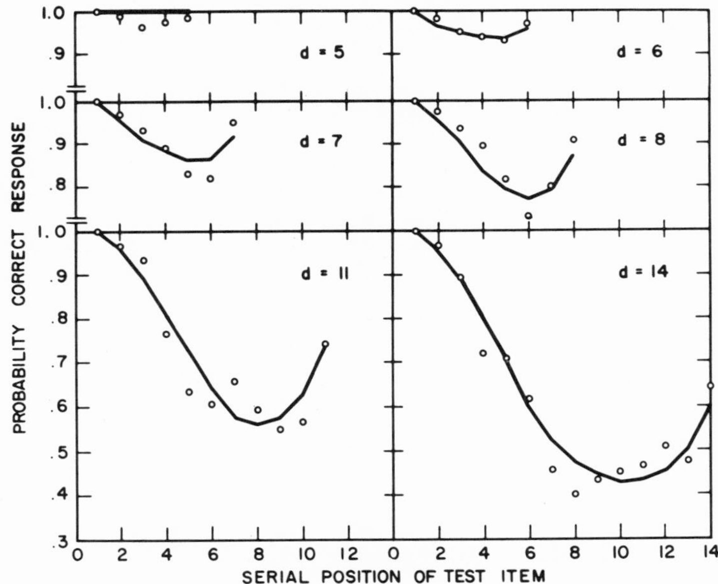

Fig. 25. Observed and theoretical probabilities of a correct response as a function of serial position (Experiment 8).

color of a small patch on one side; four colors (black, white, blue, and green) were used. The cards were presented to the subject at a rate of one card every 2 seconds. The subject named the color of each card as it was presented; once the color of the card had been named it was turned face down on a table so that the color was no longer visible, and the next card was presented. After presentation of the last card in a display, the cards were in a straight row on the table; the card presented first was to the subject's left and the most recently presented card to the right. The trial terminated when the experimenter pointed to one of the cards on the table and the subject attempted to recall the color of that card. The subject was instructed to guess the color if uncertain and to qualify the response with a confidence rating. The confidence ratings were the numerals 1 through 4. The subjects were told to say 1 if they were positive; 2 if they were able to eliminate two of the four possible colors as being incorrect; 3 if one of the four colors could be eliminated as incorrect; and 4 if they had no idea at all as to the correct response.

It is important to note that only one position is tested in a display on each trial. The experiment involved 20 female subjects who participated in five daily sessions, each lasting for approximately 1 hour. Over the course of the five sessions, a subject was given approximately 400 trials. The display size, d, was varied from trial to trial and took on the following values: $d = 3$, 4, 5, 6, 7, 8, 11, and 14. Details of the experimental procedure are presented in Phillips, Shiffrin, and Atkinson (1967).

Figure 25 presents the probability of a correct response at each serial position for displays of size 5, 6, 7, 8, 11, and 14. For displays of sizes 3 and 4, the probability correct was 1.0 at all positions. The circles in the figure are the observed points; the solid lines are predicted curves which will be explained shortly. The serial positions are numbered so that item 1 designates the last item presented (the newest item), and item d designates the first item presented (the oldest item). The most apparent features of the curves are a fairly marked S-shaped recency portion and a smaller, quite steep primacy portion. For all display sizes, the probability of a correct response is 1.0 at serial position 1.

1. *Theory*

We must first decide whether a subject will set up and use a rehearsal buffer in this situation. Despite the fact that the continuous procedure has been dropped, it is still unlikely that the subject will engage in a significant amount of long-term coding. This is true because the task is still one of high "negative transfer"; the stimuli, which are the positions in the display, are constantly being re-paired with new responses as a session continues. Too much LTS encoding would undoubtedly lead to a high degree of interference among lists. It is only for a relatively weak and decaying LTS trace that a temporal search of long-term memory may be expected to keep the various lists separate. This difficulty in LTS transfer leads to the adoption of short-term strategies. Another reason for using a rehearsal buffer in this task depends upon the small list lengths employed; for small list lengths, there is a high probability that the item will be in the buffer at the moment of test. Thus the adoption of a rehearsal buffer is an efficient strategy. There is some question concerning just what the unit of rehearsal is in this situation. For example, the subject could assign numbers to positions in the display and then rehearse the number-color pairs. Most likely, however, the subject uses the fact that the stimuli always remain before her to combine STS rehearsal with some form of visual mnemonic. That is, the unit of rehearsal is the response alone; as the subject rehearses the responses, she "mentally" places each response upon the appropriate card before her. This might therefore be a situation where the a-v-l and visual short-term stores are used in conjunction with each other. In any case, it seems reasonable that the units of rehearsal are the names (or perhaps the abbreviations) of the colors.

We might ask how the buffer will act in this situation. As noted earlier, in reference to the "overt-covert" experiment, the fact that items are read aloud as they are presented will tend to cause the subject to enter each item into the buffer. Furthermore, an S-shaped recency effect would not be unexpected. Indeed, if the units of rehearsal are the responses themselves, then the subject might tend to keep them in consecutive order to ease the visual memory task; if all items enter the buffer and are kept in consecutive order, then the oldest items will tend to be deleted first. That is, when a new item enters the buffer there will be a tendency to eliminate the oldest item from the buffer to make room for it. One other question that should be considered is the size of the buffer the subject would be expected to use in this task. There are a number of reasons why the buffer size should be larger here than in the continuous tasks of Section IV. First, the subject is not continually being interrupted for tests as in the previous studies; more of the subject's attention may therefore be allotted to rehearsal. Second, rehearsal of color names (or their abbreviations) is considerably easier than number-letter combinations. Equivalent to rehearsing "32-G, 45-Q" might be "Black, White, Black, Green" (or even a larger set if abbreviations are used). The magnitude of the difference may not be quite as large as this argument would lead us to expect because undoubtedly some time must be allotted to keeping track of which response goes on which position, but the estimate of the buffer size nevertheless should be larger in this situation than in the continuous tasks.

The STS part of the model for this experiment is similar to that used in the "overt" experiment in Section IV,D in that every item is entered in the buffer when it is presented. There is one new factor, however, that must be considered. Since each trial starts with the buffer empty, it will be assumed that the first items presented enter the buffer in succession, without knocking any item out, until the buffer is filled. Once the buffer is filled, each item enters the buffer and knocks out one of the items currently there. If the most recently presented item is in slot r of the buffer, and the oldest item is in slot 1, then the probability that the item in slot i of the buffer will be the one eliminated is

$$\frac{\delta(1-\delta)^{i-1}}{1-(1-\delta)^r}.$$

This is the same equation that was used to describe the knock-out process for the overt-covert study (Experiment 4). The larger δ, the greater the tendency to delete the oldest item in the buffer when making room for a new one.

The first set of long-term storage and retrieval assumptions that will be considered are essentially identical to those used in the previous sections. Information will be assumed to enter LTS during the entire period an item resides in the buffer at a rate θ per inter-item interval. This process must be qualified with regard to the first few items presented on each trial before the buffer is filled; it is assumed that the subjects divide their attention equally among the items in the buffer. Thus, if the rate of transfer is θ when there is only one item in the buffer, and the buffer size is r, then the rate of transfer will be θ/r when the buffer is filled. That is, since attention must be divided among r items when the buffer is full, each item receives only $1/r$th as much transfer as when the buffer only holds a single item. In general, information on each item will be transferred to LTS at rate θ/j during the interval in which there are j items in the buffer. The effect of this assumption is that more information is transferred to LTS about the items first presented in a list than about later items that are presented once the buffer is full.

The LTS decay and retrieval processes must now be examined. In earlier experiments we assumed that information decayed solely as a result of the number of items intervening between study and test; in other words, only the retroactive interference effect was considered. Because the previous tasks were continuous, the number of items preceding an item's presentation was effectively infinite in all cases. For this reason the proactive effects were assumed to be constant over conditions and did not need explicit inclusion in the model. In the present experiment the variation in list size makes it clear that proactive interference effects within a trial will be an important variable. The assumption that will be used is perhaps the simplest version of interference theory possible: each preceding and each succeeding item has an equal interfering effect. To be precise, if an amount of information I has been transferred to LTS for a given item, then every other item in the list will interfere with this information to the extent of reducing it by a proportion τ. Thus, if there were d items in the list, the item of interest would have an amount of information in LTS at the time of test equal to $I(\tau^{d-1})$. Clearly, the longer the list the greater the interference effect.

The model can now be completed by specifying the response process which works as follows. An item in the buffer at the time of test is responded to correctly. If the item is not in the buffer, then a search is made in LTS. The probability of retrieving the appropriate response is, as in our other models, an exponential function of this information and equals $1 - \exp[-I(\tau^{d-1})]$; if a retrieval is not made, then the subject guesses.

2. *Data Analysis*

The parameter values that gave the best fit to the data of Fig. 25 using a minimum χ^2 criterion were as follows: $r = 5$, $\delta = .38$, $\theta = 2.0$, and $\tau = .85$.[20] Remember that r is the buffer size, δ determines the probability of deleting the oldest item in the buffer, θ is the transfer rate to LTS, and τ is the proportional loss of information caused by other items in the list. The theoretical curves generated by these parameter estimates are shown in Fig. 30 as solid lines. The predictions are quite accurate as indicated by a χ^2 value of 44.3 based on 42 degrees of freedom. It should be emphasized that the curves in the figure were all fit simultaneously with the same parameter values.

The primacy effect in the curves of Fig. 25 is predicted because more information is transferred to LTS for the first items presented on each trial. There are two reasons for this. First, the transfer rate on any given item is higher the fewer items there are in the buffer; thus the initial items, which enter the buffer before it is filled, accumulate more information in LTS. Second, the initial items cannot be knocked out of the buffer until the buffer is filled; thus the time period that initial items reside in the buffer is longer on the average than the time for later items. The recency effect is predicted because the last items presented in a list tend to be still in the buffer at the time of test; the S-shape arises because the estimate of δ indicates a fairly strong tendency for the oldest items in the rehearsal buffer to be eliminated first when making room for a new item.

Having estimated a set of parameter values that characterizes the data in Fig. 25, we now use these estimates to predict the confidence rating data. Actually, it is beyond the scope of this paper to analyze the confidence ratings in detail, but some of these data will be considered in order to illustrate the generality of the model and the stability of the parameter estimates. The data that will be considered are presented in Fig. 26; graphed is the probability of giving confidence rating R_1 (most confident) for each list size and each serial position. The observed data is represented by the open circles. It is clear that these results are similar in form to the probability correct curves of Fig. 25. The model used to fit these data is quite simple. Any item in the buffer is given an R_1. If the item is not in the buffer, then a search is made of LTS. If the amount of information in LTS on the item is $I(\tau^{d-1})$ then the probability of giving R_1 is an exponential function of that information: namely the

[20] For details on the method of parameter estimation see Phillips, Shiffrin, and Atkinson (1967).

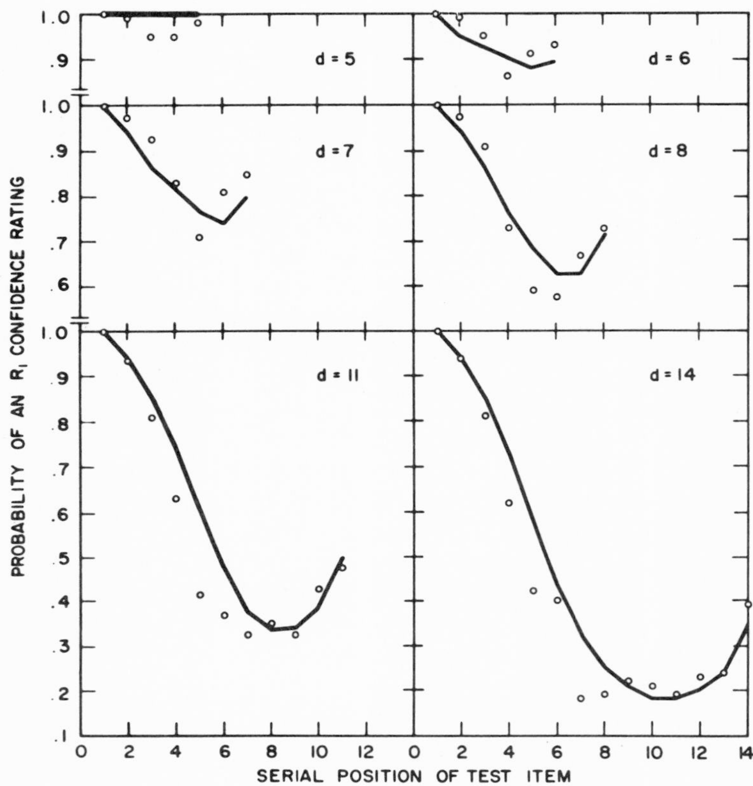

FIG. 26. Observed and predicted probabilities of confidence rating R_1 as a function of serial position (Experiment 8).

function $1 - \exp[-c_1 I(\tau^{d-1})]$, where c_1 is a parameter determining the subject's tendency to give confidence rating R_1. This assumption is consistent with a number of different viewpoints concerning the subject's generation of confidence ratings. It could be interpreted equally well as an assignment of ratings to the actually perceived amount of information in LTS, or as a proportion of the items that are recovered in an all-or-none fashion.[21] In any event, the predictions were generated using the previous parameter values plus an estimate of c_1. The predicted curves, with c_1 equal to .66, are shown in Fig. 26. The predictions are not as accurate as those in Fig. 25; but, considering that only one new parameter was estimated, they are quite good.

[21] The various possibilities may be differentiated through an analysis of conditional probabilities of the ratings given correct and incorrect responses, and through ROC curve (Type II) analyses (Bernbach, 1967, Murdock, 1966) but this will not be done here.

3. *Discussion*

In developing this model a number of decisions were made somewhat arbitrarily. The choice points involved will now be considered in greater detail. The assumption that the amount of transfer to LTS is dependent upon the number of items currently in the buffer needs elaboration. Certainly if the subject is engaged in coding or other active transfer strategies, the time spent in attending to an item should be directly related to the amount of transfer to LTS. On the other hand, the passive type of transfer which we assume can occur in situations where the subject makes use of a rehearsal buffer may not be related to the time spent in rehearsing an item per se, but rather to the total period the item resides in the buffer. That is, direct attention to an item in STS may not be necessary for some transfer to take place; rather a passive form of transfer may occur as long as the item remains in STS. Thus in situations where the rehearsal buffer is used and active transfer strategies such as coding do not occur, it could reasonably be expected that the amount of information transferred to LTS would be related solely to the total time spent in the buffer, and not to the number of items in the buffer at the time. In practice, of course, the actual transfer process may lie somewhere between these two extremes. Note that even if the transfer rate for an item is assumed to be a constant (unrelated to the number of items currently in the buffer) the first items presented for study still would have more information transferred to LTS than later items; this occurs because the items at the start of a list will not be knocked out of the buffer until it is filled and hence will reside in the buffer for a longer time on the average than later items. For this reason, the primacy effect could still be explained. On the other hand, the primacy effect will be reduced by the constant transfer assumption; in order to fit the data from the current experiment with this assumption, for example, it would be necessary to adjust the retrieval scheme accordingly. In modeling the free verbal-recall data that follows, a constant transfer assumption is used and accordingly a retrieval scheme is adopted which amplifies more strongly than the present one small differences in LTS strength.

We now consider the decay assumption in greater detail. The assumption is that the information transferred to LTS for a particular item is reduced by a proportion τ for every other item in the list. There are a number of possibilities for the form of this reduction. It could be actual physical interference with the trace, or it could be a reduction in the value of the current information as a result of subsequent incoming information. An example of this latter kind of interference will be helpful. Suppose, in a memory experiment the first item is GEX-5, and the subject stores "G__-5" in LTS. If tested now on GEX, the subject would give the correct response 5. Suppose a second item GOZ-3 is presented and the subject stores "G__-3" in LTS. If he is now tested on either GEX or GOZ his probability of a correct response will drop to .5. Thus the actual information stored is not affected, but its value is markedly changed.

The assumption that every other item in a list interferes equally is open to question on two counts. First of all, it would be expected that an item about which a large amount of information is transferred would interfere more strongly with other items in LTS than an item about which little information is transferred. Certainly when no transfer occurs for an item, that item cannot interfere with other LTS traces. However, the equal interference assumption used in our analysis may not be a bad approximation. The second failing of the equal interference assumption has to do with separation of items. If the list lengths were very long, it might be expected that the number of items separating any two items would affect their mutual interference; the greater the separation, the less the interference. The list lengths are short enough in the present experiment, however, that the separation is probably not an important factor.

4. *Some Alternative Models*

It is worth considering some alternatives to the interference process of the model just presented, henceforth referred to as Model I in this subsection. In particular it is important to demonstrate that the effects of the interference-decay assumption, which could be viewed as a structural feature of memory, can be duplicated by simple search processes. For example, any limited search through the information in LTS will give poorer performance as the amount of that information increases. In order to make the concept of the search process clear, Model II will adopt an all-or-none transfer scheme. That is, a single copy of each item may be transferred to LTS on a probabilistic basis. If a copy is transferred, it is a perfect copy to the extent that it always produces a correct response if it is retrieved from LTS. The short-term features of the model are identical to those of Model I: each item enters the buffer; when the buffer is filled each succeeding item enters the buffer and knocks out an item already there according to the δ-process described earlier.

The transfer assumption for Model II is as follows. If an item is one of the j items in the buffer, then the probability that a copy of that item will be placed in LTS between one item's presentation and the next is θ/j. Therefore, the transfer depends, as in Model I, upon the number of other items currently in the buffer. No more than one copy may be placed in LTS for any one item. The retrieval assumptions are the following. A correct response is given if the item is in the buffer when tested. If it is not in the buffer, then a search is made in LTS. If a copy of the item exists in LTS and is found, then a correct response is given; otherwise a random guess is made. As before, we assume that the information pertinent to the current list is distinguishable from that of earlier lists; thus, the search is made only among those copies of items in the current list. The central assumption of Model II is that exactly R selections are made (with replacement) from the copies in LTS; if the tested item has not been found by then, the search ends. The restriction to a fixed number of searches, R, is perhaps too strong, but can be justified if there is a fixed time period allotted to the subject for responding. It should be clear that for R fixed, the probability of retrieval decreases as the list length increases; the longer the list the more copies in LTS, and the more copies the less the probability of finding a particular copy in R selections. Model II was fit to the data in the same fashion as Model I. The parameter values that gave the best predictions were $r = 5$, $\delta = .39$, $\theta = .72$, and $R = 3.15$. The theoretical curves generated by these parameters are so similar to those for Model I that Fig. 25 adequately represents them, and they will not be presented separately. Whereas the χ^2 was 44.3 for Model I, the χ^2 value for Model II was 46.2, both based on 42 degrees of freedom. The similarity of the predictions serves to illustrate the primary point of introducing Model II: effects predicted by search processes and by interference processes are quite similar and consequently are difficult to separate experimentally.

The search process described above is just one of a variety of such mechanisms. In general there will be a group of possible search mechanisms associated with each transfer and storage assumption; a few of these processes will be examined in the next section on free-verbal-recall. Before moving on to these experiments, however, we should like to present briefly a decay and retrieval process combining some of the features of interference and search mechanisms. In this process the interference does not occur until the search begins and is then caused by the search process itself. The model (designated as Model III) is identical in all respects to Model II until the point where the subject begins the search of LTS for the correct copy. The assumption is that the subject samples copies with replacement, as before, but each unsuccessful search may disrupt the sought-after copy with probability R'. The search does not end until the appropriate copy is found or until all copies in LTS have been examined. If the copy does exist in LTS, but is disrupted at any time during the search process, then when the item is finally retrieved, the stored information will be such that the subject will not be able to recall at better than the chance level. The parameter values giving the best fit for this model were $r = 5$, $\delta = .38$, $\theta = .80$, and

$R' = .25$. The predicted curves are again quite similar to those in Fig. 25 and will not be presented. The predictions are not quite as accurate, however, as those of Models I and II, the χ^2 value being 55.0.[22]

B. Free-Verbal-Recall Experiments

The free-verbal-recall situation offers an excellent opportunity for examining retrieval processes, because the nature of the task forces the subject to engage in a lengthy search of LTS. The typical free-verbal-recall experiment involves reading a list of high-frequency English words to the subject (Deese & Kaufman, 1957; Murdock, 1962). Following the reading, the subject is asked to recall as many of the words as possible. Quite often list length has been a variable, and occasionally the presentation time per item has been varied. Deese and Kaufman, for example, used lists of 10 and 32 items at 1 second per item. Murdock ran groups of 10, 15, and 20 items at 2 seconds per item, and groups of 20, 30, and 40 items at 1 second per item. The results are typically presented in the form of serial position curves: the probability of recall is plotted against the item's position in the list. The Murdock (1962) results are representative and are shown in Fig. 27. It should be made clear that the numbering of serial positions for these curves is opposite from the scheme used in the previous section; that is, the first item presented (the oldest item at the time of test) is labeled serial position 1. This numbering procedure will be used throughout this section to conform with the literature on free-verbal-recall; the reader should keep this in mind when comparing results here with those presented elsewhere in the paper. The primacy effect in Fig. 27 is the rise on the left-hand portions of the curves and the recency effect is the larger rise on the right-hand portions of the curves. The curves are labeled with the list length and the presentation rate per item. Note that the curves are quite similar to those found in Experiment 8 of the previous section; an effect not seen in Experiment 8 (because of the short list lengths used) is the level asymptotic portions of the curves which appear between the primacy and recency effects for the longer lists.

The form of the curves suggests that a buffer process could explain the results, with the words themselves being the units of rehearsal. The recency effect would be due to the probability that an item is still in the buffer at test; this probability goes to near zero after 15 items or so and the recency effect accordingly extends no further than this. The primacy effect would arise because more information accrued in LTS for the first few items presented in the list. Whether a buffer strategy is reasonable in the free-recall situation, however, is worth further discussion. It can hardly be maintained that high-frequency English words are difficult to

[22] For a more detailed account of Models I, II, and III, and a comparison among models, see Atkinson and Shiffrin (1965).

code; on the other hand, the task is not a paired-associate one and cues must be found with which to connect the words. One possibility is that upon seeing each word the subject generates a number of associates (from LTS) and tries to store the group of words; later during testing a search which retrieves any of the associates might in turn retrieve the desired word. We tend to doubt that this strategy, used by itself, will greatly improve performance.[23] To the extent that coding occurs, it

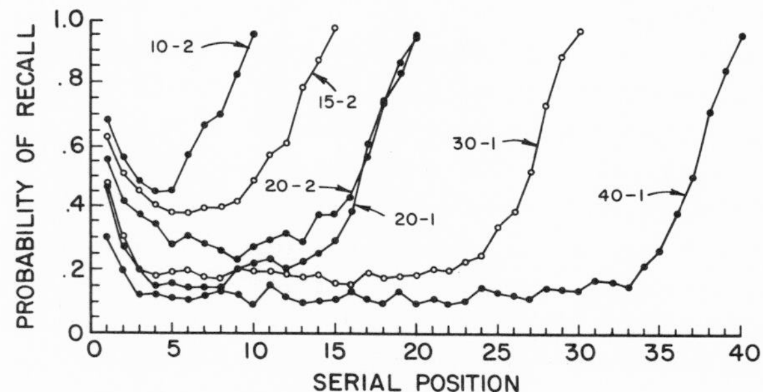

FIG. 27. Probability of correct recall as a function of serial position for free verbal recall. After Murdock (1962).

probably involves connecting words within the presented list to each other. This technique would of course require the consideration of a number of words simultaneously in STS and therefore might be characterized reasonably well by a buffer process. Whether or not coding occurs in the free-recall situation, there are other reasons for expecting the subjects to adopt a buffer strategy. The most important reason is undoubtedly the improvement in performance that a rehearsal buffer will engender. If the capacity of the buffer is, say, 4 or 5 words, then the use of a buffer will assure the subjects of a minimum of four or five items correct on each list (assuming that all of the items may be read out of the buffer correctly). Considering that subjects report on the average only about 8 or 9 items, even for long lists, the items stored in the buffer are an important component of performance.

It will be assumed, then, that the subjects do adopt a rehearsal strategy. The comparability of the curves in Fig. 25 to those in Fig. 27

[23] B. H. Cohen (1963) has presented free-recall lists containing closely related categories of words, e.g., north, east, south, west. Indeed, the recovery of one member of a category usually led to the recovery of other members, but the total number of categories recalled did not exceed the number of separate words recalled from noncategorized lists.

might indicate that a model similar to any of the models presented in the previous section could be applied to the current data. There are, however, important differences between the two experimental paradigms which must be considered: the free-recall situation does not involve pairing a response with a stimulus for each list position, and has the requirement of multiple recall at the time of test. The fact that explicit stimulus cues are not provided for each of the responses desired would be expected to affect the form of the search process. The multiple-response requirement raises more serious problems. In particular, it is possible that each response that is output may interfere with other items not yet recalled. The problem may be most acute for the case of items still in the buffer; Waugh and Norman (1965) have proposed that each response output at the time of test has the same disrupting effect upon other items in the buffer as the arrival of a new item during study. On the other hand, it is not clear whether a response emitted during test disrupts items in LTS. It might be expected that the act of recalling an item from LTS would raise that item's strength in LTS; this increase in strength is probably not associated, however, with the transfer of any new information to LTS. For this reason, other traces will most likely not be interfered with, and it shall be assumed that retrieval of an item from LTS has no effect upon other items in LTS.

Because there is some question concerning the effects of multiple recall upon the contents of the buffer, and because this section is primarily aimed at LTS processes, the part of the free-recall curves that arise from the buffer will not be considered in further analyses. This means that the models in this section will not be concerned with the part of the curve making up the recency effect; since the data in Fig. 27 indicate that the recency effect is contained in the last 15 items (to the right in the figure) of each list, these points will be eliminated from the analyses. Unfortunately, the elimination of the last 15 items means that the short list lengths are eliminated entirely. The problem of obtaining data for short list lengths not contaminated by items in the buffer at the time of test has been circumvented experimentally by a variation of the counting-backward technique. That is, the contents of the buffer can be eliminated experimentally by using an interfering task inserted between the end of the list and the start of recall. We now turn to a consideration of these experiments.

A representative experiment is that by Postman and Phillips (1965). Words were presented at a rate of one per second in all conditions. In one set of conditions three list lengths (10, 20, and 30) were used and recall was tested immediately following presentation. This, of course, is the usual free recall procedure. The serial position curves are shown in the top panel of Fig. 28 in the box labeled "O second." The same list lengths were used for those conditions employing an intervening task; immediately following presentation of the list the subjects were required to count backwards by three's and four's for 30 seconds. Following this intervening task, they were asked to recall the list. The results are shown in the lower panel in Fig. 28. If the intervening task did not affect the contents of LTS but did wipe out all items in the buffer, then the recency

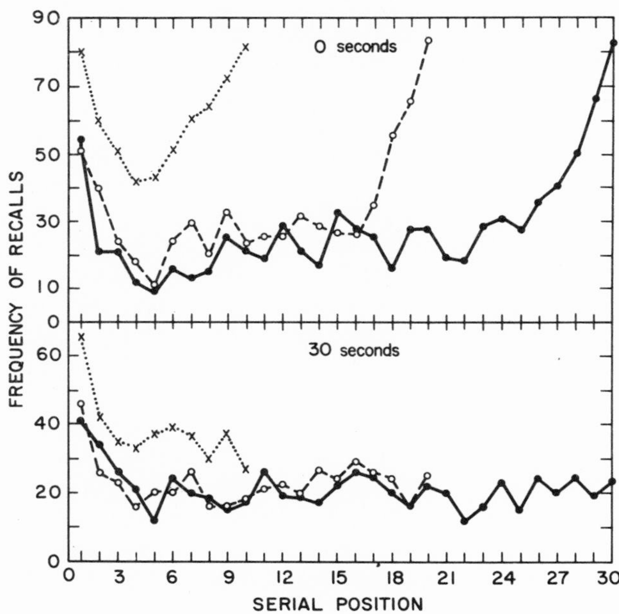

FIG. 28. Probability of correct recall as a function of serial position for free verbal recall with test following 0 seconds and 30 seconds of intervening arithmetic. After Postman & Phillips (1965).

effects would be expected to disappear with the curves otherwise unchanged. This is exactly what was found. The primacy effects and asymptotic levels remain unchanged while the recency effect disappears. It is clear, then, that normal free-recall curves (without intervening arithmetic) from which the last 15 points have been deleted should be identical to curves from experiments using intervening arithmetic. The following data have therefore been accumulated: Murdock's data with the last 15 points of each list deleted; data reported by Deese and Kaufman (1957) using a free-recall paradigm, but again with the last 15 points of each list deleted; the data reported by Postman and Phillips (1965); and some data collected by Shiffrin in which an intervening task was used to eliminate the contents of the buffer.[24] All of these serial position curves have the same form; they show a primacy effect followed by a level asymptote. For this reason the results have been presented in Table I. The first three points of each curve, which make up the primacy

TABLE I

OBSERVED AND PREDICTED SERIAL POSITION CURVES FOR VARIOUS FREE-VERBAL-RECALL EXPERIMENTS

List	Point 1 Obs.	Point 1 Pred.	Point 2 Obs.	Point 2 Pred.	Point 3 Obs.	Point 3 Pred.	Asymptote Obs.	Asymptote Pred.	Asymptote Number of points
M-20-1	.46	.45	.27	.37	.20	.29	.16	.22	2
M-30-1	.38	.35	.30	.28	.21	.22	.19	.17	12
M-20-2	.55	.61	.42	.51	.37	.41	.31	.32	2
M-40-1	.30	.29	.20	.23	.13	.18	.12	.14	22
M-25-1	.38	.39	.23	.32	.21	.25	.15	.19	7
M-20-2.5	.72	.66	.61	.56	.45	.46	.37	.35	2
D-32-1	.46	.33	.34	.27	.27	.21	.16	.16	14
P-10-1	.66	.62	.42	.52	.35	.42	.34	.32	7
P-20-1	.47	.45	.27	.37	.23	.29	.22	.22	17
P-30-1	.41	.35	.34	.28	.27	.22	.20	.17	27
S-6-1	.71	.74	.50	.64	.57	.52	.42	.40	3
S-6-2	.82	.88	.82	.79	.65	.66	.66	.52	3
S-11-1	.48	.60	.43	.50	.27	.40	.31	.31	8
S-11-2	.72	.76	.55	.66	.52	.54	.47	.42	8
S-17-1	.55	.49	.33	.40	.26	.32	.22	.24	14
S-17-2	.68	.66	.65	.56	.67	.45	.43	.35	14

effect, are given in the table. The level portions of the curves are then averaged and the average shown in the column labeled "asymptote." The column labeled "number of points" is the number of points which have been averaged to arrive at the asymptotic level.[25] The column labeled "list" gives the abbreviation of the experimenter, the list length, and the presentation rate for each of the serial position curves. (M = Murdock, 1962; D = Deese and Kaufman, 1957; P = Postman and Phillips, 1965; S = Shiffrin.)

[24] The Shiffrin data are reported in more detail in Atkinson and Shiffrin (1965).

[25] For the Postman-Phillips and Shiffrin lists the number of points at asymptote are simply list length, d, minus 3. For the Murdock and the Deese-Kaufman lists the number of points is $d - 15 - 3$ because the last 15 points in these lists have been eliminated.

1. *Theoretical Analysis*

Having accumulated a fair amount of parametric data in Table I, we should now like to predict the results. The first model to be considered is extremely simple. Every item presented enters the subject's rehearsal buffer. One by one the initial items fill up the buffer, and thereafter each succeeding item knocks out of the buffer a randomly chosen item. In conditions where arithmetic is used following presentation, it is assumed that the arithmetic operations knock items from the buffer at the same rate as new incoming items. This is only an approximation, but probably not too inaccurate. Information is assumed to be transferred to LTS as long as an item remains in the buffer, in fact as a linear function of the total time spent in the buffer (regardless of the number of other items concurrently in the buffer). If an item remains in the buffer for j seconds, an amount of information equal to θ times j is transferred to LTS. Call the amount of information transferred to LTS for an item its *strength*. When the subject engages in a search of LTS during recall it is assumed that he makes exactly R searches into LTS and then stops his search (the number of searches made might, for example, be determined by the time allowed for recall). On each search into LTS the probability that information concerning a particular item will be found is just the ratio of that item's strength to the sum of the strengths of all items in the list. Thus, items which have a greater LTS strength will be more likely to be found on any one search. The probability that the information in LTS will produce a correct recall, once that information has been found in a search, is assumed to be an exponential function of the strength for that item.

There are just three parameters for this model: r, the buffer size; θ, the parameter determining the rate per second at which information on a given item is transferred to LTS while the item resides in the rehearsal buffer; and R the number of searches made.[26] The probability of a correct response from the buffer is zero for the results in Table I because the contents of the buffer have been emptied experimentally by intervening arithmetic, or because the recency data (which represents recovery from the buffer) has been omitted. The parameters giving the best fit to the data were as follows: $r = 4$, $\theta = .04$, and $R = 34$. The predictions also are presented in Table I. The predictions are rather remarkable considering that just three parameters have been used to predict the results from

[26] It is important to remember that θ for this model is defined as the *rate per second* of information transfer, and thus the time measures listed in Table I need to be taken into account when applying the model. For example, an item that resides in the buffer for three item presentations will have 3θ amount of information in LTS if the presentation rate is one item per second, and 7.5θ if the presentation rate is 2.5 seconds per item.

four different experiments employing different list lengths and different presentation rates. Some of the points are not predicted exactly but this is largely due to the fact that the data tends to be somewhat erratic; the predictions of the asymptotic values (where a larger amount of data is averaged) are especially accurate.

2. *Some Alternative Models*

A number of decisions were made in formulating the free-recall model that need to be examined in greater detail. First consider the effect of an arithmetic task upon items undergoing rehearsal. If the arithmetic caused all rehearsal and long-term storage operations to cease immediately, then the probability of recalling the last item presented should decrease toward chance (since its LTS strength will be negligible, having had no opportunity to accumulate). The serial position curve, however, remains level and does not drop toward the end of the list. One possible explanation is that all transfer to LTS takes place when the item first enters the buffer, rather than over the period the item remains in the buffer; in this case the onset of arithmetic would not affect the formation of traces in LTS. While this assumption could handle the phenomenon under discussion, we prefer to consider the LTS trace as building up during the period the item remains in the buffer. Recall that this latter assumption is borne out by the accuracy of the earlier models and, in particular, the U-shaped functions presented in Fig. 12 for the multiple-reinforcement experiment. The explanation of the level serial position curve implied by our model is that the arithmetic operations remove items from the buffer in a manner similar to that of new entering items. Two sources give this assumption credibility. First, Postman and Phillips (1965) found that short periods of arithmetic (15 seconds) would leave some of the recency effect in the serial position curve, suggesting that some items remained in the buffer after brief periods of arithmetic. Second, the data of Waugh and Norman (1965) suggest that output operations during tasks such as arithmetic act upon the short-term store in the same manner as new incoming items.

Another choice point in formulating the model occurred with regard to the amount of LTS transfer for the first items in the list. The assumption used in an earlier model let the amount of transfer depend upon the number of other items concurrently undergoing rehearsal, as if the attention allotted to any given item determines the amount of transfer. An alternative possibility is that the amount of transfer is determined solely by the length of stay in the buffer and is therefore independent of the number of items currently in the buffer. Another assumption resulting in this same independence effect is that the subject allots to items in the buffer only enough attention to keep them "alive"; when the number of items in the buffer is small, the subject presumably uses his spare time for other matters. A free-verbal-recall experiment by Murdock (1965) seems to support a variant of this latter assumption. He had subjects perform a rather easy card-sorting task during the presentation of the list. The serial position curve seemed unaffected except for a slight drop in the primacy effect. This would be understandable if the card-sorting task was easy enough that the buffer was unaffected, but distracting enough that extra attention normally allotted to the first few items in the list (before the buffer is filled) is instead allotted to the card-sorting task. In any case, it is not clear whether the transfer rate should or should not be tied to the number of items concurrently in the buffer. The model that we have proposed for free-recall (henceforth referred to as Model I in this subsection) assumed a constant transfer process; a model using a variable transfer assumption will be considered in a moment.

The search process used in Model I is only one of many possibilities. Suppose, for example, that the strength value for an item represents the number of bits of information stored about that item (where the term "bits" is used in a nontechnical sense). A search might then be construed as a random choice of one bit from all those bits stored for all the items in the list. The bits of information stored for each item, however, are associated to some degree, so that the choice of one bit results in the uncovering of a proportion of the rest of the information stored for that item. If this proportion is small, then different searches finding bits associated with a particular item will result in essentially independent probabilities of retrieval. This independent retrieval assumption was used in the construction of Model I. On the other hand, finding one bit in a search might result in all the bits stored for that item becoming available at once; a reasonable assumption would be that this information is either sufficient to allow retrieval or not, and a particular item is retrieved the first time it is picked in a search or is never retrieved. This will be called the dependent retrieval assumption.

It is interesting to see how well the alternate assumptions regarding transfer and search discussed in the preceding paragraphs are able to fit the data. For this reason, the following four models are compared:[27]

Model I: Transfer to LTS is at a constant rate θ regardless of the number of other items concurrently in the buffer, and independent retrieval.

Model II: Transfer to LTS is at a variable rate θ/j where j is the number of other items currently in the buffer, and independent retrieval.

Model III: Constant LTS transfer rate, and dependent retrieval.

[27] These models and the related mathematics are developed in Atkinson and Shiffrin (1965).

Model IV: Variable LTS transfer rate, and dependent retrieval. Model I, of course, is the model already presented for free-verbal-recall. The four models were all fit to the free-verbal-recall data presented in Table I, and the best fits, in terms of the sums of the squared deviations, were as follows: Model I: .814; Model II: 2.000; Model III: .925; Model IV: 1.602 (the lowest sum meaning the best predictions). These results are of interest because they demonstrate once again the close interdependence of the search and transfer processes. Neither model employing a variable transfer assumption is a good predictor of the data and it seems clear that a model employing this assumption would require a retrieval process quite different from those already considered in order to fit the data reasonably well.

Perhaps the most interesting facet of Model I is its ability to predict performance as the presentation rate varies. A very simple assumption, that transfer to LTS is a linear function of time spent in the buffer, seems to work quite well. Waugh (1967) has reported a series of studies which casts some light on this assumption; in these studies items were repeated a variable number of times within a single free-recall list. The probability of recall was approximately a linear function of the number of repetitions; this effect is roughly consonant with an assumption of LTS transfer which is linear with time. It should be noted that the presentation rates in the experiments we analyzed to not vary too widely: from 1 to 2.5 second per item. The assumption that the subject will adopt a buffer strategy undoubtedly breaks down if a wide enough range in presentation rates is considered. In particular, it can be expected that the subject will make increasing use of coding strategies as the presentation rate decreases. M. Clark and G. Bower (personal communication) for example, have shown that subjects proceeding at their own pace (about 6–12 seconds a word) can learn a list of 10 words almost perfectly. This memorization is accomplished by having the subject make up and visualize a story including the words that are presented. It would be expected that very slow presentation rates in free-recall experiments would lead to coding strategies similar to the one above.

One last feature of the models in this section needs further examination. Contrary to our assumption, it is not true that successive lists can be kept completely isolated from each other at the time of test. The demonstration of this fact is the common finding of intrusion errors: items reported during recall which had been presented on a list previous to the one being tested. Occasionally an intrusion error is even reported which had not been reported correctly during the test of its own list. Over a session using many lists, it might be expected that the interference from previous lists would stay at a more or less constant level after the presentation of the first few lists of the session. Nevertheless, the primacy and asymptotic levels of the free-recall serial position curves should drop somewhat over the first few lists. An effect of this sort is reported by Wing and Thomson (1965) who examined serial position curves for the first, second, and third presented lists of a session. This effect is undoubtedly similar to the one reported by Keppel and Underwood (1962); namely, that performance on the task used by Peterson and Peterson (1959) drops over the first few trials of a session. The effects in both of these experiments may be caused by the increasing difficulty of the search process during test.

C. Further Considerations Involving LTS

The models presented in the last section, while concerned with search and retrieval processes, were nevertheless based primarily upon the concept of a rehearsal buffer. This should not be taken as an indication that rehearsal processes are universally encountered in all memory experiments; to the contrary, a number of conditions must exist before they will be brought into play. It would be desirable at this point then to examine some of the factors that cause a subject to use a rehearsal buffer. In addition, we want to consider a number of points of theoretical interest that arise naturally from the framework developed here. These points include possible extensions of the search mechanisms, relationships between search and interference processes, the usefulness of mnemonics, the relationships between recognition and recall, and coding processes that the subject can use as alternatives to rehearsal schemes.

Consider first the possible forms of search mechanisms and the factors affecting them. Before beginning the discussion two components of the search process should be emphasized: the first component involves locating information about an item in LTS, called the "hit" probability; the second component is the retrieval of a correct response once information has been located. The factor determining the form of the search is the nature of the trace in long-term store. The models considered thus far have postulated two different types of traces. One is an all-or-none trace which allows perfect recall following a hit; the other is an unspecified trace which varies in strength. The strength notion has been used most often because it is amenable to a number of possible interpretations: the strength could represent the "force" with which a particular bond has been formed, the number of bits of information which have been stored, or the number of copies of an item placed in memory. It should be emphasized that these different possibilities imply search processes with different properties. For example, if the strength represents the force of a connection, then it might be assumed that there is an equal chance of hitting any particular item in a search, but the probability of giving a correct answer following a hit would depend upon the strength. On the other hand, the strength might represent the number of all-or-none copies stored in LTS for an item, each copy resulting in a correct response if hit. In this case, the probability of a hit would depend upon the strength (the number of copies) but any hit would automatically result in a correct answer. A possibility intermediate to these two extremes is that partial copies of information are stored for each item, any one partial copy allowing a correct response with an intermediate probability. In this case, the probability of a hit will depend on the number of partial copies, and the probability of a correct response following a hit will depend on the particular copy that has been found. A different version of this model would assume that all the partial copies for an item become available whenever any one copy is hit; in this version the probability of a correct answer after a hit would depend on the full array of copies stored for that item. In all the search processes where the retrieval probability following a hit is at an intermediate level, one must decide whether successive hits of that item will result in independent retrieval probabilities. It could be assumed, for example, that failure to uncover a correct response the first time an item is hit in the search would mean that the correct response could not be recovered on subsequent hits of that item.[28] This outline of some selected search processes indicates the variety of possibilities; a variety which makes it extremely difficult to isolate effects due to search processes from those attributable to interference mechanisms.

Other factors affecting the form of the search are at least partially controlled by the subject; a possible example concerns whether or not the searches are made with replacement. Questions of this sort are based upon the fact that all searches are made in a more or less ordered fashion; memory is much too large for a completely random search to be feasible. One ordering which is commonly used involves associations: each item recovered leads to an associate which in turn leads to another associate. The subject presumably exercises control over which associates are chosen at each stage of the search and also injects a new starting item whenever a particular sequence is not proving successful.[29] An alternative to the associate method is a search along some partially ordered dimension. Examples are easy to find; the subject could generate letters of the

[28] For a discussion of partial and multiple copy models, see Atkinson and Shiffrin (1965).

[29] Associative search schemes have been examined rather extensively using free-recall methods. Clustering has been examined by Deese (1959), Bousfield (1953), Cofer (1966), Tulving (1962), and others; the usual technique is to determine whether or not closely associated words tend to be reported together. The effect certainly exists, but a lack of parametric data makes it difficult to specify the actual search process involved.

alphabet, considering each in turn as a possible first letter of the desired response. A more general ordered search is one that is made along a temporal dimension; items may be time-tagged or otherwise temporally ordered, and the subject searches only among those items that fall within a particular time span. This hypothesis would explain the fact that performance does not markedly deteriorate even at the end of memory experiments employing many different lists, such as in the free-verbal-recall paradigm. In these cases, the subject is required to respond only with members of the most recent list; if performance is not to degenerate as successive lists are presented, the memory search must be restricted along the temporal dimension to those items recently stored in LTS. Yntema and Trask (1963) have demonstrated that temporal information is available over relatively long time periods (in the form of "time-tags" in their formulation) but the storage of such information is not well understood.

We now turn to a brief discussion of some issues related to interference effects. It is difficult to determine whether time alone can result in long-term interference. Nevertheless, to the extent that subjects engage in a search based upon the temporal order of items, interference due to the passage of time should be expected. Interference due to intervening material may take several forms. First, there may be a reduction in the value of certain information already in LTS as a result of the entry of new information; the loss in this case does not depend on making any previous information less accessible. An example would be if a subject first stores "the simulus beginning with D has response 3" and later when another stimulus beginning with D is presented, he stores "the stimulus beginning with D has response 1." The probability of a correct response will clearly drop following storage of the second trace even though access to both traces may occur at test. Alternatively, interference effects may involve destruction of particular information through interaction with succeeding input. This possibility is often examined experimentally using a paired-associate paradigm where the same stimulus is assigned different responses at different times. DaPolito (1966) has analyzed performance in such a situation. A stimulus was presented with two different responses at different times, and at test the subject was asked to recall both responses. The results indicated that the probability of recalling the first response, multiplied by the probability of recalling the second response, equals the joint probability that both responses will be given correctly. This result would be expected if there was no interaction of the two traces; it indicates that high strengths of one trace will not automatically result in low strengths on the other. The lack of an interaction in DaPolito's experiment may be due to the fact that subjects knew they would be tested on both responses. It is interesting to note that there are search mechanisms that can explain this independence effect and at the same time interference effects. For example, storage for the two items might be completely independent as suggested by DaPolito's data; however, in the typical recall task the subject may occasionally terminate his search for information about the second response prematurely as a result of finding information on the first response.

Within the context of interference and search processes, it is interesting to speculate about the efficacy of mnemonics and special coding techniques. It was reported, for example, that forming a visual image of the two words in a paired-associate item is a highly effective memory device; that is, one envisages a situation involving the two words. Such a mnemonic gains an immediate advantage through the use of two long-term systems, visual and auditory, rather than one. However, this cannot be the whole explanation. Another possibility is that the image performs the function of a mediator, thereby reducing the set of items to be searched; that is, the stimulus word when presented for test leads naturally to the image which in turn leads to the response. This explanation is probably not relevant in the case of the visual-image mnemonic for the following reason: the technique usually works best if the image is a very strange one. For example, "dog-concrete" could be imaged as a dog buried to the neck in concrete; when "dog" is tested, there is no previously well-learned association that would lead to this image. Another explanation involves the protection of the stored information over time; as opposed to the original word pairs, each image may be stored in LTS as a highly distinct entity. A last possibility is that the amount of information stored is greatly increased through the use of imagery—many more details exist in the image than in the word pair. Since the image is highly cohesive, the recovery of any information relevant to it would lead to the recovery of the whole image. These hypotheses are of course only speculations. At the present time the relation of the various search schemes and interference processes to mnemonic devices is not well understood. This state of affairs hopefully will change in the near future since more research is being directed toward these areas; mediation, in particular, has been receiving extensive consideration (e.g., Bugelski, 1962; Runquist & Farley, 1964).

Search processes seem at first glance to offer an easy means for the analysis of differences between recognition and recall. One could assume, for example, that in recall the search component which attempts to locate information on a given item in LTS is not part of the recognition process; that is, one might assume that in recognition the relevant information in LTS is always found and retrieval depends solely on matching the stored information against the item presented for test.

Our analysis of free-verbal recall depended in part upon the search component to explain the drop in performance as list length increased. Thus if the free recall task were modified so that recognition tests were used, the decrement in performance with list length might not occur. That this will not be the case is indicated by the position-to-color memory study (Experiment 8) in which the number of responses was small enough that the task was essentially one of recognition; despite this fact, the performance dropped as list length increased. One possible explanation would be that search is necessary even for recognition tasks; i.e., if the word "clown" is presented, all previous times that that word had been stored in LTS do not immediately spring to mind. To put this another way, one may be asked if a clown was a character in a particular book and it is necessary to search for the appropriate information, even though the question is one of recognition. On the other hand, we cannot rule out the possibility that part of the decrement in performance in free recall with the increase of list length may be due to search changes, and part to other interference mechanisms. Obviously a great deal of extra information is given to the subject in a recognition test, but the effect of this information upon search and interference mechanisms is not yet clear.

We now turn to a consideration of LTS as it is affected by short-term processes other than the rehearsal buffer. It has been pointed out that the extent and structure of rehearsal depends upon a large number of factors such as the immediacy of test and difficulty of long-term storage. When rehearsal schemes are not used in certain tasks, often it is because long-term coding operations are more efficacious. These coding processes are presumably found in most paired-associate learning paradigms; depending upon conditions, however, the subject will probably divide his attention between coding and rehearsal. Atkinson and Shiffrin (1965) have presented a paired-associate learning model based upon a rehearsal-buffer. Whether a rehearsal strategy would be adopted by the subject in a given paired-associate learning experiment needs to be determined in each case. The answer is probably no for the typical fixed-list learning experiment, because the items are usually amenable to coding, because the test procedure emphasizes the importance of LTS storage, and because short study-test intervals are so infrequent that maintenance of an item in STS is not a particularly effective device. If these conditions are changed, however, then a paired-associate model based upon a rehearsal buffer might prove applicable.

It is important to note the distinction between coding models and rehearsal models. Rehearsal models actually encompass, in a rough sense, virtually all short-term processes. Coding, for example, may be considered as a type of rehearsal involving a single item. The buffer process is a special type of rehearsal in which a fixed number of items are rehearsed for the primary purpose of maintaining them in STS. A pure coding process is one in which only a single item is considered at a time and in which the primary purpose is the generation of a strong LTS trace; almost incidentally, the item being coded will be maintained in STS through the duration of the coding period, but this is not a primary purpose of the process. These various processes, it should be emphasized, are under subject control and are brought into play as he sees fit; consequently there are many variations that the subject can employ under appropriate conditions. One could have a coding model, for example, in which more than one item is being coded at a time, or a combination model in which several items are maintained via rehearsal while one of the items is selected for special coding.

At the other extreme from the buffer strategy, it might be instructive to consider a coding process that acts upon one item at a time. Although such a process can be viewed as a buffer model with a buffer containing only one item, the emphasis will be upon LTS storage rather than upon the maintenance of the item in STS. The simplest case occurs when the presentation rate is fairly slow and the subject attempts to code each item as it is presented for study. However, the case that seems most likely for the typical paired-associate experiment, is that in which not every item is coded, or in which it takes several presentation periods to code a single item. The first case above could be conceptualized as follows: each item is given a coding attempt during its presentation interval, but the probability of finding a code is ξ. The second case is a bit more complex. One version would have a single item maintained in STS over trials until a code is found. It could be supposed that the probability of a code being found during a single presentation interval is ξ; having once coded an item, coding attempts are focused on the next presented item. This model has something in common with the buffer models in that some items will remain in STS over a period of several trials. This will produce a short-term decay effect as the interval between presentation and test is increased.

It is worth considering the form of the usual short-term effects that are found in a paired-associate learning. Figure 29 presents data from a paired-associate experiment by Bjork (1966). Graphed is the probability of a correct response for an item prior to its last error, as a function of the number of other items intervening between its study and subsequent test. The number of intervening items that must occur before this curve reaches the chance level can be taken as a measure of the extent of the short-term effect. It can be seen that the curve does not reach chance level until after about 20 items have been presented. If the coding model mentioned above were applied to this data, a short-term effect would be

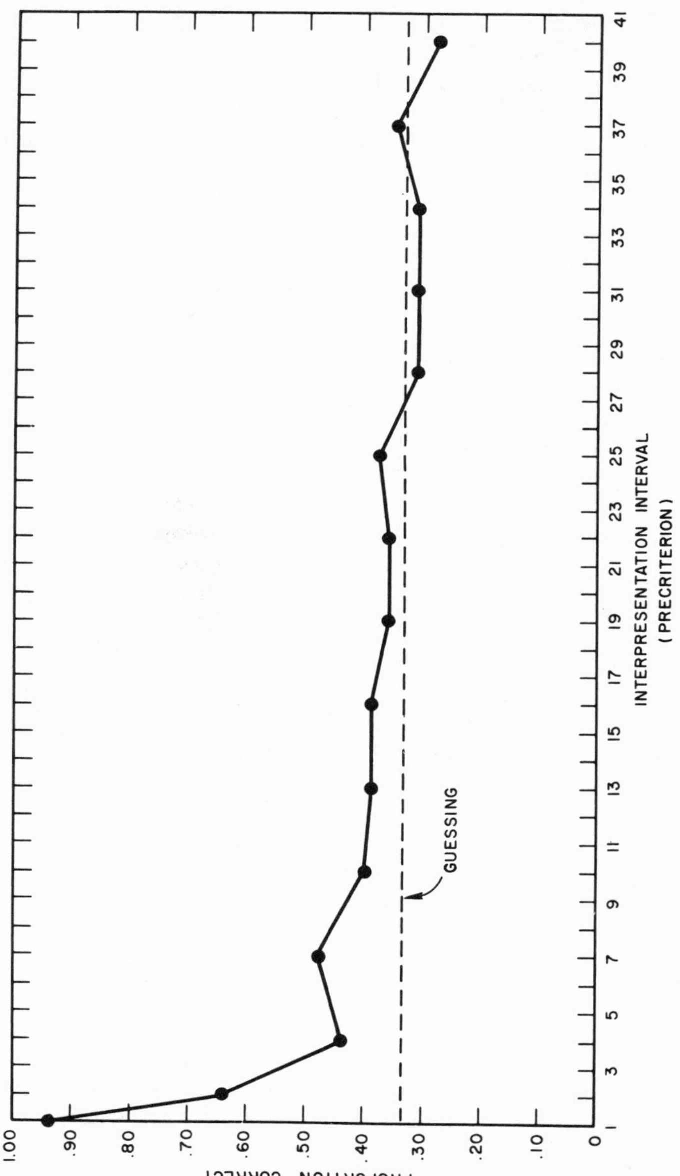

FIG. 29. Probability of a correct response prior to the last error as a function of lag. After Bjork (1966).

predicted due to the fact that some items are kept in STS for more than one trial for coding. It hardly seems likely, however, that any item will be kept in STS for 20 trials in an attempt to code it. Considerations of this sort have led a number of workers to consider other sources for the "short-term" effect. One possibility would be that the effect is based in LTS and is due to retroactive interference. A model in which this notion has been formalized was set forth by Restle (1964) and subsequently developed by Greeno (1967). For our purposes Greeno's presentation is more appropriate. He proposes that a particular code may be categorized as "good" or "bad." A good code is permanent and will not be interfered with by the other materials presented in the experiment. A bad code will be retrievable from LTS for a time, but will be subject to interference from succeeding items and will eventually be useless. Employing this model, the short-term effects displayed in Fig. 29 are due to those items that were assigned bad codes (i.e., codes that were effective for only a short period of time). The interesting feature of this model is its inclusion of a short-term memory effect based not upon features of STS, but upon processes in LTS.[30] One other useful way in which this LTS interference process has been viewed employs Estes' stimulus fluctuation theory (Estes, 1955a, 1955b). In this view, elements of information in LTS sometimes become unavailable; it differs from the above models in that an unavailable element may become available again at a later time. In this sense, fluctuation theory parallels a number of the processes that are expected from search considerations. In any case, the theory has been successfully applied in a variety of situations (Izawa, 1966). There is a great deal more that can be said about paired-associate learning and long-term processes in general, but it is beyond the scope of this paper to enter into these matters. We should like to reemphasize, however, the point that has just been made; namely, that short-term decay effects may arise from processes based in LTS as well as mechanisms in STS; considerable care must be taken in the analysis of each experimental situation in order to make a correct identification of the processes at play.

VI. Concluding Remarks

The first three sections of this paper outlined a fairly comprehensive theoretical framework for memory which emphasized the role of control processes—processes under the voluntary control of the subject such as

[30] It is this short-term effect that is probably captured by the intermediate state in various Markov models for paired-associate learning (Atkinson & Crothers, 1964; Bernbach, 1965; Bjork, 1966; Calfee & Atkinson, 1965; Kintsch, 1965, 1967; Young, 1966). Theorists using these models have been somewhat noncommital regarding the psychological rationale for this intermediate state, but the estimated transition probabilities to and from the state suggest to us that it represents effects taking place in LTS.

rehearsal, coding, and search strategies. It was argued that these control processes are such a pervasive and integral component of human memory that a theory which hopes to achieve any degree of generality must take them into account. Our theoretical system has proved productive of experimental idea. In Sections IV and V a particular realization of the general system involving a rehearsal buffer was applied to data from a variety of experiments. The theoretical predictions were, for the most part, quite accurate, proving satisfactory even when based upon previously estimated parameter values. It was possible to predict data over a range of experimental tasks and a wide variety of independent variables such as stimulus-set size, number of reinforcements, rehearsal procedures, list length, and presentation rate. Perhaps even more impressive are the number of predictions generated by the theory which ran counter to our initial intuitions but were subsequently verified.

It should be emphasized that the specific experimental models we have considered do not represent a general theory of the memory system but rather a subclass of possible models that can be generated by the framework proposed in the first half of the paper. Paired-associate learning, for example, might best be described by models emphasizing control processes other than rehearsal. These models could be formulated in directions suggested by stimulus sampling theory (Estes, 1955a, 1955b, 1968), models stressing cue selection and coding (Greeno, 1967; Restle, 1964), or queuing models (Bower, 1967b).

Finally, it should be noted that most of the ideas in this paper date back many years to an array of investigators: Broadbent (1957, 1958) and Estes (1955a, 1968) in particular have influenced the development of our models. The major contribution of this paper probably lies in the organization of results and the analysis of data; in fact, theoretical research could not have been carried out in the manner reported here as little as 12 years ago. Although conceptually the theory is not very difficult to understand, many of our analyses would have proved too complex to investigate without the use of modern, high-speed computers.

References

Atkinson, R. C., Brelsford, J. W., Jr., & Shiffrin, R. M. Multi-process models for memory with applications to a continuous presentation task. *Journal of Mathematical Psychology*, 1967, **4**, 277–300.

Atkinson, R. C., & Crothers, E. J. A comparison of paired-associate learning models having different acquisition and retention axioms. *Journal of Mathematical Psychology*, 1964, **1**, 285–315.

Atkinson, R. C., & Shiffrin, R. M. Mathematical models for memory and learning. Technical Report No. 79, Institute for Mathematical Studies in the Social Sciences, Stanford University, 1965. (To be published in D. P. Kimble (Ed.), *Proceedings of the third conference on learning, remembering and forgetting*. New York: New York Academy of Sciences.)

Averbach, E., & Coriell, A. S. Short-term memory in vision. *Bell System Technical Journal*, 1961, **40**, 309–328.

Averbach, E., & Sperling, G. Short-term storage of information in vision. In C. Cherry (Ed.), *Information theory*. London and Washington, D.C.: Butterworth, 1961. Pp. 196–211.

Barbizet, J. Defect of memorizing of hippocampal-mammillary origin: A review. *Journal of Neurology, Neurosurgery, and Psychiatry*, 1963, **26**, 127–135.

Battig, W. F. Evidence for coding processes in "rote" paired-associate learning. *Journal of Verbal Learning and Verbal Behavior*, 1966, **5**, 171–181.

Bernbach, H. A. A forgetting model for paired-associate learning. *Journal of Mathematical Psychology*, 1965, **2**, 128–144.

Bernbach, H. A. Decision processes in memory. *Psychological Review*, 1967, **74**, 462–480.

Binford, J. R., & Gettys, C. Nonstationarity in paired-associate learning as indicated by a second guess procedure. *Journal of Mathematical Psychology*, 1965, **2**, 190–195.

Bjork, R. A. Learning and short-term retention of paired-associates in relation to specific sequences of interpresentation intervals. Technical Report No. 106, Institute for Mathematical Studies in the Social Sciences, Stanford University, 1966.

Bousfield, W. A. The occurrence of clustering in the recall of randomly arranged associates. *Journal of General Psychology*, 1953, **49**, 229–240.

Bower, G. H. Application of a model to paired-associate learning. *Psychometrika*, 1961, **26**, 255–280.

Bower, G. H. A multicomponent theory of the memory trace. In K. W. Spence and J. T. Spence (Eds.), *The psychology of learning and motivation: Advances in research and theory*, Vol. I. New York: Academic Press, 1967. Pp. 229–325. (a)

Bower, G. H. A descriptive theory of memory. In D. P. Kimble (Ed.), *Proceedings of the second conference on learning, remembering and forgetting*. New York: New York Academy of Sciences, 1967. Pp. 112–185. (b)

Brelsford, J. W., Jr., Shiffrin, R. M., & Atkinson, R. C. Multiple reinforcement effects in short-term memory. *British Journal of Mathematical and Statistical Psychology*, 1968, in press.

Brelsford, J. W., Jr., & Atkinson, R. C. Short-term memory as a function of rehearsal procedures. *Journal of Verbal Learning and Verbal Behavior*, 1968, in press.

Brelsford, J. W., Jr., Keller, L., Shiffrin, R. M., & Atkinson, R. C. Short-term recall of paired-associates as a function of the number of interpolated pairs. *Psychonomic Science*, 1966, **4**, 73–74.

Broadbent, D. E. The role of auditory localization in attention and memory span. *Journal of Experimental Psychology*, 1954, **47**, 191–196.

Broadbent, D. E. Successive responses to simultaneous stimuli. *Quarterly Journal of Experimental Psychology*, 1956, **8**, 145–152.

Broadbent, D. E. A mechanical model for human attention and immediate memory. *Psychological Review*, 1957, **64**, 205–215.

Broadbent, D. E. *Perception and communication*. Oxford: Pergamon Press, 1958.

Broadbent, D. E. Flow of information within the organism. *Journal of Verbal Learning and Verbal Behavior*, 1963, **4**, 34–39.

Brown, J. Some tests of decay theory of immediate memory. *Quarterly Journal of Experimental Psychology*, 1958, **10**, 12–21.

Brown, R., & McNeill, D. The "tip of the tongue" phenomenon. *Journal of Verbal Learning and Verbal Behavior*, 1966, **5**, 325–337.

Bugelski, B. R. Presentation time, total time, and mediation in paired-associate learning. *Journal of Experimental Psychology*, 1962, **63**, 409–412.

Buschke, H. Retention in immediate memory estimated without retrieval. *Science*, 1963, **140**, 56–57.

Buschke, H., & Lim, H. Temporal and interactional effects in short-term storage. *Perception and Psychophysics*, 1967, **2**, 107–114.

Calfee, R. C., & Atkinson, R. C. Paired-associate models and the effects of list length. *Journal of Mathematical Psychology*, 1965, **2**, 254–265.

Cofer, C. N. Some evidence for coding processes derived from clustering in free recall. *Journal of Verbal Learning and Verbal Behavior*, 1966, **5**, 188–192.

Cohen, B. H. Recall of categorized word lists. *Journal of Experimental Psychology*, 1963, **66**, 227–234.

Cohen, R. L., & Johansson, B. S. The activity trace in immediate memory; a reevaluation. *Journal of Verbal Learning and Verbal Behavior*, 1967, **6**, 139–143.

Conrad, R. Acoustic confusions in immediate memory. *British Journal of Psychology*, 1964, **55**, 1, 75–84.

Conrad, R., & Hille, B. A. The decay theory of immediate memory and paced recall. *Canadian Journal of Psychology*, 1958, **12**, 1–6.

DaPolito, F. J. Proactive effects with independent retrieval of competing responses. Unpublished doctoral dissertation, Indiana University, 1966.

Deese, J. Influence of inter-item associative strength upon immediate free recall. *Psychological Reports*, 1959, **5**, 305–312.

Deese, J., & Kaufman, R. A. Serial effects in recall of unorganized and sequentially organized verbal material. *Journal of Experimental Psychology*, 1957, **54**, 180–187.

Estes, W. K. Statistical theory of distributional phenomena in learning. *Psychological Review*, 1955, **62**, 369–377. (a)

Estes, W. K. Statistical theory of spontaneous recovery and regression. *Psychological Review*, 1955, **62**, 145–154. (b)

Estes, W. K. A technique for assessing variability of perceptual span. *Proceedings of the National Academy of Sciences of the U.S.*, 1965, **4**, 403–407.

Estes, W. K. Reinforcement in human learning. In J. Tapp (Ed.), *Current problems in reinforcement*. New York: Academic Press, 1968, in press.

Estes, W. K., & Taylor, H. A. A detection method and probabilistic models for assessing information processing from brief visual displays. *Proceedings of the National Academy of Sciences of the U.S.*, 1964, **52**, No. 2, 446–454.

Estes, W. K., & Taylor, H. A. Visual detection in relation to display size and redundancy of critical elements. *Perception and Psychophysics*, 1966, **1**, 9–16.

Estes, W. K., & Wessel, D. L. Reaction time in relation to display size and correctness of response in forced-choice visual signal detection. *Perception and Psychophysics*, 1966, **1**, 369–373.

Freedman, J. L., & Landauer, T. K. Retrieval of long-term memory: "Tip-of-the-tongue" phenomenon. *Psychonomic Science*, 1966, **4**, 309–310.

Greeno, J. G. Paired-associate learning with short-term retention: Mathematical analysis and data regarding identification of parameters. *Journal of Mathematical Psychology*, 1967, **4**, 430–472.

Harley, W. F., Jr. The effect of monetary incentive in paired-associate learning using a differential method. *Psychonomic Science*, 1965, **2**, 377–378. (a)

Harley, W. F., Jr. The effect of monetary incentive in paired-associate learning using an absolute method. *Psychonomic Science*, 1965, **3**, 141–142. (b)

Hart, J. T., Jr. Recall, recognition, and the memory-monitoring process. Unpublished doctoral dissertation, Stanford University, 1965.

Hebb, D. O. Distinctive features of learning in the higher animal. In J. F. Delafresnaye (Ed.), *Brain mechanisms and learning.* London and New York: Oxford University Press, 1961. Pp. 37–46.

Hellyer, S. Supplementary report: Frequency of stimulus presentation and short-term decrement in recall. *Journal of Experimental Psychology*, 1962, **64**, 650–651.

Hintzman, D. L. Classification and aural coding in short-term memory. *Psychonomic Science*, 1965, **3**, 161–162.

Hintzman, D. L. Articulatory coding in short-term memory. *Journal of Verbal Learning and Verbal Behavior*, 1967, **6**, 312–316.

Izawa, C. Reinforcement-test sequences in paired-associate learning. *Psychological Reports*, Monograph Supplement, 3-V18, 1966, 879–919.

Katz, L. A technique for the study of steady-state short-term memory. *Psychonomic Science*, 1966, **4**, 361–362.

Keppel, G., & Underwood, B. J. Proactive inhibition in short-term retention of single items. *Journal of Verbal Learning and Verbal Behavior*, 1962, **1**, 153–161.

Kintsch, W. Habituation of the GSR component of the orienting reflex during paired-associate learning before and after learning has taken place. *Journal of Mathematical Psychology*, 1965, **2**, 330–341.

Kintsch, W. Memory and decision aspects of recognition learning. *Psychological Review*, 1967, **74**, 496–504.

Lambert, W. E., & Jakobovitz, L. A. Verbal satiation and changes in the intensity of meaning. *Journal of Experimental Psychology*, 1960, **60**, 376–383.

Landauer, T. K. Rate of implicit speech. *Perceptual and Motor Skills*, 1962, **15**, 646–647.

Madsen, M. E., & Drucker, J. M. Immediate memory by missing scan and modified digit span. *Psychonomic Science*, 1966, **6**, 283–284.

Melton, A. W. Implications of short-term memory for a general theory of memory. *Journal of Verbal Learning and Verbal Behavior*, 1963, **2**, 1–21.

Miller, G. A. The magical number seven, plus or minus two: Some limits on our capacity for processing information. *Psychological Review*, 1956, **63**, 81–97.

Milner, B. The memory defect in bilateral hippocampal lesions. *Psychiatric Research Reports*, 1959, **11**, 43–58.

Milner, B. Neuropsychological evidence for differing memory processes. Abstract for the symposium on short-term and long-term memory. *Proceedings of the 18th international congress of psychology, Moscow*, 1966. Amsterdam: North-Holland Publ., 1968, in press.

Milner, B. Amnesia following operation on the temporal lobes. In O. L. Zangwill and C. W. M. Whitty (Eds.), *Amnesia.* London and Washington, D.C.: Butterworth, 1967. Pp. 109–133.

Montague, W. E., Adams, J. A., & Kiess, H. O. Forgetting and natural language mediation. *Journal of Experimental Psychology*, 1966, **72**, 829–833.

Murdock, B. B., Jr. The serial position effect of free recall. *Journal of Experimental Psychology*, 1962, **64**, 482–488.

Murdock, B. B., Jr. Effects of a subsidiary task on short-term memory. *British Journal of Psychology*, 1965, **56**, 413–419.

Murdock, B. B., Jr. The criterion problem in short-term memory. *Journal of Experimental Psychology*, 1966, **72**, 317–324.

Peterson, L. R. Short-term verbal memory and learning. *Psychological Review*, 1966, **73**, 193–207. (a)

Peterson, L. R. Short-term memory. *Scientific American*, 1966, **215**, 90–95. (b)

Peterson, L. R., & Peterson, M. Short-term retention of individual verbal items. *Journal of Experimental Psychology*, 1959, **58**, 193–198.

Peterson, L. R., Wampler, R., Kirkpatrick, M., & Saltzman, D. Effect of spacing presentations on retention of a paired-associate over short intervals. *Journal of Experimental Psychology*, 1963, **66**, 206–209.

Phillips, J. L., Shiffrin, R. M., & Atkinson, R. C. The effects of list length on short-term memory. *Journal of Verbal Learning and Verbal Behavior*, 1967, **6**, 303–311.

Posner, M. I. Components of skilled performance. *Science*, 1966, **152**, 1712–1718.

Postman, L. The present status of interference theory. In C. N. Cofer (Ed.), *Verbal learning and verbal behavior*. New York: McGraw-Hill, 1961. Pp. 152–179.

Postman, L. Does interference theory predict too much forgetting? *Journal of Verbal Learning and Verbal Behavior*, 1963, **2**, 40–48.

Postman, L. Short-term memory and incidental learning. In A. W. Melton (Ed.), *Categories of human learning*. New York: Academic Press, 1964. Pp. 145–201.

Postman, L., & Phillips, L. W. Short-term temporal changes in free recall. *Quarterly Journal of Experimental Psychology*, 1965, **17**, 132–138.

Restle, F. Sources of difficulty in learning paired associates. In R. C. Atkinson (Ed.), *Studies in mathematical psychology*. Stanford, Calif.: Stanford University Press, 1964. Pp. 116–172.

Runquist, W. N., & Farley, F. H. The use of mediators in the learning of verbal paired associates. *Journal of Verbal Learning and Verbal Behavior*, 1964, **3**, 280–285.

Sperling, G. The information available in brief visual presentations. *Psychology Monographs*, 1960, **74** (Whole No. 498).

Sperling, G. A model for visual memory tasks. *Human Factors*, 1963, **5**, 19–31.

Sperling, G. Successive approximations to a model for short-term memory. *Acta Psychologica*, 1967, **27**, 285–292.

Sternberg, S. High speed scanning in human memory. *Science*, 1966, **153**, 652–654.

Tulving, E. Subjective organization in free recall of "unrelated" words. *Psychological Review*, 1962, **69**, 344–354.

Underwood, B. J., & Ekstrund, B. R. Studies of distributed practice: XXIV. Differentiation and proactive inhibition. *Journal of Experimental Psychology*, 1967, **74**, 574–580.

Waugh, N. C. Presentation time and free recall. *Journal of Experimental Psychology*, 1967, **73**, 39–44.

Waugh, N. C., & Norman, D. A. Primary memory. *Psychological Review*, 1965, **72**, 89–104.

Wickelgren, W. A. Size of rehearsal group and short-term memory. *Journal of Experimental Psychology*, 1965, **68**, 413–419.

Wickelgren, W. A., & Norman, D. A. Strength models and serial position in short-term recognition memory. *Journal of Mathematical Psychology*, 1966, **3**, 316–347.

Wing, J. F., & Thomson, B. P. Primacy-recency effects in free recall. *Proceedings of the* 1965 *annual convention of the American Psychological Association*. Pp. 57–58.

Yntema, D. B., & Mueser, G. E. Remembering the present state of a number of variables. *Journal of Experimental Psychology*, 1960, **60**, 18–22.

Yntema, D. B., & Mueser, G. E. Keeping track of variables that have few or many states. *Journal of Experimental Psychology*, 1962, **63**, 391–395.

Yntema, D. B., & Trask, F. P. Recall as a search process. *Journal of Verbal Learning and Verbal Behavior*, 1963, **2**, 65–74.

Young, J. L. Effects of intervals between reinforcements and test trials in paired-associate learning. Technical Report No. 101, Institute for Mathematical Studies in the Social Sciences, Stanford University, 1966.

MEDIATION AND CONCEPTUAL BEHAVIOR[1]

Howard H. Kendler and Tracy S. Kendler

UNIVERSITY OF CALIFORNIA,
SANTA BARBARA, CALIFORNIA

Psychology has its fashions and fads. Its entire history has been punctuated by the appearance of theorists and methodologists, who if they did not act like messiahs were at least perceived as such. Repeatedly psychologists have been offered methodological prescriptions and eternal truths that, if taken and accepted, would lead to the promised land where behavior would be both comprehensible and controllable. For discussion purposes we can assign the role of messiah to such recent intellectual leaders as Hull, Tolman, and Wertheimer. We all know these "messiahs" failed but the extent of their failures is debatable. If one surgically dissects their ideas in isolation from the historical context from which they emerged, and the range of phenomena for which they were intended, their failures are magnified. However, if their efforts are

[1] The preparation of this paper was facilitated by the following grants: National Science Foundation grant GB-1447, Office of Naval Research Contract Nonr-4222(04), and Public Health Service grant HD-01361. Appreciation is expressed to the following graduate students who are currently participating in this research program: Barbara Basden, Linda Fry, Eber Hampton, and George Watson.

viewed within the framework of a developing and expanding empirical science, their successes become more apparent and their failures more understandable.

Regardless of how we view the contributions of the "messiahs," a general reaction against them and their style was adopted about two decades ago by large segments of the psychological community. With it came a more realistic appraisal of the state of psychological theory and knowledge, but this realism failed to dim the persistent hope among psychologists that some innovation would transform our disorderly array of facts into some systematic consistency. As a result, the search for a global theory was redirected into a pursuit of some method or idea or gadget that would prove our salvation. In short, we did not abandon our search for salvation, we merely sought it in a different place.

Mathematical models, operant conditioning, information theory, decision processes, transformational grammar, computer simulation, attention, and mediation were some of the concepts and ideas that attracted the allegiance and energy of sizable groups of psychologists in their pursuit of systematizing some problem areas of psychology. We would like to discuss the last concept, mediation, not because it is distinguished by powerful techniques or unique methods that will lead psychology to the promised land, but because it is a particularly effective vehicle for focusing on problems that have *both* empirical and theoretical significance.

I. The Meaning of Mediation

A discussion of mediation raises several difficulties. It does not represent a highly articulated system. It possesses neither a leading spokesman nor a specific methodology. It does not represent a revolutionary innovation or an extension of a single traditional approach. And finally, the term *mediation* is vague simply because it has been used in a variety of ways. In order to reach firm ground upon which experimental results can be presented, we would like to start clarifying the term mediation by first dismissing some trivial and misleading conceptions.

The concept of mediation, can be, and often is, assigned to any position that assumes that there are intervening physiological or theoretical processes operating between an organism's environment and his behavior. To equate mediation with this global view makes the concept as simple as it is empty. Obviously a body, with receptors, a central nervous system, and effectors, intervenes between stimulation and behavior. Equally obvious is the possibility of postulating intervening theoretical mechanisms to account for the behavior of organisms. As we see it, the purpose of a *mediational* conception (note the indefinite article) is not to acknowledge the influence of physiological processes on behavior, or the feasibility of formulating a behavior theory, but instead to systematize environmental-behavior relationships in order to integrate and predict the facts of psychology. Even the most extreme "black box" psychologist would not deny the existence of blood and guts, or even nerve cells. He may question the wisdom of considering them when analyzing behavior, but he certainly does not deny their existence. Similarly, the antitheoretical radical positivist does not deny the possibility of hypothesizing intervening processes; he merely questions the strategy of doing so. Thus we would dismiss the general intervening conception of mediation as being trivial. It packs so much into the mediational framework that nothing is really excluded. It is our contention that mediational theory achieves significance only in comparison to an articulated nonmediational formulation.

An example of this sort of overgeneralized mediational formulation is the S-O-R conception of stimulus-response psychology. Our intention is not to be critical of Dashiell (1928) and Woodworth (1958) because their espousal of the S-O-R formulation had some significance in that they were arguing for the inclusion of certain processes, such as *set*, which they felt were being ignored. But we do not think the S-O-R formulation represents an important model of a mediational formulation. Let us examine it briefly.

Woodworth insisted upon enlarging the S-R paradigm to include an intervening link, the organism (O), because "The O inserted between S and R makes explicit the obvious role of the living and active organism in the process; O receives the stimulus and makes the response. This formula suggests that psychologists should not limit their investigations to the input of stimuli and the output of motor responses. They should ask how the input of stimuli can possibly give rise to the output; they should observe intervening processes if possible or at least hypothesize them and devise experiments for testing the hypothesis" (Woodworth, 1958, p. 31).

The basic point here is obvious; variations in behavior are not perfectly correlated to variations in stimuli. The solution is to identify these intervening processes or postulate intervening variables, as did Tolman and Hull. But as has already been suggested, this line of reasoning is primarily methodological rather than substantive.

In a certain sense Watson and, perhaps to a lesser extent, Hull, represent a halfway point between a global, methodologically oriented mediational approach and a substantive, experimentally oriented mediational conception.

Without trying in any way to disparage the contributions of John B. Watson, it should be recognized that he was primarily a methodologist, and only secondarily an empiricist. His attempt to formulate a theory of thought based on mediated implicit speech movements did not result from empirical considerations but instead emerged from his persistent concern with translating subjective psychological problems into objective experimental procedures. His mediational theory had its roots in methodological considerations, not empirical ones. Although Watson's views may be important in the historical analysis (Goss, 1961) of psychological mediation, it failed to lead to any systematic findings on which a mediational theory could be based.

Although Clark Hull's mediational formulation with its emphasis on the r_g-s_g mechanism was more precise and had a firmer empirical base than Watson's peripheralistic analysis of thought, it nevertheless resembled Watson's conception in that it was primarily polemic. Whereas Watson was concerned with persuading the public that subjective psychological problems could be experimentally attacked by objective experimental techniques, Hull was interested in demonstrating to psychologists how principles of conditioning could be applied to complex problem-solving behavior. In both cases the mediational process served as a device to demonstrate the generality of an approach. The mediational mechanism did not emerge from the demands of an ongoing research program but instead from the methodological and theoretical challenges of opposing viewpoints. It is interesting and somewhat amusing (or perhaps depressing) to note that one of the most ingenious applications of his mediational anticipatory goal response mechanism was applied to a phenomenon that probably does not exist.

In 1935 and again in 1952 Hull offered an explanation of insightful problem-solving. He began by defining the behavior in question as the ability of organisms to produce novel combinations of behavior segments suitable for problem solution. The theoretical mechanism that purportedly mediated this behavior was the anticipatory goal response (r_g) which produced a stimulus (s_g) that tended to elicit the correct initial response segment leading to problem solution. The theory seemed to be designed to meet the challenge presented by Maier's demonstration that rats could "reason" (1929). To illustrate his theory Hull designed an experimental paradigm made up of runways typical of rat research. It was characteristic of him not to be satisfied merely to show, as Watson may have been, that it is possible for his theory to cope with intelligent behavior. Instead, he provided a number of deductions about subsidiary behavior in the alleys that would test the validity of his premises. The logic of the analysis has been criticized (Deutsch, 1956), but it is even more embarrassing to the formulation that subsequent experiments by

Koronakos (1959) and Gough (1962) show that rats do not produce the anticipated insightful solutions. When the same experimental paradigm was adapted to children we found that the probability of such solutions was very low in children 5 years of age but increased monotonically with age (T. S. Kendler & Kendler, 1967).

The discrepancy between his theory and the facts did not faze Hull because he viewed his efforts more as a theoretical exercise than as an attempt to explain a specific experimental fact. The problem for him was to invent a theoretical mechanism, based on conditioning principles, that could explain inferential behavior of the sort that was reported by Maier. If rats were incapable of such behavior the theory would still have relevance for those organisms (e.g., monkeys, humans) who could infer.

The reason we cite the extraempirical considerations that encouraged Watson and Hull to adopt their particular brand of mediational formulation is not to question their efforts (in our estimation it is extremely difficult to formulate compelling arguments *against* any general research strategy), but instead to identify an historical characteristic associated with mediational formulation. And this characteristic is that mediational formulations have been generated primarily to illustrate the generality of particular methodological and theoretical approaches.

Times have changed, however. A more pragmatic concern with methodology and theory has encouraged contemporary researchers to view mediation primarily within an empirical framework. Contemporary mediational formulations possess three major characteristics. First, mediational theory has an external structure to surround the mediational mechanism. In other words, there is something to mediate between. Second, there are *specific* mediational mechanisms. Although mediation is a general term, experimental results are providing information about the psychological characteristics of mediational mechanisms. Third, mediational theory has been formulated to apply to systematic sets of data; it has been created by the demands of the data, not the aspirations of the theorist.

The relevance of these three characteristics to our general analysis can be clarified by extending our discussion. The importance of an external framework on which to anchor mediational mechanisms should be obvious if we want to retain some of the common language origins of mediation. One dictionary defines mediation as "The state or action of anything mediating between two things." It is not accidental that mediational conceptions have been associated with the stimulus-response (S-R) approach in this country and classical conditioning theory in Soviet Russia. Both of these approaches involve clear specifications of the independent and dependent variable in psychological experiments.

Stimulus-response language forces its user to represent experimental results in terms of the relationships between S's and R's. Having this external structure allows for the hypothesizing of mediational mechanisms.

According to its three distinguishing characteristics, mediational theory need not be limited to an S-R formulation. In this connection it is interesting to compare the Gestalt conception of the *behavioral environment* with the S-R mediational mechanism. Koffka, in his *Principles of Gestalt Psychology*, offers an interesting anecdote to introduce the concept of *behavioral environment*:

> "On a winter evening amidst a driving snowstorm a man on horseback arrived at an inn, happy to have reached a shelter after hours of riding over the windswept plain on which the blanket of snow had covered all paths and landmarks. The landlord who came to the door viewed the stranger with surprise and asked him whence he came. The man pointed in the direction straight away from the inn, whereupon the landlord, in a tone of awe and wonder, said: 'Do you know that you have ridden across the Lake of Constance?' At which the rider dropped stone dead at his feet." (Koffka, 1935, pp. 27–28.)

The point of this story, aside from its amusing punch line, is to emphasize the difference between the rider's geographical (physical) environment (the lake) and his behavioral environment (a plain). His behavior occurred in the behavioral environment, for if he had known that it was a lake the rider would never have taken that route.

It is doubtful that Koffka fully appreciated the relevance of his story. Not only does the anecdote differentiate between the geographical and behavioral environments, but it also directs our attention to a possible source of difficulty. Koffka attributes the death of the stranger to "sheer fright" after learning that he risked his life when riding over a frozen lake. The fear is inferred from his sudden collapse. But perhaps the death had nothing to do with the fear; it was just a coincidence that it occurred at that very moment. In fact we cannot be sure, on the basis of the evidence offered, that the rider was ever fearful. Of course the problem here is to measure the behavioral environment independent of the behavior that one seeks to explain. Gestalt theory, as many critics have noted, has not been very successful in doing this. On the other hand, S-R psychologists have been encouraged, perhaps even forced, by their language system to develop definitions of mediating events which include manipulable stimulus variables. In this way they avoid tautological "explanations."

A blanket criticism of Gestalt explanation or a blanket endorsement of S-R theories is not intended because the quality of their interpretations varies a good bit from phenomenon to phenomenon. The major interest now is to specify an essential characteristic of mediational theory, viz., the presence of an outer framework to support the mediational mechanism. By doing so, we have noted a similarity between S-R mediational theory and the behavioral (psychological) environment of Gestalt psychology. The implication of this analysis is that Gestalt theory and mediational S-R theory would be structurally similar if the behavioral environment of the Gestalt theory were more closely tied to the physical environment.

The second essential characteristic that we have specified for mediational theory is that it possesses a specific mediational mechanism. One such mechanism that has been used a great deal is the implicit response-produced cue. Four basic assumptions are made. First, an implicit response can be elicited by an external stimulus or just emitted. Second, this implicit response produces an implicit cue. Third, an overt instrumental response can become associated with this implicit cue. Fourth, principles of association based on conditioning and discrimination learning can apply to the relationships between an overt stimulus and an implicit response, an implicit stimulus and an implicit response, and an implicit stimulus and an overt response.

There are many ways of conceptualizing these implicit stimuli and response events. We prefer to view them initially as theoretical concepts with conceptual properties similar to known empirical relationships between stimuli and responses in conditioning and discrimination learning. No doubt the epistemological status of these hypothetical events can be modified as our knowledge increases. In some situations these implicit stimuli and responses will be coordinated to introspective reports, language behavior, muscular movements, perceptual responses, etc. In addition these mediating events need *not* be conceptualized only in terms of stimulus-response relationships observed in simple learning situations. As we learn more about verbal processes, perception, motivation, and other processes, it would be possible to incorporate these new facts and ideas in mediational mechanisms. In short, S-R mediational theory has its origins in the facts and theories of conditioning and discrimination learning but its future is not limited to them. In a sense it is an expanding theory in that it can make relevant analyses of specific phenomena while possessing potentialities for much wider application.

The third characteristic of contemporary mediational theory is that it has been generated by systematic research programs instead of being primarily a theoretical and methodological gimmick. No attempt will be made to validate this statement by surveying modern mediational formulations (e.g., Berlyne, 1965; Osgood, 1957). Instead, our comments about mediational theory will be limited to the research program with which we have been involved for the past decade.

II. An Experimental Analysis of Reversal and Nonreversal Behavior

A. Visual Stimuli

It is important to note that the mediational mechanism was initially introduced into our formulation only in response to the demands of some data. An experiment (H. H. Kendler & Vineberg, 1954) was designed to determine the influence the learning of simple concepts (concepts based on one stimulus attribute) had upon the learning of a compound concept (concepts based on two stimulus attributes) which involved combinations of simple concepts. Initially subjects were required to learn two simple concepts successively. Following this, they learned the test concept, which was a compound concept. One group had learned both of the simple concepts of which the test concept was composed, the second group had learned only one, while the third group had learned neither of these simple concepts. The results of the study indicated that the rate of learning the test (compound) concept was directly related to the number of simple concepts appropriate to the test concept that had been learned. This finding could be easily handled by a single-unit S-R formulation that assumed that the rate of conditioning the compound concept was a simple function of the degree to which each component had been conditioned. Nevertheless, such a formulation would fail to describe all the results. With one particular compound concept it was found that the acquisition of the two simple concepts on which it was based was not sufficient to produce the learning of the compound concept. It appeared that the advantage derived from the acquisition of the appropriate simple concepts did not stem from merely learning them in the sense of attending to appropriate stimulus attributes and then making the appropriate sorting responses. Instead, the advantage accruing from learning the appropriate simple concepts resulted from the opportunity it gave the *S* to represent them by a verbal response that could transfer to the task of learning the compound concept.

The importance of the mediating representational response in the concept identification behavior of college students led us to question Buss's (1953) simple single-unit analysis of why college students find it easier to make a reversal than a nonreversal shift.

Figure 1 schematically represents these two kinds of shifts. In the first discrimination the *S*s are confronted with a pair of stimuli that differ in two dimensions; size (large and small) and brightness (black and white). In order to receive reinforcements consistently, *S* has to choose the large stimulus whether it is black or white. After learning this discrimination, the *S*s are confronted with one of two new discriminations with the same stimuli. In a reversal shift the *S*s must reverse their preference; in order to receive reinforcement consistently they must now respond to the small stimuli, the *opposite* of what they had been doing previously. In a nonreversal shift, perhaps described more precisely as an extra-dimensional shift, the subject is required to shift his response to the dimension that was previously irrelevant. In this figure, responses to the black instance of the brightness dimension are reinforced in the non-reversal shift. The reversal-nonreversal experimental technique, it should be noted, describes the transfer between two discriminations.

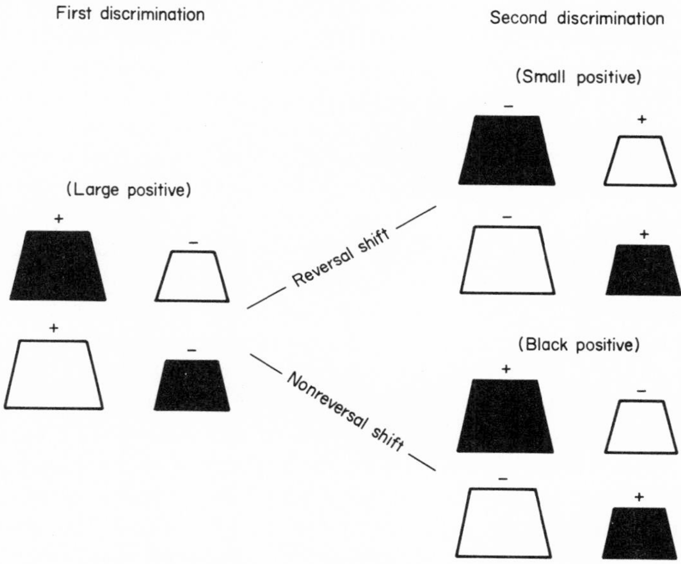

FIG. 1. Examples of a reversal and a nonreversal shift.

These discriminations can vary in difficulty from simple to complex. Thus it is possible to test humans of widely different ages as well as animals of different species with the same kind of problem.

Buss attributed the fact that college students find it easier to execute a reversal shift than a nonreversal shift to the retarding influence of intermittent reinforcements. For example, in Fig. 1, when an *S* is making a nonreversal shift from large positive to black positive, he is reinforced when choosing the large black stimulus in preference to the small white stimulus. This fortuitous reinforcement of the choice of the large stimulus helps maintain the previously correct size discrimination and hence retards the learning of the brightness discrimination. The reversal shift group, on the other hand, receives no reinforcement of the previously correct responses, since they are 100% nonreinforced.

Although Buss's explanation seemed reasonable, it was really inappropriate. Buss was blinded by a single-unit S-R theory which he applied indiscriminately to his data. Although the reversal shift was executed more rapidly than the nonreversal shift, his data suggested that the reason for this relationship was the rapidity with which the reversal shift was executed, not the slowness with which the nonreversal shift was achieved. Anyone familiar with the initial reversal learning of rats is

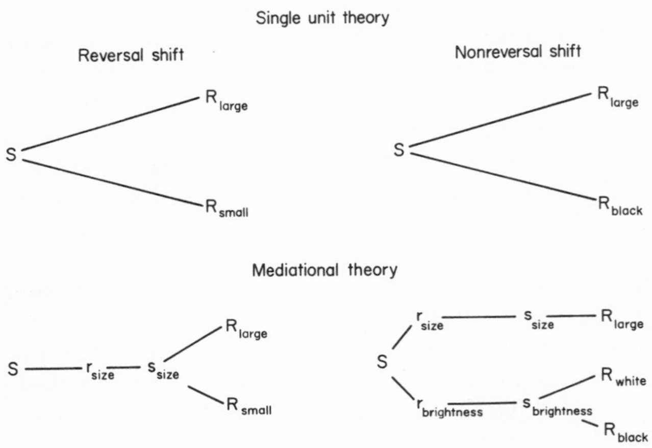

Fig. 2. A single unit and mediational S-R analysis of a reversal and a nonreversal shift.

aware of its slowness. The rapidity with which Buss's *S*s executed a reversal shift suggested that some special factor was operating to accelerate it. Extrapolating from the formulation suggested by H. H. Kendler and Vineberg (1954), a mediational analysis was offered to explain Buss's results. According to a mediational representation, a reversal shift enables the *S* to utilize the same mediated response. Only the overt response has to be changed. A nonreversal shift, on the other hand, requires the acquisition of a *new* mediated response, the cues of which have to be attached to a *new* overt response. Some misunderstanding (e.g., Bogartz, 1965) resulted from the labeling of Fig. 2. Labeling the mediating responses in terms of physical dimensions (brightness, size) did not imply that the subjects were actually making such implicit verbal responses. These labels were used to identify the physical referents of the mediational responses but the exact nature of the response, whether it was a verbal response naming a dimension (e.g., brightness), or a specific verbal label (e.g., black or white), or a perceptual attending response, or something else, was left unspecified.

Because the old mediational sequence has to be discarded and a new one formed, it would be expected that the nonreversal shift should be executed more slowly than a reversal shift. The reason for this deduction was not stated precisely when originally proposed. The statement made was that "... at the completion of the learning the first concept the implicit cues appropriate to the second concept would be present for *S*s in the reversal group; they would merely be connected to the 'wrong' sorting response" (H. H. Kendler & D'Amato, 1955, p. 165). Implied in such a prediction is that the sorting responses would extinguish more rapidly than the mediating responses that elicited the implicit cues. Admittedly, however, at this stage of the research program we felt no great concern to make a fine-grained analysis of the reversal shift mechanism. We simply made the general assumption that a mediating response appropriate to the pre- and postreversal shift occurred, and this mediating response was the source of positive transfer in reversal learning. The strategy governing the research program was that there was merit in leaving the conceptual properties of the mediating response open-ended. More data, rather than premature speculation, would be the best guide for filling in the structure of the mediational process.

According to a single-unit S-R theory, which we interpreted primarily in terms of the principal assumptions of Spence's theory of discrimination learning (1936), a nonreversal shift should be faster than a reversal shift if the fortuitous reinforcements were eliminated. The reason for this is that at the time of the shift the difference between the competing habits in the reversal shift (large to small) is greater than it is for the competing habits (large to black) in the nonreversal shift.

The conflicting interpretations of the single-unit and mediational theories were tested in a group of crucial experiments in which the effects of intermittent reinforcements were controlled or eliminated. In all of these studies (e.g., Buss, 1956; Harrow & Friedman, 1958; H. H. Kendler & D'Amato, 1955) it was found that, with college students, a reversal shift was executed more rapidly.

The finding that college students execute a reversal shift more rapidly than a nonreversal shift raised the question of whether lower animals would behave differently. According to a single-unit theory they should. Typically, the initial reversal shift in discrimination learning is a difficult task. But there was no good available evidence at that time comparing reversal and nonreversal shifts at the infrahuman level, so Kelleher (1956) did his PhD thesis on this problem. He found that rats did, in fact, execute a nonreversal shift more rapidly. Since Kelleher's study other investigators have confirmed and extended his finding to a number of different species. In all of these experiments (e.g., Brookshire, Warren, & Ball, 1961; Mackintosh, 1962; Schade & Bitterman, 1966; Tighe,

1964) the infrahuman *S*s, which included fish, pigeons, chickens, rats, and monkeys, found it easier to execute a nonreversal than a reversal shift when no overlearning was given. Even with considerable overlearning, rats (Tighe, Brown, & Youngs, 1965) and monkeys (Tighe, 1964) continued to perform the nonreversal shift more easily.

B. Developmental Implications

The next step in the research program was to understand the discontinuity between the behavior of rats and college students. Somewhere on a hypothetical biological continuum there should be a point between the rat and college student where a transition is made from single-unit to mediational control. Is this transition from single-unit to mediational control phylogenetic, ontogenetic, or both? This question led us to use the reversal-nonreversal shift technique with young children.

Experiments with nursery school (T. S. Kendler, Kendler, & Wells, 1960) and with kindergarten children (T. S. Kendler & Kendler, 1959) gave us some insight about this so-called transition point. As a group, nursery school children found a nonreversal shift to be easier than a reversal shift; to put it bluntly, they behaved more like rats than college students. Kindergarten children executed a reversal and nonreversal shift at approximately the same rate. An analysis of their data suggested that those who learned the first discrimination rapidly executed a reversal shift more rapidly than a nonreversal shift whereas slow learners found the nonreversal shift easier. Evidence (Heal, Bransky, & Mankinen, 1966; Smiley & Weir, 1966) now suggests that the behavior we observed with kindergartners may have been influenced by dimensional dominance; the children with a preference for the relevant dimension learned the first discrimination rapidly and executed a reversal shift quickly and a nonreversal shift slowly while the children with a preference for the irrelevant dimension learned the first discrimination and reversal shift slowly and a nonreversal shift relatively rapidly. Although this a reasonable hypothesis, before it can be accepted more sensitive techniques of measuring dimensional preference and a better method of estimating the effects of eliminating subjects who are unable to learn the first discrimination must be devised. But regardless or whether or not the dimensional preference hypothesis can explain our results with kindergartners, it cannot explain, as will be seen, the developmental changes in the tendency to execute reversal shifts.

The difference between the shift performance of nursery school and kindergarten children suggested an interesting developmental trend but the results were not conclusive. A systematic study over a wider age range was needed. Such a study required an experimental procedure applicable to various ages and species that would provide a quantitative measure of developmental change. The optional shift adapted from Buss (1956) met these requirements nicely. As we shall see, the experimental task illustrated in Fig. 3 is simple enough to be learned by 3-year-old children and adaptable enough to yield meaningful results in subjects ranging from rats to college students. The essence of the procedure is to require a shift in which the subject has a number of options, one of which is a reversal of his previous response. With such a procedure, developmental differences will be revealed by the percent of individuals of different age groups who will select the available options.

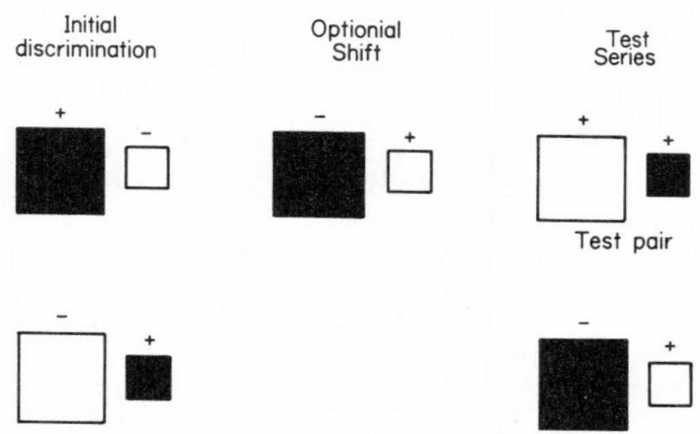

FIG. 3. An example of the three phases of the optional shift procedure.

The first investigation was with children who ranged from 3 to 10 years of age. The stimuli used are illustrated in Fig. 3. In all of our experiments the various possible reinforçement patterns were presented in a counterbalanced design; the figure presents one of these patterns for illustrative purposes. The initial discrimination is similar to the reversal nonreversal shift procedure previously described. The procedure begins to differ on the second discrimination, the optional shift, which is presented immediately after criterion is reached in the initial discrimination. Only one stimulus pair is presented and the reward pattern is reversed; to reach criterion the subject must shift his response. But the shift is optional because both dimensions are now relevant and redundant; he may respond to either dimension or to both. In the final phase of the experiment the test pair, on which any choice is rewarded, is alternated with the training pair on which only the correct choice is rewarded (small-white). From responses to the test pair we may infer the basis of the optional shift. If S selects the large white square 8 or more times out of 10, then his response during the entire test series, including the nontest pair, is primarily to white regardless of size. From such a response pattern we infer that since he shifted from black to white, he made an *optional reversal shift*. If he chooses the small black square at least 8 of 10 times, then during the entire test series he responds predominantly to the small stimulus, regardless of its color. Such a pattern requires a shift from black to small, and constitutes an *optional extradimensional shift*. Should he fail to choose either member of the test pair consistently, he is considered to have made a nonselective shift.

There are two avenues of theoretical analysis relevant to this experimental situation, each one yielding a different set of predictions. Which analysis is applicable depends on whether the choice behavior of *S* is mediated by a system of symbolic responses. Symbolic mediation should make an optional reversal shift the most likely response for the same reason that it makes reversal easier than extradimensional shift. If a symbolic dimensional response occurs, it institutes a habit family hierarchy which increases the probability of response to all members of that hierarchy (Hull, 1934; Maltzman, 1955). The overt choice response to the positive stimulus gains in relative strength because it is reinforced. When reinforcement ceases, the difference between the strengths of the dominant response and other members is that hierarchy decrease. Since the only feasible alternative response in the hierarchy is to the previously negative stimulus, this response occurs and is rewarded. The relevant mediator is maintained and *S* makes an optional reversal.

C. Single-Unit S-R Theory

What are we to expect if there is no symbolic dimensional response which mediates the choice? The answer to this question takes us into the vortex of a number of current controversies which recently seemed on the verge of settlement, only to reappear in a new, more sophisticated guise. Although the predictions we made in the previous studies were based primarily on Spence's discrimination learning theory (1936, 1952), any form of continuity theory would predict that reversal shifts would be more difficult than nonreversal shifts. At the time the research was initiated it seemed unnecessary to labor the point. Now, however, the basic tenets of continuity theory are again being challenged. The assumption that all of the stimuli that impinge on the sensorium of the organism become associated with the response is contested by attention theorists like Broadbent (1961) and Sutherland (1959). The validity of the assumption that learning is a gradual incremental process is denied by so many prominent learning theorists there is no need to cite examples. Under these circumstances it is necessary to delineate more precisely the simpler processes that we believe accounts for the behavior when no symbolic dimensional mediator occurs, in order once more to put them to the test. For present purposes we shall outline the theory as it applies to the experimental situation presented in Fig. 3. It is assumed that:

1. The visual stimulus complex can be analyzed into four major

components, large, small, black, and white. Each discriminandum therefore consists of a compound of two of these components, e.g., large-black or small-white.

2. Every reinforced approach response to a given stimulus compound increases the excitatory tendency for each component to produce that response in an amount that is a constant proportion of the difference between its current tendency and its upper asymptote.

3. Each nonreinforced response to a stimulus compound decreases the excitatory tendency for each component to produce that response in an amount that is a constant proportion of the difference between its current tendency and its lower asymptote.

4. The strength of the excitatory tendency of a given stimulus compound is equal to the sum of the weighted component excitatory tendencies. In this example we have assumed the weight of all components to be equal.

5. The probability of approaching a given compound is a positive function of the magnitude of the composite excitatory tendencies.

6. In the case of mutually exclusive approach responses, the one with the greater excitatory tendency will prevail, provided the difference exceeds the required threshold.

The theory can be applied to each of the three phases of the optional shift procedure (Fig. 3). In the initial discrimination, when only responses to black are rewarded, the excitatory tendency of that component would increase. Since responses to white are never rewarded, the excitatory tendency of white would decrease. The excitatory tendencies of the irrelevant components (large and small), which are reinforced about half the time, would each tend to stabilize at some value between their respective upper and lower asymptotes. The stabilization value depends on the relation between the incremental and decremental rate.

The application of the theory to the second phase of the optional shift procedure, the phase in which both dimensions are relevant and the reward pattern is reversed, is illustrated in Fig. 4. For esthetic reasons the illustration assumes that the incremental and decremental rates are equal and constant for each of the four components. It also assumes that the stabilization values of the irrelevant components have been reached by the end of the criterion run of the initial discrimination. The predictions that follow do not require that the incremental and decremental rates be equal nor that the irrelevant components reach their stabilization value before the shift. They do require that, at the time of the shift, the excitatory tendencies of the two irrelevant components are less than the positive stimulus and greater than the negative component.

During the second phase (optional shift) no responses to the large black square are reinforced, consequently there should be a gradual decrease in the excitatory tendencies of the large and black components. The magnitude of the decrease depends on the number of nonreinforced trials. Conversely, responses to the small white compound, which are always reinforced, result in gradually increasing excitatory tendencies for both the small and white components. Criterion is attained when the combined excitatory strength of small and white sufficiently exceeds that of large and black.

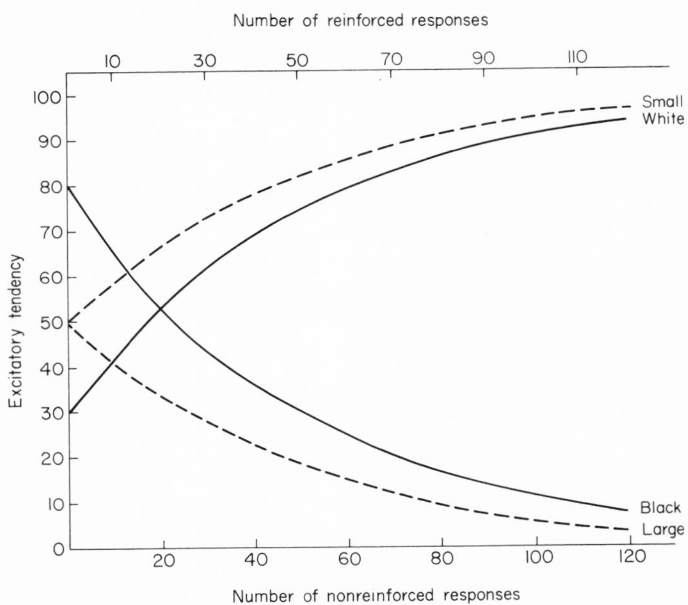

FIG. 4. An illustration of the hypothetical increase and decrease of the excitatory tendencies of each stimulus component during the second phase of the optional shift procedure.

What we wish to predict are the choices made to the test pair during the third phase of the optional shift procedure. The test pair contains the same stimulus components reshuffled. The choice that confronts *S* is between a small black compound and a large white compound. According to the theory, if criterion is attained on phase two before all of the components have reached their respective asymptotes, the composite excitatory strength of the small black compound should exceed that of the large white compound. If the difference between the excitatory strengths of the two test compounds sufficiently exceeds the difference threshold, small-black would be chosen more frequently than large-white. However, the theory also predicts that the difference between the excitatory strengths of the test compounds should decrease as the number of training trials increases. If criterion on the second phase is reached when this difference is less than the required threshold, S should distribute his choices randomly between the two compounds that compose the test pair. Without specifying the several parameters and the difference threshold, the theory cannot specify whether the shift should be primarily nonselective or extradimensional. If, however, both nonselective and extradimensional shifts are considered as nonreversal shifts, then the theory predicts that optional nonreversal shifts should be more probable than optional reversal shifts.

To avoid misunderstanding, we must pause for a brief comment. It is not essential to continuity theory that the asymptotes for all the excitatory tendencies be equal. In fact we are at present devising a formulation which would define dimensional dominance in terms of the relative difference between the upper and lower asymptotes of the stimulus components that comprise each of the dimensions. We have evidence that dimensional dominance so defined can be demonstrated in rats. This point is raised here because the prediction about the relative frequency of reversal and nonreversal (extradimensional or nonselective) shifts depends on the relative asymptotic values of the stimuli involved. In fact, if the asymptotes are sufficiently different there is a limited set of conditions in which the theory would predict that optional reversal would be more likely than optional nonreversal shifts. Specifying these conditions would require too much detail for the present but the predictions about these conditions are about to be tested experimentally. Meanwhile, it will not lead us too far astray to assume equal asymptotes since all indications are that for the data to be presented the experimental conditions are within the range required to predict that nonreversal shifts should exceed reversal shifts.

D. Developmental Changes

Mediational and single-unit theory produce distinctively different predictions, yet we expected to find evidence for both. Single-unit theory should effectively predict rat behavior, mediational theory should predict mature human behavior, and for children the relative effectiveness of either theory should depend on the age of the children.

Figure 5 presents the results of two studies relevant to these predictions. To the left are the results of an experiment on rats using the stimulus compounds shown in Fig. 3 (T. S. Kendler, Kendler, & Silfen, 1964). Twenty-three out of the 24 rats made optional nonreversal shifts (i.e., either extradimensional or nonselective shifts). The overwhelming tendency for rats to make optional nonreversal shifts was confirmed by Tighe and Tighe (1966). They used the optional shift procedure to measure the effects of overlearning on rats and children. For stimuli they used horizontal versus vertical stripes placed on flat versus raised squares. There was no overlearning effect among rats but for each learning condition and each dimension the proportion of nonreversers was much greater than reversers. The proportions of optional reversal, extradimensional, and nonselective shifters for all experimental groups of rats combined were .10, .46, and .44 respectively. The results of both

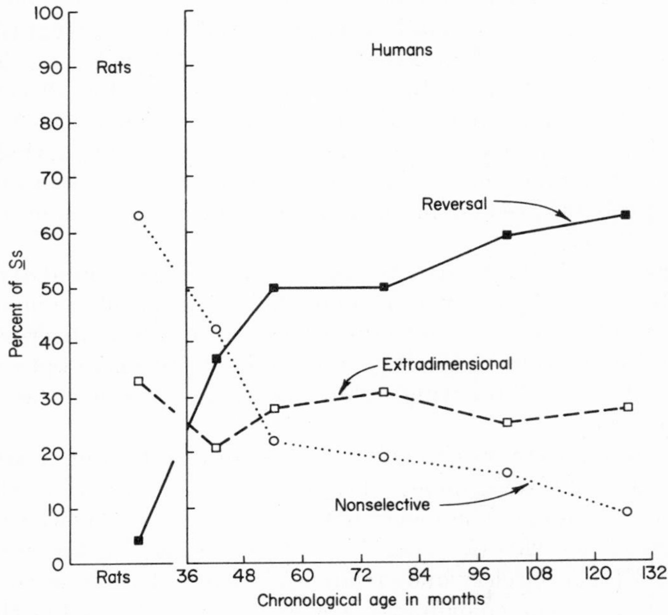

FIG. 5. The percent of *S*s responding in each optional shift category for 90–120-day-old rats and children of different ages.

of these experiments are in good agreement with those obtained from other reversal-nonreversal shift procedures and with the proposed continuity theory.

On the right side of Fig. 5 are the results we obtained with children using the same stimuli (T. S. Kendler, Kendler, & Learnard, 1962). Although the stimuli were the same for the rats and the children, the procedure differed in some inevitable ways. The rats were run for 20 trials a day, were maintained on an ad libitum diet, and were reinforced with food for a correct response. Most of the children completed the entire experiment in a single session, were not systematically deprived of anything, and obtained a token marble for correct choices. Doubtless these procedural variations had some effect, although it seems unlikely that they would in themselves account for the observed species differences. Nevertheless, the effect of the procedural differences will require further analysis. Be that as it may, the procedure for all of the human subjects was identical yet there was a statistically significant, monotonic increase in optional reversers between the youngest and eldest children. Returning to Fig. 5, it will be noted that at the upper age level the most probable response was the predicted optional reversal. The general trend of these results got some small measure of confirmation from the Tighe and Tighe study. They found that for children shift behavior depended on both overlearning and dimension. Nevertheless, for all conditions combined, the proportion of optional reversers was .56 for the 3-year-old group and .78 for the 4-year-olds. In the main the children in their study, as in ours, were much more likely than rats to make optional reversals and this probability was, in turn, greater among the elder than the younger children.

As an aside it should be stressed that in gathering this kind of developmental data it is important that, once you have specified your population, *no* child be eliminated for failure to learn the initial discrimination. Since children who learn slowly are more likely to make optional nonreversal shifts, eliminating slow learners biases the sample inappropriately.

To the human data we can add a new set of results (Fig. 6) which not only replicates the developmental trend among children but extends its generality and range. The generality of the trend was tested by using three dimensions, size (approx. 7.0 versus 3.5 cm^2), color (red versus green), and form (circle versus triangle) in each of three combinations (size-color, size-form, color-form). The range was extended at the upper end by including sixth grade and college students. The other two groups were kindergarten and second-grade children. The procedure was the same as in the previous study except for an automatic apparatus which effectively reduced the possibility of untoward experimenter influence to which children are susceptible. Figure 6 presents the proportion of optional reversers at each age level for each of the dimension pairs individually, and all dimension pairs combined. There were 96 *S*s at each grade level; 32 for each dimension pair. The mean C.A. for each grade level is presented on the figure. There was no overlap in C.A. between the grade levels.

It can be seen that for each dimension pair there is a monotonic increase in percent of optional reversers with increasing age. A multiple χ^2 analysis (Sutcliffe, 1957) indicates that the variability attributable to grade level is highly significant ($\chi^2 = 27.35$, $df = 3$, $p < .001$). The variability attributable to dimension pair is also significant ($\chi^2 = 6.15$,

$df = 2$, $p = .05$) but since the confidence level is not high it should be replicated for confirmation. The interaction between dimension pair and grade level falls far short of significance ($\chi^2 = 5.89$, $df = 6$, $.25 < p < .50$).

Since there is no significant interaction, it is reasonable to combine the results of the several dimension-pairs to provide a more stable estimate of the nature of the developmental trend. Four points are, of

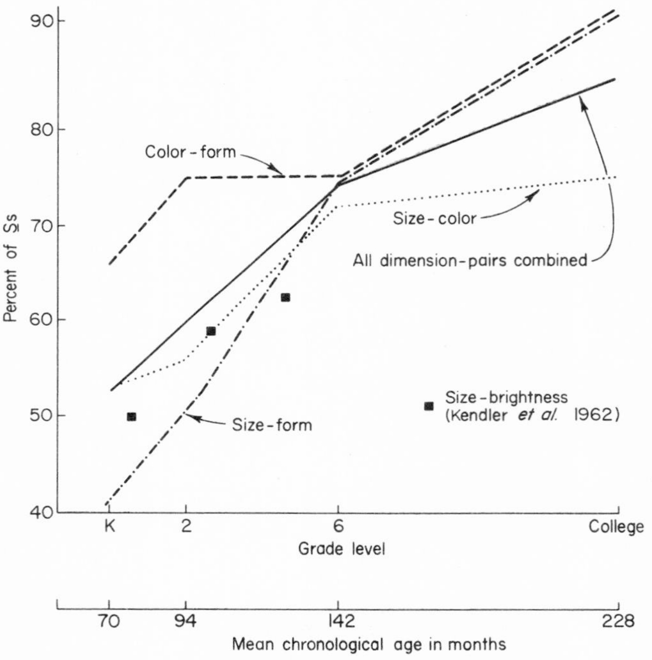

FIG. 6. The percent of *S*s who made optional reversal shifts at each developmental level.

course, insufficient to determine the nature of the function, but visual inspection of the combined results suggests a regular, growth-type function which continues to increment gradually well past sixth grade (about 12 years of age), possibly up to college age. A more complete characterization must await more data, particularly at the younger age levels. Of the five age levels in Fig. 5, three overlap the range of the present study. When the results of those three ages are plotted on the coordinates of Fig. 6 they conform quite well to the newer set of results, particularly, as one might expect, to those of the size-color groups.

Figure 7 shows the trends for extradimensional shifts and for nonselective shifts for the three dimension pairs combined. The individual trends for each dimension pair are not presented because the number of instances at each point are too small to provide stable configurations. The combined data show that between kindergarten and college age the most probable nonreversal shift is extradimensional, but both types of

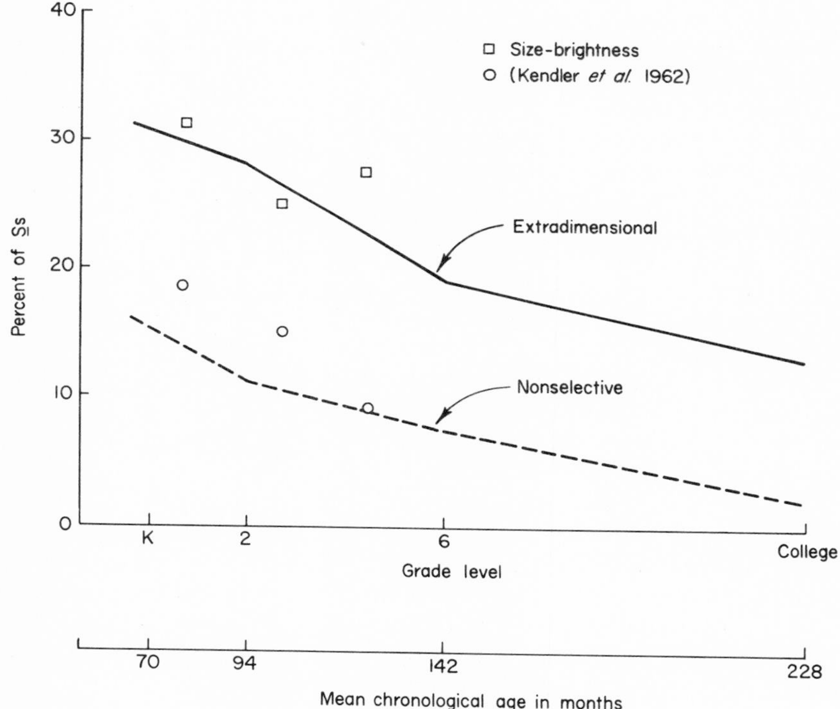

FIG. 7. The percent of *S*s who made extradimensional and nonselective shifts at each developmental level.

nonreversal shift decrease steadily with age. These results also show good agreement with the previous findings.

Taken together, all of the data presented are consonant with the following conclusions about reversal-nonreversal shift behavior. The continuity type of discrimination learning theory accounts for infrahuman shift behavior. Mediational formulation fits college student behavior. The probability that a child's choice will fit one formulation or the other depends on his age; the younger he is the more likely he is to behave according to the single-link theory. Conversely, the older he is the more probable it is that he will behave according to the mediational formulations.

A methodological aside is in order at this point. The studies cited in Figs. 5, 6, and 7 are, in strict parlance, developmental rather than experimental. Some reflections from Nagel (1957) will make plain the sense in which we use the term *developmental*. For Nagel the term *development* refers to a process that occurs over time, a process which consists of changes that yield relatively permanent but novel increments in structure and functioning. Embryologists and evolutionists would add another limitation that is particularly meaningful to psychologists. Developmental change must also eventuate in modes of organization not previously manifested, resulting in a system with an increased capacity for *self-regulation*, a larger measure of relative independence from environmental fluctuations. "The connotation of development involves two essential components: the notion of a system possessing a definite structure and a definite set of preexisting capacities; and the notion of a sequential set of changes in the system yielding relatively permanent but novel increments not only in its structure but in its mode of operation as well." (Nagel, 1957 p. 17).

The research and the theoretical interpretations of the results we have described qualify as developmental in the deepest sense. We start with a model of a relatively simple system with a definite structure. Structure in this sense refers to a conception of the nature of the processes or mechanisms that produce the observed behavior. This structure consists of a system that is sensitive to a range of external stimuli and capable of making differential responses to them. It has the capacity to modify the stimulus-response connections on the basis of reward contingencies, in a particular manner. Operating within such a system, it should be harder to learn a reversal shift than a nonreversal shift or, given the option, nonreversal should be more likely than reversal shifts. This prediction has been tested and confirmed on a range of infrahuman organisms. Having described our initial system and its capacities and noted that it applies to a wide range of organisms, we can begin to deal with the set of sequential changes in this system which eventuates in a new mode of organization resulting in increased capacity for self-regulation. We have hypothesized that as human beings mature the system of relatively simple S-R association changes to a system that includes one or more mediating links which results in a new structure with an increased capacity for self-regulation. This is because the mediating links are of such a character that they produce self-generated stimulation which enters into the control of behavior, resulting in a new and different mode of operation. This changed mode expresses itself in a marked change in overt behavior in which reversal shift becomes more probable than nonreversal shifts. The change with species and with age depicted in Figs. 5, 6, and 7 qualify as a developmental law, potentially capable of mathematical expression.

Development is one of the important facts of life with which psychologists must eventually deal. And developmental laws have an appealing regularity psychologists cannot afford to ignore, but they also have some important limitations. The major limitation is that developmental laws are not causal. As Nagel (1961) points out, they cannot be causal for two reasons. In the first place though developmental laws may state a necessary condition for the occurrence of some event, they do not state the sufficient conditions. It may, for example, be true that the child has to have the capacities associated with the unmediated response system before he can move to the stage in which his response is influenced by symbolic mediation, but the first stage of the developmental change does not cause the second. Moreover, developmental laws generally state relations between events separated by a temporal interval of some duration. In consequence, since something may intervene after the earlier event to prevent the realization of the later event, the sequential order is not likely to be invariant. It is plain that the earlier event does not cause the later event since infrahumans do not progress from one system to another as humans do. This is not to imply that animals are incapable of mediation. We know that mediational links occur in infrahuman organisms. For example, there is some evidence that rats make intradimensional shifts (to new stimuli on the same dimension) more easily than extradimensional shifts (Shepp & Eimas, 1964). Such data could be explained by the establishment of an observing or scanning response which maximizes the stimulation received from the relevant dimension. But this kind of mediating response is not of the same order as the hypothetical symbolic mediator since it does not result in new modes of organization which increase the capacity of the system for self-regulation. The behavior is still primarily under control of the external visual stimulus. However, we do not deny that some forms of symbolic mediation can be taught to infrahuman organisms. Later on, some instances of such mediation will be cited. The developmental law merely shows that human beings, in their natural habitat, become increasingly likely as they mature to make optional reversals. Strictly speaking, this generalization should be limited to the natural American habitat. There is, however, some recent evidence that a similar type of development may characterize Liberian children (Cole, 1968). No such developmental progression has been demonstrated for infrahuman *S*s, at least in the laboratory habitat, not even for monkeys whose habitat included considerable learning set training (Tighe, 1964).

If, however, stage one does not cause stage two, we are left with the necessity to explain what does. Or, put more generally, given that developmental laws are important and useful, it is nevertheless necessary, if we are to explain or control behavior, to seek causal laws to supplement the developmental findings, and ultimately to organize the developmental and causal laws in a conceptual framework. The proposed theoretical formulation led us to postulate that the observed developmental changes are due to the intervention of a mediating process. Our next problem was and continues to be the investigation of the nature and operation of this mediational mechanism, and of how it enters into human development.

III. The Nature of Mediation

The mediating mechanism could be theoretically conceptualized and empirically analyzed in a number of different ways. Although, as has been noted, the research program was initiated by an analysis that suggested the importance of verbal processes in human concept identification problems (H. H. Kendler & D'Amato, 1955; H. H. Kendler & Vineberg, 1954), the nature of the mediational response was left open-ended as revealed by the following quotations:

"Some mediating events can be conceivably and probably will be coordinated to introspective reports, language behavior, muscular movements, and other observable events" (H. H. Kendler & Kendler, 1962, p. 6).

"... the mediating link is conceived of as a perceptual or verbal response, often covert, to the relevant dimension which produces cues that determine the overt response" (T. S. Kendler, Kendler, & Learnard, 1962, p. 572).

This open-endedness was deliberate because no compelling reason existed to identify the mediated response with one, and only one, psychological mechanism. Although verbal processes seemed to be important, there were obvious reasons for avoiding the restrictive assumption that verbal and mediational processes were one and the same. Several sources of data (e.g., Harlow, 1949, 1959) suggested that animals were able to solve a two-choice discrimination problem just as rapidly as our human subjects were executing a reversal shift. Rats, after being subjected to successive reversals, learn to reverse after making only one error (Dufort, Guttman, & Kimble, 1954). Similarly, monkeys in learning set problems solve a new discrimination in one trial. And at the time that our research program was initiated (H. H. Kendler & Kendler, 1962), the overlearning reversal effect (ORE) was considered to be a valid, reliable phenomenon. Thus three sets of data all suggested that animals could be trained to make rapid reversals. Having made the assumption that a rapid reversal required some mediational mechanism and knowing that nonverbal organisms could behave in a somewhat similar fashion, we felt obligated not to limit mediational mechanisms to verbal processes.

In spite of our reluctance to equate mediational processes with verbal behavior for the reasons already offered, the investigation of the influence of verbal factors on reversal behavior was encouraged for two reasons:

1. The hypothesis that verbal factors were involved in the increasing tendency for children to respond in a reversal manner as they grow older was intuitively obvious and appealing. It also seemed relatively easy to test the assumption that children, as they mature, acquire representational responses that mediate between the stimuli of the discrimination task and the overt choice. Although animals exhibit behavior similar to the rapid reversals of humans, we could find no evidence that non-articulate organisms after learning a discrimination for the *first time* could reverse rapidly. Perhaps verbal mediation was required for an initial rapid reversal, while a more primitive form of mediation was required for successive reversals, learning sets, and the ORE.

2. In spite of the many indeterminacies involved in the S-R mediational analysis of reversal shift behavior, the conceptualization was nevertheless challenged. House and Zeaman (1962, 1963) offered an *observing response* interpretation of the ability of older children and adults to execute a reversal shift more rapidly than a nonreversal shift. Their formulation assumes that a rapid reversal does not result from the addition of response-produced interoceptive stimulation but is due instead to the acquisition of observing responses that make effective certain features (e.g., size) of the exteroceptive stimulation. If verbal labels facilitate a reversal shift, as some studies had suggested (e.g., H. H. Kendler & Kendler, 1961; T. S. Kendler, Kendler, & Wells, 1960), then they do so, according to their line of reasoning, not because the words provide a mediating response that generates an implicit cue appropriate to both original and reversal learning, but instead because the label encourages the *S* to make the observing response which is required for a reversal shift. Mackintosh (1965) offered a related perceptual theory that emphasizes central attention mechanisms instead of peripheral orienting acts to account for a variety of data from animal discrimination studies as well as reversal shift behavior.

The issues involved in this apparent "controversy" between our S-R mediational formulation and the observing response conception of House and Zeaman (1962), and the attention theory of Mackintosh (1965) are much more complex than they appear initially. A complete discussion of the differences would not only take into consideration large portions of the history of experimental psychology, but also sociological and cultural pressures that inevitably shape the course of science (Basalla,

1967). But some of the differences can be pinpointed if they are translated into a common form of discourse, such as S-R language (H. H. Kendler, 1965). Let us first distinguish an S-R mediational mechanism from an observing reponse formulation (Spence, 1960). We have already characterized the former in terms of a representative sequence (S-r-s-R) in which the environmental stimulus (S) evokes an implicit response (r) which in turn produces an implicit stimulus (s) to which the overt response (R) becomes associated. An observing response may be represented by the following sequence:

$$S_1\text{-}R_1 \rightarrow s_2\text{-}R_2$$

In this representation the subject orients (R_1) his receptors to a certain portion of the environment (S_1), and as a result, his receptors are presumably exposed to a component (s_2) of the stimulus pattern (S_1). The similarity between the S-R mediational conception and the observing response formulation is obvious; a similar sequence of stimulus and response events occur, differing only in that the first response of the S-R mediational formulation represents a general class of responses whereas the initial response in the observing response formulation is a specific receptor-orienting reaction. The observing response formulation can be considered as one example of the larger classification of S-R mediational formulations.

Even with relatively simple stimulus compounds (S_1) slight differences in orienting responses (R_1) can produce different patterns of stimulation (s_2). This point escaped Mackintosh (1965) when he noted "if rats are trained on a discrimination between a black horizontal and white vertical rectangle, there is no conceivable way in which they could orient themselves so as to look at the orientation differences between the stimuli without thereby seeing the brightness difference (and vice versa)" (p. 143).

Although this analysis is superficially true, the important consideration is not whether they can avoid being stimulated by brightness differences when observing orientation, or vice versa, but whether they are being stimulated by the *same* stimulus pattern when observing brightness or orientation differences. When discriminating brightness differences, the subject will presumably fixate on the center of the rectangles while he will tend to fixate on the periphery of the rectangles when observing differences in orientation. Analyzing incoming stimulation at the site of the receptors should reveal whether different patterns of stimulation do in fact result from different orienting responses.

An attention theory can be represented in the following fashion:

$$S\text{-}s\text{-}R$$

The physically defined stimulus pattern (S) confronting the organism is filtered and organized to produce an effective stimulus (s) which is directly connected to the response (R). This conception is, in a certain sense, a two-stage formulation in that the first stage refers to some input process that transforms the pattern of physical stimulation while the second stage involves the association of the response to the effective stimulus. Presumably, principles of attention and perceptual organization determine how the physical stimulation is transformed into the effective pattern of stimulation. It might be argued that this perceptual formulation is not a two-stage conception, because in any behavioral situation external stimulation must be transformed into patterns of neural impulses. Such an argument overlooks an important psychological difference. In some situations, the perceptual problem of the transformation of the physical stimulus (S) into the effective stimulus (s) is relatively insignificant, as is the case for many discrimination tasks used by S-R psychologists. In a black-white discrimination task with rats, involving alternative alleys, the perceptual transformation problems are minimized. However, with more complicated discrimination tasks, the problems of perceptual transformation become crucial. To explain the results obtained in these complex perceptual discrimination tasks within the framework of this S-s-R model, it becomes essential to formulate principles that govern the transformation of S into s.

Although the observing response and perceptual formulation are functionally equivalent in that external stimulation is transformed into an effective stimulus pattern, the intervening processes which accomplish this end are quite different. The observing response is a response mechanism that selects out a certain portion of the environmental stimulation so that it strikes the organism's sensorium. Attention, on the other hand, is a sensory input and/or central mechanism which determines how a particular pattern of stimuli striking the receptors will be organized into an effective stimulus compound. Both Mackintosh (1965) with his perceptual model and Schoenfeld and Cumming (1963) in their analysis of the role of perception in behavior theory fail to distinguish sharply between observing response and attention mechanisms. One obvious reason is that our experimental techniques and knowledge of perception have not developed sufficiently to convert the theoretical distinction made into an empirical difference. But advances in our knowledge of neural patterns of stimulation in visual receptors (e.g., Ratliff, 1965) promise to make this distinction between observing responses and attention more relevant in the future.

At the present time, however, it is impossible to design a crucial experiment to test the relative merits of an S-R mediational formulation as compared to either an observing response or selective-attention conception in the kind of discrimination problem that has been reviewed up to now. There are two primary reasons for this. First, the implicit response in the S-R mediational formulation was, as has already been indicated, never limited to verbal processes. Second, the theoretical difference between S-R mediational and observing or attention formulations reflects to some extent the controversy between learning and perceptual models of behavior (H. H. Kendler, 1952). Recent evidence that has emphasized the control of sensory input by central processes (e.g., Melzack & Wall, 1965) has made it more difficult to distinguish between these two kinds of models. In analyzing any complex chain of behavior, it is difficult, if not impossible, to isolate perceptual from learning processes. If a definitive evaluation of the relative merits of the S-R mediational and observing or attention formulations is to be made, further conceptual articulations of both viewpoints is required. This point can be illustrated by referring to a specific experiment. In a study by Katz (1963), children received differential verbal training to associate nonsense syllables with four highly similar forms. After this they were exposed to a simple perceptual discrimination task and were instructed to indicate whether two of the four forms, presented briefly, were perceptually the same or different. Katz reports that children who had associated a common, as opposed to different, label to the two forms perceived the stimuli as identical more often than did the *S*s who had learned to label them with distinctive nonsense syllables. In addition, the *S*s who had a common label for two forms found it more difficult to discriminate between the two forms than did *S*s who had learned distinctive labels. Thus the results were interpreted to support the idea that words can determine what we actually perceive (Whorf, 1956). If two familiar shapes have a common label, we tend to perceive them as identical; if they have distinctive labels, we tend to perceive them as different. But another interpretation is possible.[2] A common label encourages the *S* to attend to the similar portion of the two shapes; distinctive labels encourage them to look at portions of the shapes that are obviously different. Although labels can influence our perceptions, they do not change them. They just encourage different perceptual orienting responses.

In spite of the difficulty or impossibility of evaluating the relative merits of the two formulations as they apply to reversal behavior, the controversy nevertheless directs attention to some empirical problems that may be valuable to explore. One implication that may be drawn from perceptual formulations is that a reversal shift should be rapid when an organism is observing or attending to the appropriate stimulus dimension. If this is so, why cannot it be demonstrated unequivocally,

[2] We are indebted to Dr. E. J. Gibson for alerting us to this interpretation.

as it has with adult humans, that a rapid reversal is possible after an infrahuman organism has learned a discrimination *for the very first time*? It is difficult to believe that the unique ability of older children and human adults to execute initial rapid reversals is due either to their reinforcement histories or perceptual sensitivities as compared with younger children and lower animals. Instead, our guess is that the difference is related to some superior cognitive ability of adult humans and older children as compared to younger children and lower animals. It is interesting to note that Piaget (Flavell, 1963) suggests that the logical operation of reversibility begins to develop in children when they are about 7 years of age. It may be that verbal processes are fundamental to this cognitive ability, or it may be that such verbal processes are an expression of this superior cognitive ability. In any case, it seems strategic to investigate how the verbal processes influence reversal behavior.

This problem has already been explored in this research program but the major technique has been to determine the influence of verbal labeling responses on reversal shifts in a two-choice discrimination task involving stimulus displays that varied in brightness, size, and shape (e.g., H. H. Kendler & Kendler, 1961; T. S. Kendler, 1964; T. S. Kendler, Kendler, & Wells, 1960). The difficulty of interpreting these results in relationship to the relative merits of an S-R mediational formulation of a perceptual (attention or observing response) conception has already been alluded to.

Verbal Stimuli

Since it seems to be difficult, perhaps impossible, to manipulate experimentally verbal responses without simultaneously affecting observing responses, we decided to try an indirect approach. An experimental situation was arranged in which the influence of observing responses was minimized. A discrimination problem was used involving different kinds of verbal material with an unchanging observing response. Variations observed in the speed of reversing in such a situation can be attributed to differences in verbal material.

The discrimination task was a simple one (see Table I). Eight items were presented individually to *S* who was required to associate each with one of two button-pressing responses. For the *word* group the eight items consisted of two groups of four words, each of which represented an instance of one concept (e.g., clothing). For the *trigram* group the eight items were unrelated three-consonant trigrams which had to be separated into two categories predetermined by the *E*. After the criterion of initial learning was reached, some of the *S*s in each group (R) were trained on a reversal shift; correct responding demanded that *S* shift his sorting response for each item. The expectation was that the word-reversal group would reverse more rapidly than the trigram-reversal group because the words have a tendency to evoke a common mediating representational response (e.g., clothing, vegetable) that would be appropriate for initial and reversal learning.

The rest of the *S*s were trained on a half-reversal shift (HR). In a half-reversal shift the sorting responses for half the items of each group are shifted, while the response to the other half remains as it was prior to the shift. For example, if the trigrams HBF, WZG, FCM, and BTP were associated with the same motor response, then following the shift HBF

TABLE I

VERBAL MATERIAL

Words	Trigrams	Words	Trigrams
Shirt	HBF	Bee	CJW
Hat	WZG	Ant	LNP
Dress	FCM	Fly	DLZ
Pants	BTP	Mosquito	WGC
Pea	DHX	Bed	SFM
Potato	GKN	Chair	KXF
Carrot	XRH	Desk	QZG
Bean	LJS	Table	HKB

and WZG would be shifted to the other response while the previous sorting response for FCM and BTP would be retained.

With conceptually linked words a reversal shift would be expected to be easier than a half-reversal shift because the preexperimentally learned representational responses provide cues that are appropriate for the reversal shift and inappropriate for the half-reversal shift.

The influence of the two kinds of shifts on the sorting responses of trigrams would depend on the method by which the trigrams were originally grouped. If each of the trigrams was associated directly with the correct sorting response, then a half-reversal shift should be executed more rapidly than a reversal shift. This would follow because a half-reversal shift, assuming single unit associations, requires a change in response to only four items whereas in a reversal shift the response of each of the eight items has to be shifted. However, it is likely that at least some *S*s would invent mnemonics that would represent some or all of the trigrams in each of the sorting groups. These mnemonics should facilitate a reversal shift but interfere with a half-reversal shift. To the extent that mnemonic representational responses are used, the superiority of a half-reversal shift over a reversal shift with trigrams would be reduced and ultimately reversed. Nevertheless, the ready accessibility of representational responses for words as compared with trigrams suggests that the difference between reversal and half-reversal shifts will be greater for the words than for the trigrams.

This expectation was confirmed, as shown in Fig. 8. An analysis of variance of postshift learning showed both a significant effect between

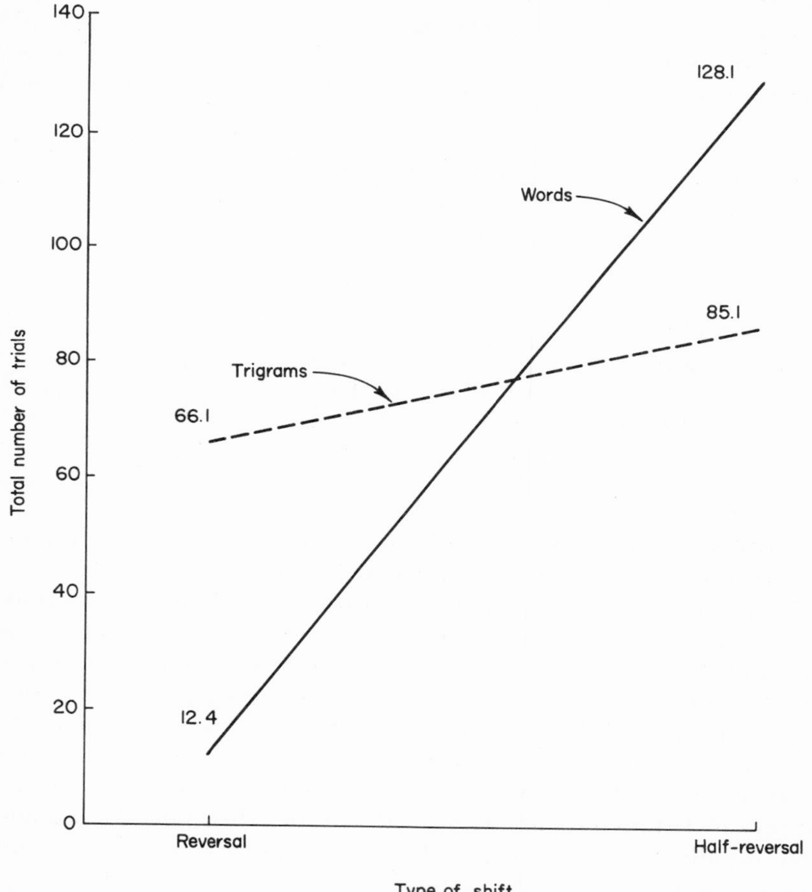

FIG. 8. The interaction between type of shift and verbal material.

shifts (reversal and half-reversal) and a significant interaction between shifts and verbal material (both $p < .001$). Individual comparisons between these means indicated that all the differences were significant ($p < .01$) except the one between the reversal and half-reversal for the trigrams, although the direction of this difference was in favor of a more rapid execution of a reversal shift.[3] The fact that no significant difference between these two groups was observed suggests that *S*s combined both single-unit and mediational functioning when sorting the trigrams. This suggestion gains some support from the *S*s' reactions to a series of questions asked at the end of the experiment. Some *S*s developed mnemonics for classifying two or three trigrams of one group while connecting the remaining item or items directly to the appropriate sorting response.

In the experiment just described, a comparison was made between half- and full-reversal shifts but these two shifts represent only two of the four possible shifts. A one-quarter and three-quarter reversal shift are also possible. In a one-quarter shift, one of the four items initially categorized is shifted to the other category while in a three-quarter shift three items are shifted. It was decided to determine the parametric relationships involving the four kinds of shifts and the two types of verbal material (words and trigrams).

In attempting to predict the relative ease of executing the four kinds of shifts with conceptual words, two general conceptions of postshift behavior seemed relevant. The first was based on the expected difficulty of categorizing the eight words following the shift. The classification required for both a one-quarter and three-quarter shift involves categories possessing three items from one concept and one from the other (e.g., *shirt*, *hat*, *dress*, and *pea*; *potato*, *carrot*, *bean*, and *pants*). Such a category is not uncorrelated with the concept initially learned (e.g., clothing) since it can be represented by the conceptual term, vegetable, with one qualification (all vegetables except pants). According to this line of reasoning, a one-quarter and three-quarter reversal shift should be more difficult than a full-reversal shift but easier than a half-reversal shift since the one-quarter and three-quarter shift represents intermediate points between the complete retention of the conceptual categories and their complete abandonment.

But this analysis ignores the problem of the extinction of the categorizing responses used during initial learning. Although the classifications required to be learned in both a one-quarter and three-quarter shift are of equal difficulty, the three-quarter shift requires the shifting of the responses for six items while responses for only two items have to be changed for a one-quarter shift. If it can be assumed that prior to the shift *S*s are representing the two categories with the appropriate conceptual terms (e.g., clothing, vegetables), then it can be further assumed

[3] Bogartz (1965) with CVC trigrams obtained similar results. With criterion training a reversal shift was faster than a half-reversal but not significantly so. With overlearning the direction of the difference was the same but at a significant level.

that these mediated representational responses suffer extinction effects during the postshift stage when some of the categorizing responses appropriate to initial learning are no longer reinforced. The three-quarter shift group would experience three times as many nonreinforcements of responses that were initially correct as compared to the one-quarter group, while receiving only one-third as many reinforcements. Thus it would be expected that the mediational representational responses for the three-quarter group would have a greater likelihood of being extinguished and therefore not accessible during postshift learning.

Considering the process of extinction, the prediction would be that with the words a three-quarter shift should be more difficult than the one-quarter shift. A full-reversal shift should be more rapid than both. Predicting the order of the difficulty of the four kinds of shifts with trigrams is difficult because the previous comparison between half-reversal and full-reversal shifts suggested that the *S*s, to varying degrees, were responding simultaneously to the categories of the trigrams in a mediated and single-unit fashion. The absence of a significant difference between half- and full-reversal shifts with trigrams would lead one to expect that the four kinds of shifts would be executed at approximately equal rates. In any case, the shifts with words, as compared with trigrams, provide a simpler task to analyze because they are based upon strong verbal habits.

The results are reported in Fig. 9. The analysis of variance revealed a significant effect of shifts ($p < .001$). The F of the interaction between type of shift and kind of verbal material failed to be significant at the .05 level by .01. The full reversal shift with words was significantly easier ($p < .01$) than any of the other shifts. All other comparisons failed to yield a significant difference. Figure 9 *suggests* that the postshift behavior with the conceptual words was influenced by the extinction effects of the representational responses utilized during the initial categorizing stage. At the end of the experimental session each subject described the classificatory system he used. It is interesting to note that 70% of the *S*s in the one-quarter group used the category name while only 30% of the *S*s in the three-quarter group behaved similarly. In addition, 30% of the *S*s in the three-quarter group failed to solve the postshift problem while all *S*s of the one-quarter group were successful. All *S*s in the full-reversal group solved the postshift problem and all used the category name. In the one-half reversal group only 10% failed but none used the category names; they memorized what words were associated with each of the two keys. It would seem reasonable to conclude therefore that mediated representational responses can undergo extinction effects.

Although this is not a revolutionary finding, it has some relevance to the debate (e.g., Miller, 1965) that is raging about the relationship between principles of conditioning, discrimination learning, and language behavior. Perhaps it is an inevitable characteristic of a theoretical controversy that it be expressed initially in its most extreme form. Unfortunately, however, if a question is oversimplified, so, typically,

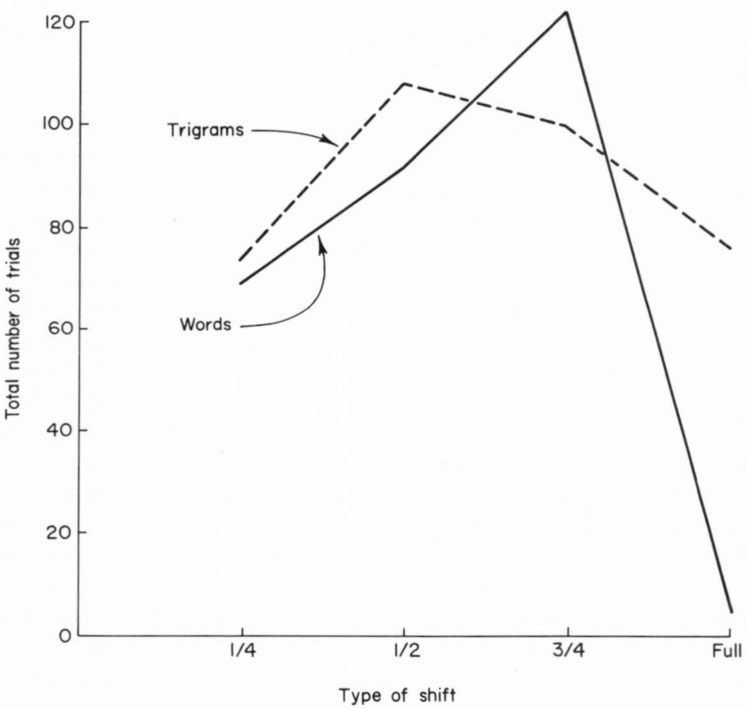

FIG. 9. The interaction between type of shift and verbal material.

will be its answer, as a review of the heredity-environment controversy in psychology will prove. The appropriate question is not whether principles of learning play a role in language behavior but what role they play and what additional theoretical principles are required for an adequate understanding of language behavior, from its acquisition to its performance. Those psychologists who are interested in behavior involving language usage in conceptual and problem-solving behavior, as well as psychologists investigating such related phenomena as verbal learning and memory, have repeatedly observed the operation of such learning processes as extinction, reinforcement, generalization, discrimination learning, and habit interference, and the importance of response-produced cues. It is our opinion that additional principles will be required to account for language acquisition and language behavior.

Regardless of what the future holds in store, it seems likely that more mileage will be obtained from questions directed at discovering both the similarities and differences between the theoretical principles that govern conditioning and discrimination learning on one hand, and those of language behavior on the other, than from prejudgments about the uniqueness of each, or their basic identity.

Returning to the summary of the verbal shift studies (H. H. Kendler, Kendler, & Sanders, 1967), a final set of data is of particular importance in throwing light on the reversal-shift mechanism. These results were obtained in a study that was designed to separate the influence of the reversal shift per se from the accessibility of appropriate representational responses. By isolating the effects of each it would be possible to discover which of the two factors contributed more to the execution of a rapid reversal shift. The method used was to have *S*s initially form two categories each containing instances of two different concepts (e.g., *shirt*, *hat*, *dress*, and *table*; *bed*, *chair*, *desk*, and *pants*). After these mixed categories were formed, two kinds of shifts were instituted; a full-reversal shift in which the mixed categories were maintained but assigned to different classifying responses or a partial-reversal shift in which the mixed categories were shifted to the preexperimental learned conceptual categories (e.g., *shirt*, *hat*, *dress*, and *pants*; *bed*, *chair*, *desk*, and *table*).

If the accessibility of an appropriate representational response were the most potent factor in postshift classifications, a partial-reversal shift should now prove easier than a reversal shift. If, however, the most important factor was the logical operation of reversing, then a full reversal shift would be faster regardless of the manner in which the words were initially categorized. The results indicated that the postshift classifications are assisted more by appropriate representational responses than by reversing previously correct responses (H. H. Kendler, Kendler, & Sanders, 1967). These findings are consistent with previous findings that a reversal shift is not executed rapidly in the absence of appropriate representational responses. These results extend this principle from situations involving trigrams to those with meaningful words that are not categorized in a conceptually consistent fashion. It should be noted, however, that the fastest postshift classification occurs when appropriate representational responses are combined with a reversal shift.

The major purpose of this series of verbal shift studies was to determine whether in a two-choice situation the execution of a reversal shift involving verbal material is facilitated by the accessibility of mediated responses that represent all the instances of a category. The results suggest that representational responses do facilitate reversal learning while simultaneously minimizing the influence of other variables. It could be argued that the advantage of conceptual instances over consonant trigrams in facilitating a reversal shift might be attributed to the greater response learning (Mandler, 1954) of the words as compared to the trigrams. But it should be recalled that when these very same words, with presumably the same degree of response learning, were present in mixed-conceptual categories, reversal learning was found to be slow. The present results also rule out the hypothesis that a reversal shift is easy for a sophisticated *S* because of the simplicity of the logical operation involved in reversing. Quite obviously, if this were the case, reversal shifts with trigrams would be as easy as reversal shifts with conceptual instances.

The present studies bear some relationship to the verbal-loop hypothesis (Glanzer & Clark, 1963) which was proposed to explain the difficulty in recalling a systematically varied set of perceptual stimuli. Essentially the verbal-loop hypothesis states that the recall of such a set of stimuli will be inversely related to the length of the verbal chain the *S* used to represent the stimuli. The same hypothesis can be applied in the present studies to the speed with which adults execute postshift learning after sorting verbal material into two groups; the shorter the verbal representation, the more rapid the shift. In this context the verbal-loop hypothesis can be thought of as identifying an important characteristic of the mediational process which influences learning in the present experimental situation.

It should be noted before proceeding to the next section that the results which demonstrate the importance of mediated representational responses in reversal learning do not deny the possibility that observing responses can also facilitate reversal shifts with perceptual stimuli.

IV. The Operating Characteristics of Representational Responses

The verbal-shift studies suggested another direction for our research program. If we view rapid reversal-shifting as a significant behavioral event, and accept the idea that the accessibility of a representational response plays a fundamental role in this phenomenon, then an analysis, both theoretical and empirical, of the operating characteristics of representational responses during reversal shifts is in order.

This portion of our research program is only in its infancy. The conceptual analysis is far from complete and some of our initial studies have encountered serious methodological difficulties. Nevertheless, some of the research will be reported in order to illustrate the direction that is being taken.

A. Associative Strength Between Representational Responses

One of the first questions we posed is a simple one. In a reversal shift problem, in which the subject uses a simple conceptual term to represent the instances of a common category, can the associative relationship between the two terms influence the speed with which the shift is executed. In other words, can the representational responses function more effectively to mediate the shift if they are highly associated with each other? This question has been raised in somewhat different forms previously. Cofer (1960) asked whether the increase in associative strength, as measured by word association norms, between antonyms for young children might be the major variable responsible for the increased ability of children, as they mature, to execute a reversal shift. Bogartz (1965) questioned whether the rapidity of reversal shifts was limited to situations in which the two sets of stimuli discriminated during initial learning represented end points on a common dimension (e.g., large-small, white-black). Typically, words that represent the end points of a common dimension are highly associated with each other.

In order to throw some light upon these questions, a verbal-shift study was done (H. H. Kendler & Watson, 1968) in which the associative strength between the two representational responses was varied. Two pilot studies had provided equivocal evidence. In each of these studies, *S*s initially sorted eight words selected from the Underwood and Richardson (1956) norms into two sense-impression categories. For half of the *S*s the conceptual names of these two categories were highly associated (e.g., LARGE-SMALL, HARD-SOFT) while for the other half they were low associates (LARGE-HARD, LARGE-SOFT, SMALL-HARD, SMALL-SOFT). Neither study produced significant differences but both were in the direction of showing faster reversals with highly associated representational responses. However, since college students execute a reversal shift rapidly, the failure to find significant results may be due to a basal effect. In order to test this possibility, the reversal shift problem was made more difficult by adding two extra sets of four words, each representing a different sense-impression category. These extra words were "irrelevant" in the sense that the *S* was required *not* to assign them to one of the two sorting categories. In other words, the irrelevant words were to be ignored during initial training. Since some *S*s sorted them into the two relevant categories during postshift training, the irrelevant words increased the average difficulty of the reversal shift. However, the results of the study with irrelevant words were similar to those of the pilot studies; although the mean of the high-associate (HA) group was lower than the mean of the low-associate group (LA), the difference, with a two-tail test, was not significant; $.10 < p < .20$.

These results, combined with those of the two pilot studies, make it difficult to draw an unequivocal conclusion about the role of associative strength in reversal-shift behavior. The three studies produced results that favored HA *S*s over LA *S*s at two-tail probabilities of .12, .24, and .19. Thus the evidence in support of rejecting the null hypothesis is not decisive but neither is the evidence compelling that associative strength plays *no* role in reversal behavior whatsoever. One explanation of the data is that associative strength, as measured by word association norms, plays a weak role in reversal-shift behavior. One possible reason for this is that a weak associative connection between the two representational responses associated cannot be maintained during the initial training trials. When the human adult represents two categories of words with simple conceptual terms he may, through practice, develop strong associations between the two regardless of their initial associative strength. As a result, the difference between the strength of the high and low associations may become attenuated during initial training. If this analysis is correct, then a concept sorting task similar to the present one, but without the initial pairing of the two representational responses, would produce a more potent effect of level of associative strength. An experiment was designed so that the *S* on each trial was presented with four words (e.g., *elephant, atom, velvet, stone*) each of which was an instance of a different sense-impression category (LARGE, SMALL, SOFT, HARD) and he was required to select one representing the "correct" concept. After learning the correct concept, he was shifted to one of the remaining three. Since only one sorting category was used, no specific associative training between any two representational responses occurred. If associative training between conceptual terms has any effect on postshift behavior, then it should influence the choice of words on the first postshift trial when the *S* abandons his previous mode of responding. The results showed a highly significant selection ($p < .001$) of high-associate words. Consequently we must conclude that although associative strength, as measured by word-association norms, between representational responses has at best a minimal effect on reversal-shift behavior, it can nevertheless be a powerful variable in a situation in which *S*s are required to shift from one conceptual category to another when there is a choice of several alternatives. These results would be inconsistent with a model that assumes that in a concept-identification problem, hypotheses are randomly sampled from a pool of tenable hypotheses. Instead, they support the idea that the selection of a new hypothesis is increased if it is highly associated with the previously correct one.

B. Characteristics of Representational Responses

In the analysis of conceptual behavior it is important to distinguish between a *common* response and a *representational* response. Although a concept may, and has, been defined as a *common* response to dissimilar stimuli, such a definition overlooks important problems. If conceptualization involved only a *common* response (e.g., button pressing) to dissimilar stimuli, then in all the reversal-shift experiments involving verbal material that have been reviewed, the speed of the reversal shifts would have been equal. In these studies reversal shifts were not instituted before a criterion of learning (two successive series of correct responses to all eight items) was reached. Obviously *common* responses by themselves are not sufficient to produce a rapid reversal. To produce a rapid reversal the common response must fulfill a representational function. The common response must in some fashion represent the characteristics shared by the instances of a conceptual group. For example, the word *clothing* represents the characteristics of *apparel* inherent in the words *shirt*, *pants*, and *hat*. In this case the representational response possesses symbolic properties that reflect the characteristics of *all* of the instances. However, sets of words can be formed, for which no accessible representational response would possess symbolic properties characteristic of all instances. For example, the representational word *nature* would apply to only four of the following five words: *grass*, *tree*, *sky*, *bird*, *desk*. A subject who was required to make a common response to this set of words could code the set as "*nature* plus *desk*." Thus, symbolic representation of a set of items is not an all-or-none affair; different proportions of a set of items can be represented by a common symbolic response, presumably varying from 0 to 100%.

In an attempt to investigate the effect of degree of representation on reversal-shift behavior, an experiment was conducted comparing groups of related with unrelated words. The related words (e.g., *shirt*, *hat*, *pants*) belong to a natural-language conceptual category (e.g., *clothing*). A group of related words illustrate a case of 100% representation. Unrelated words were selected on the basis of not sharing membership in common conceptual categories (e.g., *carrot*, *hat*, *ant*, *chair*). In terms of natural-language usage, the unrelated words illustrate 0% representation. Nevertheless, it would be expected that subjects, by techniques of "subjective organization" (Tulving, 1964), would be able to develop symbolic representational responses that would apply to some, if not all, of the words in the same sorting response. The ability to do this, however, would be expected to be a function of the number of items in the sorting category. The larger the number of unrelated words the more difficult would become the problem of representation. In contrast, increasing the size of a category of related words would not increase the difficulty of representation because each related word is associated with a common representational response. One would therefore expect that reversing two categories of related words would be uninfluenced by the number of items in each category but the difficulty of reversing two sets of unrelated words would be a function of the number of words in each set.

In an experiment conducted to test this hypothesis, the number of words in each of two sorting categories was 2, 4, 8, or 20 while each word

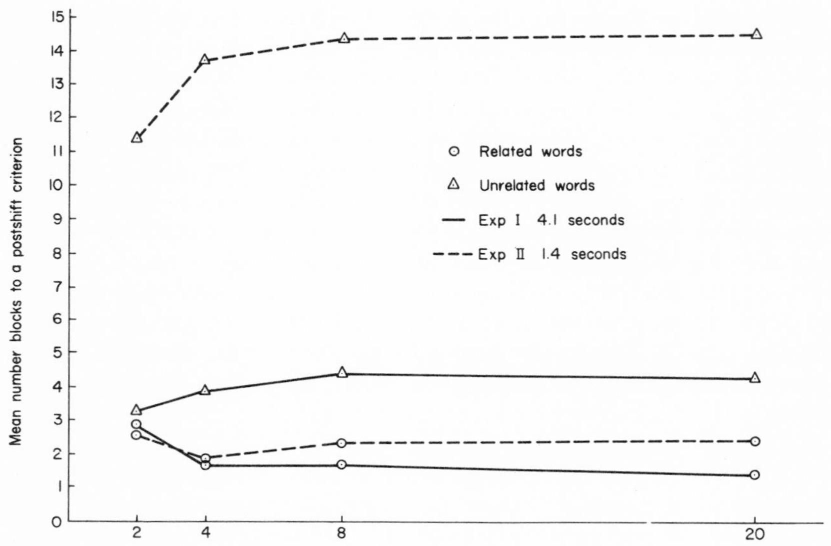

FIG. 10. Postshift performance curves for related versus unrelated words with two different stimulus exposure times.

was exposed for 4.1 seconds with an interstimulus interval of .9 second. The criterion for preshift and postshift learning was two successive blocks of correct responses to all items in each category. Thus *S*s required to sort two categories containing two words each had to make a total of at least eight successive correct responses to reach the criterion of learning. The equivalent figure for an *S* who had to sort categories of 20 words was 80. The use of mean blocks of successive correct responses made possible the comparison between the performance of groups of subjects having a different number of items in each category.

The results of this study are reported in the solid lines of Fig. 10. They show that increasing the number of related words did not increase the difficulty of executing a reversal shift. Actually the poorest performance was for the categories of two items but no overall significant difference existed among the four groups. Surprisingly, increasing the number of unrelated words also did not increase the difficulty of reversing. For the unrelated words, Group 2 exhibited the fastest reversal performance but no significant difference was found among the four groups (2, 4, 8, and 20). The overall performance of reversal-shift learning was significantly superior for the related as compared to the unrelated word groups, but no interaction effects were obtained between the number of words per category and whether or not the words were related.

Although the failure to find evidence indicating that increasing the number of unrelated words per category would retard a reversal shift was unexpected, the results are not unexplainable. It should be recalled that the *S*s reached a demanding criterion of learning (two successive blocks of correct responses) prior to the reversal shift. At the time of the shift whatever technique of "subjective organization" was used during original learning could help mediate reversal learning. One common technique was for the subject in response to a word to implicitly instruct himself to "push the opposite button." For example, when a word was exposed, the *S* would recall the previously correct response (e.g., left) and then press the other (e.g., right) button. Other investigators (Bogartz, 1965; Danks & Glucksberg, 1968) who studied reversal behavior with groups of nonsense syllables have also discovered from postexperimental interviews that some subjects use this response-switching technique.

The fact that the *S*s reversed more rapidly with related than with unrelated words suggested that the natural language conceptual terms were more effective representations for mediating reversal shifts than the rules of "subjective organization" used by the *S*s with unrelated words. One factor that would make the conceptual terms more effective than the mediated subjective organizing responses used for unrelated words is that they represent a more economical form of representation since they consist of one word (e.g., vegetable). Economy of representation would seem to have two beneficial effects. The first is that the implicit mediating responses could take place in a shorter time span. The second is that because of their brevity they would be more resistant to the effects of forgetting since that might result from the interference caused by shift in reinforcement contingencies.

If it requires a briefer time to emit representational responses for groups of related as compared to unrelated words, then it should be possible to discover an exposure time, briefer than the one used previously, that would have the effect of increasing the difficulty of reversing unrelated while simultaneously not affecting the speed of reversing related words. As the dotted lines in Fig. 10 show, this is exactly what happened when the exposure time was reduced from 4.1 seconds to 1.4

seconds while retaining the interstimulus time interval at .9 seconds. The shorter exposure time produced a significantly slower reversal of unrelated words but did not affect the speed of reversal of the related words. But as was true for the 4.1-second exposure interval, the shorter 1.4 interval did not produce any significant retarding effect on reversal shifts as the number of unrelated words increased in each category, although a suggestion in that direction is indicated by the increase in the difference in the speed of reversing categories of two and four unrelated words when the exposure interval is reduced. Intuitively, it would seem that some point should be reached where increasing the number of words in each category of unrelated words should produce a significant retarding effect on reversal shifts.

In another experiment the number of the symbolic representational responses for each sorting category was controlled by varying the number of concepts in each category while keeping constant the total number of words. Four groups of subjects were required to sort a total of 40 words into two sets of 20 each. For Group 1 all words in *each* set of 20 were drawn from one conceptual category (e.g., furniture). For Group 2, 10 words in each set were instances of one concept and 10 were instances of another (e.g., furniture and vegetable). The sets of words in Group 5 contained 4 instances from 5 concepts while each set of 20 words in Group 10 contained 2 words each from 10 conceptual categories. The expectation was that the larger the number of conceptual categories in each set of 20 words the greater would be the number of words required to represent the set. Retrospective reports collected at the end of the experiment support this expectation but the correlation was not perfect between the number of words used by the *S*s to represent each sorting category and the number of conceptual categories actually present. The mean reversal scores for Groups 1, 2, 5, and 10 were 32.2, 25.6, 55.1, and 90.9, respectively. Except for the insignificant inversion between Groups 1 and 2, reversals became increasingly difficult as the number of conceptual groups increased in each sorting category ($p < .01$).

The studies reported in this section approached the problem of identifying some of the characteristics of a representational response of a set of words that would influence its utilization in a reversal shift. The number of words in the representational response obviously plays an important role, especially when the *S* has a limited time to make a choice.

Other characteristics of representational responses, besides the number of words, no doubt, play a role in reversal shifts and other cognitive behavior that requires shifting from the utilization of one conceptual category to another. Our emphasis on the length of a representational response results primarily from the fact that this characteristic was readily amenable to experimental analysis. Perhaps the most significant aspect of the research that has just been reported is that it demonstrates that individual characteristics of representational responses can be isolated and experimentally analyzed.

C. Developmental Changes in Conceptual Organization

In the analysis of reversal and partial-reversal shifts with verbal material it became obvious that preexisting conceptual organizations exerted a powerful effect on adult human behavior. Discriminations consistent with natural language concepts were easy to perform but those that were inconsistent were most difficult.

In an attempt to trace developmental changes of natural language concepts as a child matures, an experimental methodology is being developed which can be used with children of different ages. The procedure is basically a modification of the technique that was used with verbal material with adults. Instead of words, pictures of everyday objects, from children's books, are used (e.g., *apple, pear, horse, dog*). In the first experiment conducted, four or eight pictures were used containing an equal number of instances, two or four, from two conceptual categories. After learning to sort the pictures into two conceptually consistent categories, the subjects received either a reversal or half-reversal shift. With 108 kindergarten children it was found that a reversal shift ($M = 60.5$) was executed significantly faster than a half-reversal ($M = 87.7$). With the same experimental procedure, college students executed a reversal shift in 2.8 trials while a half-reversal shift required a mean of 50.8 trials.

Although there has been a large amount of research directed at identifying the conditions that facilitate concept identification and formation, much less attention has been paid to the psychological organization of concepts and the variables that play a significant role in it. By psychological organization we refer to the relationships existing among the instances, and between the instances and the representational response which enable a concept to be used as a unitary response system. One experimental technique that can be used to measure the degree of organization is to compare the relative speed of executing reversal and half-reversal shifts. For example, the ratio of the speed of half-reversal to reversal shifts was 18.14 for college students and 1.45 for kindergartners. This ratio is not simply a result of the age difference because it will be recalled that with trigrams college students executed half-reversal and reversal shifts at approximately the same speed, the ratio being 1.29.

A basic requirement for understanding developmental changes in conceptual organization requires an experimental technique which can reflect them. Presumably the reversal-half-reversal shift technique used with natural language concepts can serve this function because it permits the systematic variation and experimental analysis of numerous relationships among the instances, and between them and the representational response. The first step, however, is to obtain some picture of the developmental changes which do occur. With such a frame of reference, it will be possible to identify experimentally specific factors and relationships associated with the observed developmental changes, and perhaps lead to the design of training techniques capable of upgrading conceptual behavior at different age levels.

V. Summary

Let us briefly summarize. We have wandered a good bit in this paper partly because investigating largely unexplored areas demands that the investigator be alert to many methodological, empirical, theoretical, and last, but not least, strategic considerations. We have tried to characterize contemporary mediational theory and then describe a research program with which we have been identified, not in an attempt to represent all mediational formulations, but instead to highlight the nature of one.

The research reported in this paper has been primarily concerned with the theoretical and experimental analysis of reversal-shift behavior. Whereas infrahuman organisms, after mastering a discrimination for the first time, find it more difficult to execute a reversal than a nonreversal shift, the order of difficulty is opposite for the adult human.

The results of a series of experiments were presented which used the optional shift procedure with rats and with humans at a wide range of developmental stages. We concluded that a single-link continuity type of discrimination learning theory could account for the rats' shift behavior. A mediational formulation was required for college students. The probability that a child's choice will fit one or the other theoretical analysis depends on his age. The younger the child, the more likely he is to behave in accordance with a single-link analysis. But with increasing age there is a steady increase in the probability that his shift will accord with the mediational analysis.

In order to explain the ability of organisms to execute rapid reversal shifts or to respond in a reversal manner in an optional-shift technique, an S-R mediational formulation has been proposed which assumes that an environmental stimulus (S) evokes an implicit response (r) which in turn produces an implicit stimulus (s) to which the overt response (R) becomes associated. The fundamental question within this formulation is the nature of the implicit response (r). One possible interpretation is that it represents an observing response, a receptor-orienting act, that exposes the subject to the significant portion of the discriminative cues. Another possibility is that the mediated implicit response is a symbolic response that represents the critical features of the discriminative cues that are correlated with reinforcement. It is difficult to isolate experimentally observing from symbolic mediated responses when geometrical patterns are used as discriminative stimuli. An indirect approach was attempted by using a verbal discrimination task. Subjects initially were required to sort verbal items into one of two categories and then execute a reversal shift. A set of experiments indicated that the rapid execution of a reversal shift depends on the accessibility of a mediated symbolic response that represents all the instances of a sorting category.

In an attempt to isolate some of the characteristics of a representational response that facilitates the execution of a reversal shift, it has been found that (1) the associative strength, as measured by word-association norms, between the two representational responses has at best a minimal effect on reversal shift behavior, and (2) more economical forms of representing a category of words facilitate reversal shifts. Although kindergarten children execute a reversal shift more rapidly than a half-reversal shift, the ratio of their half-reversal to reversal performance is smaller than that of college students.

References

Basalla, G. The spread of western science. *Science*, 1967, **156**, 611–622.

Berlyne, D. E. *Structure and direction in thinking*. New York: Wiley, 1965.

Bogartz, W. Effects of reversal and nonreversal shifts with cvc stimuli. *Journal of Verbal Learning and Verbal Bahavior*, 1965, **4**, 484–488.

Broadbent, D. E. Human perception and animal learning. In W. H. Thorpe and O. L. Zangwill (Eds.), *Current problems in animal behavior*. London and New York: Cambridge University Press, 1961. Pp. 248–272.

Brookshire, K. H., Warren, J. M., & Ball, G. G. Reversal and transfer learning following overtraining in rat and chicken. *Journal of Comparative Physiology and Psychology*, 1961, **54**, 98–102.

Buss, A. H. Rigidity as a function of reversal and nonreversal shifts in the learning of successive discriminations. *Journal of Experimental Psychology*, 1953, **45**, 75–81.

Buss, A. H. Reversal and nonreversal shifts in concept formation with partial reinforcement eliminated. *Journal of Experimental Psychology*, 1956, **52**, 162–166.

Cofer, C. N. Discussion in fundamentals of psychology: The psychology of thinking. *Annals of the New York Academy of Sciences*, 1960, **91**, p. 64.

Cole, M. Reversal and nonreversal shifts among Liberian tribal people. *Journal of Experimental Psychology*, 1968, in press.

Danks, J. H., & Glucksberg, S. Effects of level of initial training on reversal shift performance and clustering in free recall: A test of the mediated association hypothesis. *Journal of Verbal Learning and Verbal Behavior*, 1968, in press.

Dashiell, J. F. *Fundamentals of objective psychology*. Boston: Houghton, 1928.

Deutsch, J. A. The inadequacy of Hullian derivation of reasoning and latent learning. *Psychological Review*, 1956, **63**, 389–399.

Dufort, R. H., Guttman, N., & Kimble, G. A. One trial discrimination reversal in the white rat. *Journal of Comparative and Physiological Psychology*, 1954, **47**, 248–249.

Flavell, J. H. *The developmental psychology of Jean Piaget*. Princeton, N.J.: Van Nostrand, 1963.

Glanzer, M., & Clark, W. H. Accuracy of perceptual recall: An analysis of organization. *Journal of Verbal Learning and Verbal Behavior*, 1963, **1**, 289–299.

Goss, A. E. Early behaviorism and verbal mediating responses. *American Psychologist*, 1961, **16**, 285–298.

Gough, P. B. Some tests of the Hullian analysis of reasoning in the rat. Paper delivered at Psychonomic Society Convention, Saint Louis, 1962.

Harlow, H. F. The formation of learning sets. *Psychological Review*, 1949, **56**, 51–65.

Harlow, H. F. Learning set and error factor theory. In S. Koch (Ed.), *Psychology: A study of a science*, Vol. II. New York: McGraw-Hill, 1959. Pp. 492–537.

Harrow, M., & Friedman, G. B. Comparing reversal and nonreversal shifts in concept formation with partial reinforcement controlled. *Journal of Experimental Psychology*, 1958, **55**, 592–598.

Heal, L. W., Bransky, M. L., & Mankinen, R. L. The role of dimension preference in reversal and nonreversal shifts of retardates. *Psychonomic Science*, 1966, **6**, 509–510.

House, B., & Zeaman, D. Reversal and nonreversal shifts in discrimination learning in retardates. *Journal of Experimental Psychology*, 1962, **63**, 444–451.

House, B. J., & Zeaman, D. Miniature experiments in the discrimination learning of retardates. In L. P. Lipsitt and C. C. Spiker (Eds.), *Advances in child development and behavior*, Vol. 1. New York: Academic Press, 1963. Pp. 313–374.

Hull, C. L. The concept of the habit-family hierarchy and maze learning. *Psychological Review*, 1934, **41**, 33–52 and 134–152.

Hull, C. L. The mechanism of the assembly of behavior segments in novel combinations suitable for problem solutions. *Psychological Review*, 1935, **42**, 219–245.

Hull, C. L. *A behavior system*. New Haven: Yale University Press, 1952.

Katz, P. A. Effects of labels on children's perception and discrimination learning. *Journal of Experimental Psychology*, 1963, **66**, 423–428.

Kelleher, R. T. Discrimination learning as a function of reversal and nonreversal shifts. *Journal of Experimental Psychology*, 1956, **51**, 379–384.

Kendler, H. H. "What is learned?"—A theoretical blind alley. *Psychological Review*, 1952, **59**, 269–277.

Kendler, H. H. Motivation and behavior. In D. Levine (Ed.), *Nebraska symposium on motivation*. Lincoln, Nebr.: University of Nebraska Press, 1965. Pp. 1–23.

Kendler, H. H., & D'Amato, M. F. A comparison of reversal shifts and nonreversal shifts in human concept formation behavior. *Journal of Experimental Psychology*, 1955, **49**, 165–174.

Kendler, H. H., & Kendler, T. S. The effect of verbalization on reversal shifts in children. *Science*, 1961, **134**, 1619–1620.

Kendler, H. H., & Kendler, T. S. Vertical and horizontal processes in problem solving. *Psychological Review*, 1962, **69**, 1–16.

Kendler, H. H., Kendler, T. S., & Sanders, J. Reversal and partial reversal shifts with verbal material. *Journal of Verbal Learning and Verbal Behavior*, 1967, **6**, 117–127.

Kendler, H. H., & Vineberg, R. The acquisition of compound concepts as a function of previous training. *Journal of Experimental Psychology*, 1954, **48**, 252–258.

Kendler, H. H., & Watson, G. W. Conceptual behavior as a function of associative strength between representational responses. *Journal of Verbal Learning and Verbal Behavior*, 1968, in press.

Kendler, T. S. Verbalization and optional reversal shifts among kindergarten children. *Journal of Verbal Learning and Verbal Behavior*, 1964, **3**, 428–436.

Kendler, T. S., & Kendler, H. H. Reversal and nonreversal shifts in kindergarten children. *Journal of Experimental Psychology*, 1959, **58**, 56–60.

Kendler, T. S., & Kendler, H. H. Experimental analysis of inferential behavior. In L. P. Lipsitt and C. C. Spiker (Eds.), *Advances in child development and behavior*, Vol. 3. New York: Academic Press, 1967. Pp. 157–190.

Kendler, T. S., Kendler, H. H., & Learnard, B. Mediated responses to size and brightness as a function of age. *American Journal of Psychology*, 1962, **75**, 571–586.

Kendler, T. S., Kendler, H. H., & Silfen, C. K. Optional shift behavior of albino rats. *Psychonomic Science*, 1964, **1**, 5–6.

Kendler, T. S., Kendler, H. H., & Wells, D. Reversal and nonreversal shifts in nursery school children. *Journal of Comparative and Physiological Psychology*, 1960, **53**, 83–87.

Koffka, K. *Principles of Gestalt psychology*. New York: Harcourt, Brace, 1935.

Koronakos, C. Inferential learning in rats: The problem-solving assembly of behavior segments. *Journal of Comparative and Physiological Psychology*, 1959, **52**, 231–235.

Mackintosh, N. J. The effects of overtraining on a reversal and a nonreversal shift. *Journal of Comparative and Physiological Psychology*, 1962, **55**, 555–559.

Mackintosh, N. J. Selective attention in animal discrimination learning. *Psychological Bulletin*, 1965, **64**, 124–150.

Maier, N. R. F. Reasoning in white rats. *Comparative Psychology Monographs*, 1929, No. 29.

Maltzman, I. Thinking: From a behavioristic point of view. *Psychological Review*, 1955, **62**, 275–286.

Mandler, G. Response factors in human learning. *Psychological Review*, 1954, **61**, 239–244.

Melzack, R., & Wall, P. D. Pain mechanisms: A new theory. *Science*, 1965, **150**, 971–979.

Miller, G. A. Some preliminaries to psycholinguistics. *American Psychologist*, 1965, **20**, 15–20.

Nagel, E. Determinism and development. In D. B. Harris (Ed.). *The concept of development*. Minneapolis: Univ. of Minnesota Press, 1957. Pp. 15–24.

Nagel, E. *The structure of science: Problems in the logic of scientific explanation*. New York: Harcourt, Brace, 1961.

Osgood, C. E. A behavioristic analysis of perception and language in cognitive phenomena. In *Contemporary approaches to cognition*. Cambridge: Harvard University Press, 1957. Pp. 75–118.

Ratliff, F. *Mach bands*. San Francisco: Holden-Day, 1965.

Schade, A. F., & Bitterman, M. E. Improvement in habit reversal as related to dimensional set. *Journal of Comparative and Physiological Psychology*, 1966, **62**, 43—48.

Schoenfeld, W. N., & Cumming, W. W. Behavior and perception. In S. Koch (Ed.), *Psychology: A study of a science*, Vol. 5. New York: McGraw-Hill, 1963. Pp. 213–252.

Shepp, B. E., & Eimas, P. D. Intradimensional and extradimensional shifts in the rat. *Journal of Comparative and Physiological Psychology*, 1964, **57**, 357–361.

Smiley, S. S., & Weir, M. W. The role of dimensional dominance in reversal and nonreversal shift behavior. *Journal of Experimental Child Psychology*, 1966, **4**, 296–307.

Spence, K. W. The nature of discrimination learning in animals. *Psychological Review*, 1936, **43**, 427–449.

Spence, K. W. The nature of response in discrimination learning. *Psychological Review*, 1952, **59**, 89–93.

Spence, K. W. Conceptual models of spatial and nonspatial selective learning. In K. W. Spence (Ed.), *Behavior theory and learning: Selected papers*. Englewood Cliffs, N.J.: Prentice Hall, 1960. Pp. 366–392.

Sutcliffe, J. P. A general method of analysis of frequency data for multiple classification designs. *Psychological Bulletin*, 1957, **54**, 134–137.

Sutherland, N. S. Stimulus analysing mechanisms. In *Proceedings of a symposium on the mechanization of thought processes*, Vol. 2. London: H.M. Stationery Office, 1959. Pp. 575–609.

Tighe, T. J. Reversal and nonreversal shifts in monkeys. *Journal of Comparative and Physiological Psychology*, 1964, **58**, 324–326.

Tighe, T. J., Brown, P. L., & Youngs, E. A. The effect of overtraining on the shift behavior of albino rats. *Psychonomic Science*, 1965, **2**, 141–142.

Tighe, T. J., & Tighe, L. S. Overtraining and optional shift behavior in rats and children. *Journal of Comparative and Physiological Psychology*, 1966, **62**, 49–54.

Tulving, E. Intratrial and intertrial retention: Notes towards a theory of free recall verbal learning. *Psychological Review*, 1964, **3**, 219–237.

Underwood, B. J., & Richardson, J. Some verbal materials for the study of concept formation. *Psychological Bulletin*, 1956, **53**, 84–96.

Whorf, B. L. *Language, thought, and reality*. New York: Wiley, 1956.

Woodworth, R. S. *Dynamics of behavior*. New York: Holt, 1958.

AUTHOR INDEX

Numbers in italics indicate the pages on which the complete references are listed.

SUBJECT INDEX